MASK OF ASIA
THE PHILIPPINES TODAY

The Filipino, more than any other Asian, suffers most acutely from lata. Where other Asians conducted a guerrilla war to preserve their identity, the Filipino, as a tactical ruse, put on the mask of the foreigner. He did survive the latter's regime, but when the time came for taking off the mask, it had become part of his face. The greater irony is that he has put on a number of masks . . .

ADRIAN E. CRISTOBAL

MASK OF ASIA
THE PHILIPPINES TODAY

GEORGE FARWELL

FREDERICK A. PRAEGER, *Publishers*
New York • Washington • London

FREDERICK A. PRAEGER, PUBLISHERS
111 Fourth Avenue, New York, N.Y. 10003, U.S.A.
77-79 Charlotte Street, London W.1, England

Published in the United States of America in 1967
by Frederick A. Praeger, Inc., Publishers

This book is published by F. W. Cheshire in Australia
as *Mask of Asia: The Philippines*

© 1966 by George Farwell

Library of Congress Catalog Card Number: 66-21777

Printed in the United States of America

To
the late
JUAN S. ALANO
A true Filipino

Contents

Illustrations

Photographs not otherwise acknowledged are the author's.

Foreword

THE YEAR I spent among the beautiful islands of the Philippines in search of material for this book I shall always remember as one of the most dramatic, stimulating and colourful of my life. It taught me as much about the outlook and fashion of living of the West as of the aspirations, sufferings and character of south-east Asia. What I have attempted is a candid as well as sympathetic portrait of the Philippines Republic. If candour is a term that can sometimes be used against me, let it be said that I have written with equal frankness and criticism of my own country.

I would like to acknowledge the generous advice and assistance I have been given by many of the Filipinos with whom I came into close contact. Chief among these are Don Juan and Doña Ramona Alano, Mr and Mrs Lorenzo Alvero, Mr Jose Y. Ayala, Dean Conrado Benitez and Dr Francesca Benitez, Mr and Mrs Tomas Benitez, Miss Helena Z. Benitez, Mr Cesar Climaco, Don Carlos Fernandez, Dr Rodolfo Gonzalez, Mr and Mrs Gene Guillermo, Mr Teodoro M. Locsin, Datu Ayu Mandi, Miss Martirez, Mr Baldimero T. Olivera, Hadji Raja, and Colonel Salcedo. Grateful acknowledgements are also made to the Public Library of New South Wales and the Mitchell Library, Sydney; the editorial boards of *The Philippines Herald*, *The Manila Times* and the *Philippines Free Press*; and to my wife, who not only put up with a great deal of sometimes arduous travel, but typed and edited the original ms.

Money: I have used throughout, with rare exceptions, the currency of the country. The customary rate is 3·90 pesos to one United States dollar; approximately 4·50 to the Australian dollar; and approximately 11 to the pound sterling.

GEORGE FARWELL

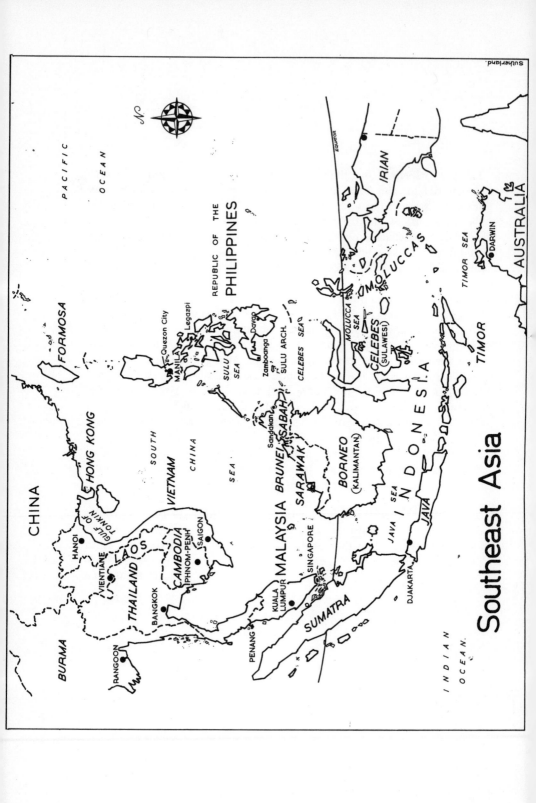

Southeast Asia

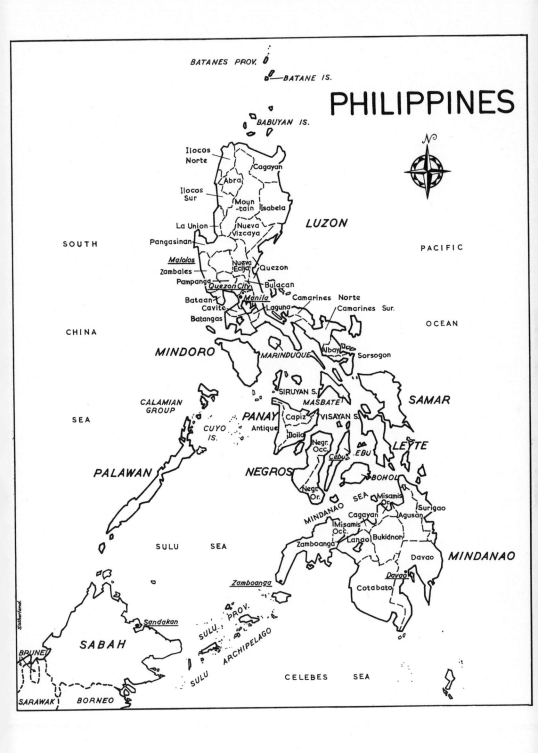

PHILIPPINES

BATANES PROV.
BATANE IS.

BABUYAN IS.

Ilocos
Norte
Cagayan
Abra
Ilocos
Sur
Moun
-tain   Isabela
La Union
Nueva
Vizcaya
Pangasinan

LUZON

Malolos
Zambales
Pampanga
Quezon City   Bulacan
Bataan   Manila
Cavite   Laguna
Batangas

Nueva
Ecija   Quezon

Camarines Norte
Camarines Sur.

MINDORO

MARINDUQUE   Albay   Sorsogon

SIRUYAN S.
MASBATE
Capiz   VISAYAN S.

PANAY
Antique
Iloilo

SAMAR

CALAMIAN
GROUP

CUYO
IS.

Negr.
Occ.
Cebu   EBU

LEYTE

PALAWAN

NEGROS

Negr.
Or.

MINDANAO

SEA
Cagayan

BOHOL

Misamis
Or.

SEA

Misamis
Occ.
Zamboanga   Lanao   Bukidnon

Surigao
Agusan

Davao

MINDANAO

SOUTH

PACIFIC

CHINA

OCEAN

SEA

Zamboanga

Davao
Cotabato

Sandakan

SULU   SEA

SULU   PROV.

SABAH

SULU   ARCHIPELAGO

BRUNEI

SARAWAK   BORNEO

CELEBES   SEA

Sutherland

MASK OF ASIA
THE PHILIPPINES TODAY

CHAPTER 1

Asia or the West?

*Once upon a time there were no people
on earth; only gods and goddesses. They
grew bored with their idle lives, so they
began to make figures out of clay. The
first batch they baked too long and came
out black. The second was underdone, too
pale and white. The third batch was just
right, brown and beautiful. These were
the Filipinos . . .*

PHILIPPINE LEGEND

ONE of the mysteries of Asia, at least from the Western viewpoint, is the
small role assigned to the Philippines in international affairs. For the outside world these islands retain a mystery that is no longer an attribute of
other Asian nations, despite their more romantic embellishments of
pagodas, cheong-sams or cherry blossom, as if these crowded peoples lived
a kind of museum existence for the benefit of tourists. Today's ideological
conflict with China, cold war manoeuvres and Indonesia's *konfrontasi*
have all obliged the more thoughtful at least of Western policy-makers to
take a closer look at the social and political realities of modern Asia. We
are no longer surprised if these are not so different from our own. The
age of patronizing Kiplings is behind us now. A Manila newspaper, in
fact, wrote recently of 'Gunga-dinism' in tones similar to that of Soekarno
defining *Necolim*. The West's colonial godsons, rebelliously or not, have
now come of age. They have inherited much of our materialist desires,
impeded only by industrial inexperience and corroding poverty.

There is no nation in the region that more urgently needs our interest
and understanding than the Philippines, which has so long remained over
the horizons of western thinking, that is, if we except American commercial interest. It may be a small nation, comparatively new to self-government, but it is also a populous one, gifted, potentially wealthy, with great
natural resources and an inventive, if sometimes disorientated people. Yet
it is seldom considered in terms of economic or military strategy; its
culture is virtually unknown and it has no readily identifiable image —
as have, say, Japan, Thailand or Malaysia.

My own attraction to this picturesque archipelago began many years
before I went there. There were complex reasons. Chief among them was
my attachment to the Pacific Ocean, especially in its tropic regions. For
me there is a vitality and charm to the sun-browned Pacific peoples that I
do not find elsewhere. I have always felt a strong affinity, for instance,

1

with Polynesians. The Malays, who are their distant cousins, have much in common with them, notably through their early feats of seamanship, their language structure, their hardy yet easy-going peasant outlook, their love of pleasure and ancient, if half-obliterated, culture. I have also known many charming and talented Filipinos. I admired their quick intelligence, erudition, courtly manners, their superb handicrafts, folk arts, traditional dances, their literature — especially the novels of Jose Rizal which have been surprisingly neglected overseas — their skills in surgery and medicine that have now made Manila the most important healing centre in south-east Asia. There is a sophistication to them that suggests affinities with the West possessed by few other Asian peoples.

It is often assumed, in fact, that the Philippines is not really part of Asia at all. Or only accidentally so. Filipinos are an island people, it is said, long ago set adrift from the Asian mainland, remote from it in temperament, history and mores. They are said to be Westerners under another skin, little Americans even, their accents those of Madison Avenue or Main Street, their manners, morals and memories harking back to feudal Spain, which conquered and changed them four centuries ago. There is no Asian tradition, no ritual art, no temples or ceremonial costume. And, in the modern context, no virus of rabid nationalism, no smouldering anti-colonial virus. Not as in neighbouring Indonesia, which is also Malay. The Philippines, after all, is a Roman Catholic country, and a Western-style democracy: the one Christian democracy in south-east Asia. Its only allies are Western powers. It subscribes to the South East Asia Treaty Organization, whose only other Asian members are the somewhat reluctant Thailand and Pakistan. It has trade agreements with the West exclusively, with the United States and, more recently, with Australia. How can this small republic, with two decades of independence, be classed as properly Asian at all? So the argument runs.

One wit has said that its people spent three hundred and fifty years in a Spanish monastery, then fifty on a Hollywood-style campus. The result is a blue-suited Filipino driving a two-tone convertible. It is a clever summary; American, of course. So clever it has deceived the outside world into believing it to be true.

Spanish domination since the sixteenth century has done much to make the Philippines face west. More than 80 per cent of its people are Catholics, so that for all but a million and a half Muslims, some Protestants and several pagan tribes, the spiritual capital is Rome. When the United States drove Spain out in 1898, the political capital shifted from Madrid to Washington. Apart from the Japanese occupation in World War Two, it remained there until independence in 1946. Hence the vogue for speaking of little Americans, or little brown Americans. It is not a phrase I care to use. Yet, in these colour-conscious times, it is used a great deal. Mainly by nationalistic Filipinos attacking those of their own kind who support American policies. Which suggests they may no longer be little Americans at all.

Nationalism, in fact, is becoming a potent force, though the new mood has been insufficiently recognized abroad.

This beautiful, densely-peopled, potentially rich chain of islands — extending, like a strung bow, one thousand miles south from Taiwan to Borneo — must soon be of crucial importance in Asia's struggle, whether nearby Vietnam's fate is settled or not. Without foreign aid its natural resources cannot be developed. Its fast expanding population needs industrial expansion to survive, or it will not even survive present threats of social anarchy. Strategically, the archipelago rests in the deceptively calm eye of a rising ideological storm. Manila Bay may be the main base for the U.S. Seventh Fleet; the huge Clark airfield may be less than two jet hours from the Asian mainland. But two low pressure belts can already be detected: westward across the China Sea, southward over Indonesia. Filipino politics are likewise generating a dangerous dynamic of their own. The struggle for the Filipino's soul has already begun. No longer is Catholicism enough to combat mass poverty. Crime waves, allied to a desperate materialism, are corroding the old stability. Communism, like the Philippine volcanoes, is still dormant, but now and again a tremor shakes the land. Which turn will the young, still immature republic make: towards Asia, or back towards the West?

All this, so far, remains a subterranean struggle. The foreigner is seldom aware of it. It is easier to build upon first assumptions.

Especially if he remains in Manila; as mostly he does. There are two Manilas, two nations here. The dominant one still has American overtones, colonial American, if such is possible. This is the familiar world, westernized. When Filipinos speak English, they do so with an American accent. They also happen to be bi-lingual. Since independence the official language has been Tagalog, a Malay dialect belonging to the largest ethnic group in Luzon. English is still the accepted language in government and commerce, despite the decree that Tagalog, now designated Pilipino, be used. Yet you cannot hope to understand even the educated Filipino, his spontaneous, unguarded reactions, unless you know his own tongue, for this is what he speaks in private life. Also, there are many Tagalog phrases, symbolically defining states of mind, that are almost untranslateable. Malay is a language of inversion. Emotion, distinctive fashions of thought have shaped it to a different structure, while the mind expressing it is different, too. In a larger sense, Pilipino unites all classes, which English never did. This was the language of the colonial masters, as Spanish was earlier. Therefore it is unwise to judge this society by its externals alone. Certainly the clothes Filipinos wear, their cars, cigarettes and styles, even their manners are mostly American. Why not? The United States has had a virtual monopoly of trade for sixty years. The Philippine constitution is based on the American model, as are Congress, the law courts, police, universities and schools.

Yet social patterns frequently reach back to older forms. These are more Spanish than most will admit these days, which is what gives the diverse and scattered islands much of their colour. In provincial towns they call their public squares *plazas*; street signs often use *avenida, calle, rua*; the quaint, high-wheeled horse cabs are *calesas* or *caratellas*. Not only the houses of the provincial well-to-do have Spanish-style gateways and court-yards, with iron grilles protecting windows. This is always a sensible precaution, the way crime is — then as now. Upper class girls are still required to take chaperones when they dine out with young men, even when they go to the downtown cinema. Older, aristocratic families often insist on speaking Castilian at home. It foxes the *nouveaux riches* as well as their maids.

And where else in Asia do you find *tangos* or *rigodons* danced at parties, or village festivals known as *fiestas*? Even the peasant is still characterized as Juan de la Cruz. The newer style is *tao*, reverting to the ancient Malay.

Above all, the religion introduced by Spain is a great shaper of life still, even if a good deal of ritual has been invested with a pagan tinge. For instance, in the nervous, perhaps neurotic, tensions of religious proces-sions, in the way flagellants in some provinces flog each other through public streets. Or in the self-crucifixion of a villager in San Pedro, Laguna, who had himself nailed to a cross four Good Fridays in succes-sion, complete with false beard, wig and crown of thorns. In modern Cebu City dancers greet the golden image of Santo Niño, brought there by Magellan in 1521, with a frenetic hopping dance known as *Pit Senyor* (hail the Lord!), a part-Spanish term that smoothes over the fact that pagan Malays, after killing the great navigator, turned the Infant Jesus into a rain god. The Spanish strain runs deep in today's Filipino; how deep none can say. There were never large numbers of Spaniards perman-ently settled here, though much inter-marriage — more fundamentally, inter-breeding — must have taken place over three centuries and a half. The *mestizo* has been largely attributed to transient government officials, the soldiery and high-living friars who shared with feudal landowners the ancient *droit de seigneur*, a right still not unknown in the sugar baronies of the Visayan islands. It is significant that the classic heroine of Filipino literature, Maria Clara, in Jose Rizal's *Noli Me Tangere*, was a friar's love-child. Today the fine distinctions between Filipinos of Spanish descent, creoles, mestizos and other racially mixed are quite impossible to unravel. An extensive Chinese strain also long precedes the coming of Spain. The late nineteenth century regime confused matters further by forcing everyone to adopt Spanish surnames from a prescribed list, because officialdom found native ones too difficult. Hence the prevalence, even among pure Malays, of common names such as Cruz, Gonzales, Rodrigo, Reyes.

There are many mysteries yet to uncover in the Filipino's past.

Meantime, valid reasons exist for a re-examination of his society less in European than in Asian terms. At grassroots level, westernized influences often become superficial. Even in cosmopolitan Manila you are almost at

4

once confronted with the climate of Asia. The proof is in its people. People; people everywhere. Not so much cast of features, skin texture, language, dress. But numbers. Millions of people; milling millions. Walk down Rizal Avenue, Ayala Boulevard, the Escolta. Stand at intersections, waiting for traffic lights to change, hemmed there by a patient, yet restive crowd, following the surge of it across hot bitumen in a lock-stepping mass, threading through the banked-up chaos of omnibuses, trucks, jeepneys, taxis, calesas, cars. Or try walking the narrower thoroughfares of Tondo, Santa Aña, Quiapo, Mandaluyong. Here is the authentic throb and thrust of Asia, the potent arterial stream, the collective force that Western powers once believed they could divert and dam. Nor is it in the capital only; not only in Manila and its city satellites, whose combined populations have swelled to three million since World War Two. Travel to other regions, to the provinces and *barrios*; to other islands; to Cebu City, Iloilo, Bacolod, Davao, Iligan. The multiplying population in these and other provincial cities in less than two decades has alarming overtones. The Philippines now has the highest rate of natural increase in Asia, and ranks fourth in population density, not far behind Taiwan, India, and Pakistan. It exerts greater pressure on limited areas available for cultivation than even Burma or India. The last census before the war, in 1939, set the population at sixteen million. By 1948 that figure had increased to nineteen. Twelve years later the total had grown, inexplicably, to twenty-seven million. This was an increase of 42·7 per cent, unless there was something wrong with the census figures. The most recent estimate, in June, 1965, put the number at 32,345,000, with a density of 108 people to every square kilometre of land.

No wonder demographers have nightmares of Asians standing on one another's shoulders in a not too remote future.

'The Philippines is one of the fastest growing countries in the world', stated an official report in 1962.[1] It added a warning that internal migration could never be large enough to relieve the pressure, while unchecked growth could lead to economic and political disaster. No one appears to have taken notice.

An American geographer put it more graphically when he wrote that 'in the time it takes to walk across Rizal Avenue, a new baby will be born somewhere in the Philippines'.[2] Certainly this broad, traffic-choked street takes some time to cross. The annual birthrate when he wrote this, in 1963, was assessed at 890,000. Today it would be one million. On present population figures, the natural increase amounts to 3·5 per cent a year. Nor does this take into account a falling death rate due, despite yearly outbreaks of cholera and gastric diseases, to increased control over malaria and tuberculosis that once made Filipinos a short-lived people.

1. *Popular Projection for the Philippines, 1960-75*, Bureau of Census and Statistics, Manila, 1962.

2 Robert E. Huke, *Shadows on the Land; An Economic Geography of the Philippines*, Manila, 1963.

These once lyrical islands are becoming a classic tableau of Malthusian excesses. In some aspects it is more alarming than in other Asian countries. In India, Japan, China, some effort at least is being made to control the chain reaction of unregulated birth. Not so in the Philippines. These peasants are also Roman Catholics; so far contraception has been as unthinkable as original sin. Which does not mean that oral contraceptives cannot be bought on Manila's blackmarket, at least by communicants among the well-to-do. *Be fruitful and multiply.* The ancient adage matches prolific nature in a tropic zone. It fails to match statistics recording this as a nation with the fifth lowest standard of living in Asia.

To view this population explosion in Christian terms only is unrealistic. It has to be seen in an Asian context, too. The Muslim and pagan minorities are as fruitful. Here matters of 'face' are involved: Asia's eternal preoccupation with face. Such attitudes are difficult to counter at intellectual levels, having deeper unconscious sources. Not to have children — even more than a man can feed — is to lose face, to imply impotence, a lack of masculinity. For the Filipino, pride and face are interchangeable terms. It is all part of his *machismo.*

Not even in overcrowded Hong Kong or Singapore have I seen so many children as in Manila. Nor in Cebu, or Davao. In late afternoons they outnumber adults in city streets, streaming out of schools, convents, cramped concrete playgrounds, pressing into already jammed suburban buses and jeepneys, bringing an hour or two of exuberance to drab thoroughfares not otherwise noted for open or smiling faces.

Sophisticated Manila is only a facade: the shiny, air-conditioned buildings of United Nations Avenue, the Escolta, Makati; the neon-lit hotels and motels along Roxas (formerly Dewey) Boulevard; the elegant boutiques and questionable night clubs (or day clubs) and sing-song bars of Mabini. Greater Manila, if you overlook exclusive suburbs like Forbes Park or Bel Air, comprises largely decayed residential areas, shanty towns and slums, a dim-lit labyrinth of backlanes, alley-ways and crowded, over-built allotments reaching away muddily for miles, without drains or sewers, often without sanitation of the most primitive kind. Here youthful voices reach their most raucous pitch, childhood's faces are older and seamier, brawls more *à la mode.* Games here are played not with foot- or tennis-balls, but with imitation guns, real knives, knuckledusters, even with steel darts fired from toy catapults, as grown hoodlums fire them from real ones around the Manila docks. In fashionable Mabini I once watched, through a restaurant window, several urchins practising expert under-arm jabs to the stomach with six-inch knives. Elsewhere, amid caseboard tenements and strung washing down back streets, the universal sport of cops and robbers gains a sharper edge when real-life cops are nervous at invading these alleys alone. Thousands of children never go to school at all. Schooling is not yet compulsory. If it were, too many parents could not afford the clothes, fares, lunches, schoolbooks. Yet numbers attending are already so large that many public schools have been forced to limit their pupils to one or two sessions daily: one set of children in the mornings, another during afternoons.

It is hard to see how this crisis can be overcome. Successive governments have been perpetually on the edge of bankruptcy. Even funds for new school buildings, for textbooks and equipment seem mysteriously to disappear. Meantime breeding accelerates. The last census, in 1960, revealed that 45 per cent of the population was under fifteen. By now large numbers of these all too pubescent teenagers will have had children of their own. Almost half the nation must now be of school age or under, which means unproductive from an industrial or rural viewpoint, setting impossible pressures on already ill-financed schools. You do not need further statistics to appreciate this ever-expanding threat to stable nationhood.

Colleges and universities are often likewise strained beyond capacity, accommodating additional students on a part-time basis, with staggered hours. Many times, along Quezon Boulevard, I have watched a tide of night students streaming out of Far Eastern University after nine o'clock, an impressive mass of eager, tired young men and women for whom a diploma offered the one promise of security.

Or did it?

Filipinos are said to have acquired their desire for education from the Americans. In a sense, this is true. Almost as soon as the United States took control, having quelled the national revolution of 1898, free schooling was introduced, to be followed by a system of higher education never known under Spain. Like the Chinese, these are a people who often tend to regard knowledge as an end in itself. A college degree, Katherine Mayo observed some forty years ago, 'is expected to act as a push button to the impossible'.[3] Even today, in the continuing atmosphere of poverty and mass competition for too few skilled jobs, a degree or diploma is regarded as essential, though the professions cannot hope to absorb all those qualified.

This was something that troubled me frequently, watching the floodtide of youth flowing down city streets. What was to happen to all these lively, earnest or scholarly young? Where were the jobs they hoped to find in later years? Where were the legal briefs, executive desks, draughtsmen's offices, laboratories and engineering projects? Already the shock of reality has struck too many. No one knows how many fledgling lawyers, science graduates, hopeful teachers have been obliged to work as clerks in government or private firms, and for a hundred pesos or less a month. It is no solace for waiters and counterhands to have a college education. Nor for the foreigner to speak lightly of the Asian's almost mystical desire for education. There is no mystique about it.

'Our people have good reasons for wanting to be educated', one univer-

3. Katherine Mayo, *The Isles of Fear*, New York, 1924.

7

sity woman told me. 'They remember the Japanese times. The brutality of the Occupation. If we do not educate ourselves, people say, we too may become animals.'

Her use of 'we' was over-modest. She happened to come of a family for whom scholarship had been a matter of course for generations. Her people were *ilustrados*. The Spanish term is again significant, especially as it was just such educated people who supported the revolution to oust Spain. *Ilustrados* also take pride in reminding the foreigner that the Philippines has the oldest university in the New World. The University of Santo Tomas was founded by the Dominican order back in 1610. It was in this massively handsome, four-square, almost medieval building that Jose Rizal studied medicine, still its pre-eminent faculty, more than eighty years ago, though the description he gave of it in his second novel, *El Filibusterismo (The Reign of Greed)*, was hardly flattering. In those days its professors were arrogantly Spanish, contemptuous of *Indio* students, and the sensitive young poet found their repressive methods intolerable. He left after his fourth year, finishing his studies in Madrid where, to his surprise, he found the atmosphere of Spain more liberal than its unhappy colony. Today the U.S.T. claims the martyred Rizal as one of its most brilliant students.

Dr Rizal, who now heads the official calendar of national heroes, was an extraordinary, many-sided personality. Doctor of medicine, graduate in philosophy and letters, poet, novelist, agriculturalist, botanist, engineer, philologist, he studied German, Italian, French and Greek during his years of exile in Europe, achieving fluency in twenty-two languages by the time he died at thirty-five. His writings made him the chief architect of the 1898 revolution he tried hard to prevent, but his death before a firing squad in Manila eighteen months earlier made that revolution inevitable. Brought up a devout Roman Catholic, with priests among his friends, he turned to freemasonry because he saw his church as the major force behind colonial repression. He left behind a body of fine writing that has become holy writ today, being studied in schools and universities, and consistently quoted by politicians whose public attitudes often deny the principles they voice. Some of the passages he wrote on the Spanish colonial order are still cause for embarrassment. '. . . Put a priest's robe as the Franciscans wear it on a carabao, and you will be lucky if the carabao does not become as lazy on account of the robe. . . . Can God be bribed and bought off, and blinded by money, nothing more nor less than a friar?'[4] '. . . The best plantations, the best tracts of land . . . are in the hands of the religious corporations, whose desideratum is ignorance and a condition of semi-starvation for the native.'[5]

Rizal, clearly, did not see the Filipino as a child of Spain. He was, in fact, the first man to crusade for the rights and integrity of his people, to dramatize the virtues of the pre-hispanic Malays, from whom he made the

4. Jose Rizal, *To The Young Women of Malolos*, National Library, Manila, 1932.
5. Jose Rizal, *The Indolence of the Filipinos*, various editions.

proud claim to be descended. The fact that he had also Chinese and Japanese ancestry only strengthens his modern claim to be called 'the father of Asian nationalism'. It remains that, throughout his life, he stressed the necessity for education if his people were ever to emancipate themselves. This is yet another reason for the Filipino drive for learning.

There is no questioning the position that Rizal, his life and work, holds amid the growing spirit of nationalism today. He has become the father figure of the republic, the martyred hero, and the thirtieth of December, the anniversary of his execution, is now a national day. It is impressive to watch this annual pilgrimage to his tomb on the Luneta, that great public park confronting, quite by chance, the American embassy. A guard of honour parades all day. The president comes to pay his homage. So does the cardinal with his escort of papal knights bearing plumed hats and ceremonial swords. So do the politicians of all parties, in formal dress, not daring to be absent. Yet, despite it all, you have the impression that few in public life really hear Rizal any more. His patriotism, his distinctively liberal ideals, his belief in the common man are lauded with great emotion by every speaker. But his own national pride runs counter to the modern concept of nationalism. Today's mood is harsher, strident, less visionary than ruthlessly pragmatic.

It is the difference of two ages.

CHAPTER 2

Complex of Islands

*This geographical unit of numberless
islands called the Philippines — this
mystical unit of numberless tongues, bloods
and cultures called a Filipino — was a
Spanish creation. There is as great a gulf
between the pre-Spanish drift of totem-and-
taboo tribes and our present existence as one
people as there is between protoplasm and a
human creature . . .*

NICK JOAQUIN

To SEE this island republic, as most do, only through the focus of a large,
cosmopolitan capital, is to misjudge its climate. The visitor, even the
diplomat or foreign investor, tends to equate it with the kind of society
he meets in Manila, with its handsome pockets of affluence, the free-
handed if sometimes perilous world of commerce, the elegant hostess and
bland senator, the lively university life and its articulate, charming people
who mostly talk English as if they had no other tongue. It is possible to
live well in a city that has not entirely forgotten the old-world courtesies
of Spain, at the chauffeur-driven level anyway, and the foreigner seldom
visits lesser regions, certainly not on foot, unless he happens to be Peace
Corps.

The true Philippines is still largely in its rural areas. This is where
80 per cent of its people live, on islands remote from one another, in
narrow valleys, small coastal settlements, introspective small towns whose
routine may have changed little in centuries. Each is a closed world of
its own, its outlook determined too often by poverty, inadequate schooling and conservative, even superstitious conduct that typifies peasant
society anywhere. This is valid even on the larger islands: Luzon, for
instance, or the Visayas, or Mindanao, which are divided into provinces
frequently jealous of another's progress, mutually distrustful, their politi-
cally-appointed governors or town mayors caught up in obscure policies
for their own advancement. A national view is rare. The basic unit is the
barrio, each small farming area surrounding towns and villages. The use
of the Spanish term has significance, suggesting how slight was the fifty
years of United States rule in altering older patterns, at least in rural
zones.

Perhaps the Spanish themselves did not transform the peasant so drasti-
cally either. Barrio is a term that stems from an older time. The Malay

10

word, *barangay*, from which it derives, was the unit of settlement under pre-hispanic sultans and *datus*. It was the ancient outrigger craft, with matting sails and seats for up to a hundred rowers, by which the first Malays reached these scattered islands. They are believed to have come by way of what is now Indonesia, the first waves arriving in the second century B.C. Each *barangay* formed a new settlement wherever landfall was made.

This complex of islands has persisted to the present day. Fragmentation may almost be said to be the natural order of society.

No one can actually tell you just how many islands there are, nor, for that matter, what constitutes an island. Even official figures vary. The most recent puts the number at 7,107. Seven thousand islands; it has a picturesque sound. But many are tiny islets, mere cays or rocks. Some even appear and disappear, the result of volcanic action. Less than one thousand are fertile enough to be inhabited, only a dozen of these with any density. The largest island, Luzon, covers 40,000 square miles and is the most industrialized, especially around the Manila area. It grows the best rice, some sugar and has fine timber in the central mountain regions. Southward is the complex of the Visayan Islands — Negros, Cebu, Panay, Samar and Leyte, among others. Sugar, copra, corn, abaca and again rice are the mainstays of a subsistence economy here. South again rise the rough-hewn mountains of Mindanao, 37,000 square miles of still largely undeveloped country, with rich timber resources, undeveloped minerals, a potential steel-making city in Iligan and most of the Muslim population, which still feels itself neglected by the self-interested and Christian north. Beyond, almost to the equator, the Sulu Archipelago trails its tiny islands like a comet's tail, remote from what government planning yet exists, inhabiting its violent dream of a piratical past.

It is not easy to bring unity to such a scattering of islands. The problems of transport alone are difficult enough. A national identity, above all, cannot readily be achieved. Without the Spanish conquest this almost haphazard grouping of islands might never have been welded together at all, for it is made up of many peoples, tribes, languages, dialects and cultures. Without the Spanish, the southern islands would undoubtedly have become part of Holland's empire, and would now be part of Indonesia. And what unity Spain did bring was often offset by its colonial policy, which was to set one people against another, conscripting Luzon and the Visayas to fight the aggressive Muslims, exploiting certain provinces, notably Pampanga and Nueva Ecija, whose leaders were bribed with lands and power to suppress rebels elsewhere. Thus, even today, people tend to think of themselves primarily as Pampangans, Ilocanos, Visayans or Batanguenos. To complicate things further, the so-called Moros of the south are themselves divided by many, almost inassimilable threads of tribal custom and tradition.

For the traveller, of course, all this makes for a great deal of variety and colour. Social life, character, scenery are as variable as the complex history of these islands. Travel twenty miles out of Manila, and you are back in the land of the carabao. There is much talk these days of mechanized farming, but it is still the slow, good-natured water buffalo that carries the poorly rewarded farmer. And, literally, carries him. You see young men, boys, old fellows sitting astride these broad-backed beasts on their way to work. You see the *carabao*, head hanging as if those wide horns were too heavy, drawing ploughs, or carts, or huge wicker baskets on sleds. In fact, pulling the nation's economy behind them. One of the worst features of the immediate post-war years, when the *tao* was hard put to make a living, was the shortage of carabao, most of them having been killed off by the Japanese to feed their armies. It took years to breed enough work animals again. Australia gave some small assistance, sending so-called wild buffalo from the Northern Territory's coastal swamps, where these once domesticated animals have acquired a big game hunting reputation for a ferocity they scarcely deserve.

North Australians would be astonished if they could see small, barefoot boys leading them along rural lands, prodding them into the rice *padis*, sitting on their necks while they wallow in muddy roadside pools.

Even along the paved Highway Three, running north through the fertile Central Provinces to Baguio, you remain close to this peasant atmosphere. The first time I drove that way was with Don Juan Alano, the 'Coconut King' of Mindanao, who spent the war years under Japanese surveillance in the Mountain Province. We left Manila at two in the morning. It was only a five hour drive, yet it spanned so much of Filipino life. First, the gaudy lights of nightclubs in suburban Bulacan, where painted hostesses beckoned to any males in sight. (Sustained protests against the wholesale drunkenness, prostitution and venereal disease fostered by these tawdry places led to their closure, at least temporarily, in 1965.) Beyond the ugly, darkened facades of new factories were rice fields, tall sugar cane, mile after mile of superb landscapes which, by day, are green and incredibly fertile, set against a backdrop of blue mountain ranges. At Malolos, on the return journey, Don Alano took me to the ornate Barosoian church overlooking the town plaza where the 1898 revolutionaries under General Aguinaldo drew up Asia's first democratic constitution. It was an event that left a lasting impression on Alano, for he remembered being carried on the shoulders of his father, a Malolos farmer, to watch the crowd of liberated peasants crowding about the church. It was a church in which, six years earlier, he had himself been christened.

The old man's devotion to this historic town was, I felt, symbolic. He was a man of resolutely democratic faith, and had spent much of his life in politics, first as secretary to Manuel (later President) Quezon when he represented the Philippines in the United States Congress, later becoming a congressman himself for five terms in pre-war Manila.* Now an almost legendary figure in Mindanao, where he has fashioned an

* See Chapter 18.

immense coconut plantation from once bandit-infested jungle, the old man has retained a reputation, rare in Filipino politics, for incorruptible idealism.

The immense, fertile plains of Pampanga and Tarlac, further north, represent the main rice bowl of Luzon. They, too, have been something of a battlefield. Here General Aguilando's armies made their last resistance against United States forces suppressing the short-lived revolution. Here a later generation of American troops, under General Douglas MacArthur, fought their way back to Manila to defeat the Japanese. It is one of history's ironies that the Filipino guerrillas, who made the reconquest easier, were the notorious Hukbalahaps, then a patriotic force. For ten years after independence, the Huks remained a threat to stable government, controlling large sectors of foothills and mountains under Communist leadership. They were silenced in 1957 by the late President Magsaysay, still a subject for hero worship, through his policy of granting land to the landless. Recently the Huks have become active again, terrorizing local farmers, diverting several battalions of the army and Philippine Constabulary, and engineering the multiple murders of local politicians.

The Huk movement is a kind of barometer. When the pointer drops to stormy, it means that the government is not doing enough for the peasants. The former President Macapagal met strong criticism in this direction.

I shall always remember one stop we made, with carburettor trouble, in Paniqui. We were in higher country here. In the fresh, misty atmosphere, I watched the deserted, pre-dawn landscape come to life. It was hardly of the twentieth century at all. Men and women passed in a shadowy, intermittent stream on their way to market. All you heard was the slap-slap of *bakyas* on the quiet road, the typical wooden sandals of the peasant's world; then the lighter clip-clip of ponies' hooves, as the small, high-wheeled *caratellas* went slowly by. They had no lamps, only the dim flames of candles held up by shawled women sitting motionless beside their menfolk at the reins. And the carabaos. The massive silhouettes of these slow-plodding beasts went on towards the rice *padis*, finding their own way, scarcely needing the lean farmers and their barefoot sons to guide them.

This was the timeless Asian scene.

The dawn world of an unchanging peasant life was different from the febrile sophistication of Angeles City, by then sixty miles behind us. Angeles, largely the creation of the USAAF's huge Clark airfield, is as far removed from the religious spirit of its Spanish founders as Los Angeles, California. It has become a nightmare of drinking dives, dance halls and accommodating hostesses, while air-conditioned supermarkets and lavish housing for servicemen's families have fostered racial antagonisms unknown elsewhere in these islands. In this unhappy little city racial strife, armed robbery, assault, murder and packed venereal clinics have produced a climate that imperils the kind of Filipino-American amity this all-important air base was designed to serve. Late in 1964, when a number of Filipino civilians were killed by base sentries, Angeles became the focal point for anti-American demonstrations which receive more detailed analysis later.

Driving up the steep mountain road towards Baguio, with its deep gorges, landslides and the rubble of old gold mines, I was reminded of the famous cable sent by the first United States governor, William H. Taft, who made the city his official summer capital at the turn of the century.

'Stood trip well, rode horseback twenty-five miles to 5,000 feet', read his exuberant cable to the Secretary of War, Elihu Root. 'Great province this, only 150 miles from Manila, with air as bracing as Adirondacks or Murray Bay stop only pines and grasslands stop temperature this hottest month in the Philippines in my cottage porch at three in the afternoon 68 stop fires are necessary night and morning.'

From the Department of War in Washington came this reply: 'Referring to telegram from you, how is horse?'

Taft weighed the best part of twenty stone.

Baguio has remained a fashionable escape for Manileños in the hottest months. The president has a residence here, the élite have their cool bungalows, United States officers a club. I do not find the place attractive, despite its upland beauty, the splendid pine trees and a prevalence of flowers usually associated with a temperate climate. It has the depressive, aimless air of an Anglo-Saxon health resort, with its indifferent guest houses, bus stations and 'scenic' walks. The only colour is to be found in the markets, where fresh vegetables, tropical fruits and marvellously ornate straw brooms stand alongside native wood carvings, masks and stark, head-hunting figurines fashioned by the Igorots.

These people are the most primitive in the Philippines. Until recently a stone-age people, who roamed the Mountain Province in nomadic fashion, treasuring the skulls of their enemies, they discovered steel and became equally ungenerous to those wanting to befriend them. They are a small people, virile, almost Indian in character, a people said to have inhabited these wild mountains for anything up to 25,000 years. They are the true aborigines. Somehow, despite the centuries of Catholic Spain, they remained a pagan people. Today the National Minorities Commission tries, not too successfully, to protect them from outside interference, a problem underlined by a *Manila Chronicle* report in 1964 which concluded: 'Land grabbing by the Christians is the common problem encountered in the establishment of settlement projects.'

Igorot is actually a general term that covers several district tribal groups: the Ifugaos, Kalinga and Aetas, each with a distinctive culture into which research is still being made. The ritual dances of the Ifugaos, with their barbaric and frenzied gong rhythms, have won world audiences in recent years through the celebrated Bayanihan Dance Company. In

14

their own setting they are even more electrifying. At the right time of year these dances can still be seen in outlying regions.

If only the Romans had found the Philippines, they must surely have added another wonder to their world. The rice terraces of this province have an air of the miraculous. To travel the spectacular, but appalling roads from Baguio to Bontoc and Banaue needs time as well as controlled nerves, but the sight of these terraces rising from steep green gorges is indeed marvellous. They are believed to have been made three thousand years ago.

They extend away mile after mile, following the contours of rough mountainsides, irrigated from a rushing, mud-coloured river, a classic example of rice culture that no one could attempt to match in such a rough-hewn region today.

To come here at the time of rice planting, or harvest time, is to recover a sense of the orphic mysteries. Through the mists of these high valleys comes the sound of nose flutes and chanting. Hour after hour, the lines of men naked except for g-strings wind up the mountain paths, chanting songs older than the Koran or the Mass, invoking their own gods, propitiating, distilling the magic necessary to ensure the seasonal crop.

The far northern regions of Luzon have an entirely different character, essentially Christian. Abra and the twin Ilocos provinces of Norte and Sur were not invaded by the Japanese, whose armies landed further south in Lingayan Gulf. Hence the destruction that left so little Spanish architecture elsewhere did not reach the centuries-old towns of the north. Vigan, the outstanding example, is almost a museum piece, one of the last replicas of colonial Spain. There are fine old churches, Spanish-style public buildings and plazas, walled gardens, monasteries, courtyards, cobblestones, affording a sense of peace seldom to be found these days in the Philippines. Perhaps the only comparable region is in Luzon's far south, where the classic volcanic cone of Mayon broods over the green and placid landscapes of Albay.

The people of Albay Province are said to be the most easy-living and tranquil of all Filipinos. In troubled, crime-haunted Manila men speak nostalgically of the fruitful landscapes around Legazpi, the gentleness and calm that, since the last devastating war, have deserted a people for whom the town fiesta, folk music and the craftsman's wheel and loom were once the only release they needed.

Not that the fiesta has by any means disappeared.

It is allied closely to to the calendar of saints. Every town, every region has its unique celebration day, much of it now far removed from orthodox religion. As in modern Mexico, the madonna, the plaster or wood-carved saint, is the focal point for ritual and procession. Some of these fiestas evoke impressive pageantry, as in the Ati-Atian festival of Kalibo, Panay Island, which commemorates an ancient peace pact between the Negritos and Malays; or the Salotsot fiesta in Ilocos Sur, where costumed kings and princes fight barbarous Moors beside the China Sea; or the

Morion Festival in the island province of Marinduque, during which masked penitents roam the streets in Holy Week costumed like Roman centurions, one of whom is beheaded in mime for declaring Christ's divinity. Here a writer friend of mine once observed the spectacular street procession on Good Friday. It re-enacted the Stations of the Cross. A large crowd applauded the splendidly-apparelled Roman soldiers as they passed. Somehow, the figure of Jesus, stumbling under his heavy cross, became lost as the crowd closed in behind the helmeted soldiers. He made his way to Calvary alone, unobserved.

'Why is it,' my friend asked, 'that we Filipinos seem always to applaud the wrong things?'

In the main, the Christian overtones of these fiestas become lost in secular joys: the brass bands, ferris wheels, chocolate wheels, fireworks, drink bars and juke boxes. And, above all, the noise. It is all so reminiscent of post-Spanish Mexico. The Indio, in both lands, reverts to more primitive joys.

Perhaps the most picturesque of all these fiestas takes place in Naga City, Bicol, during September. This is a week-long celebration, during which a novena is held in the cathedral to honour the patron of Camarines Sur. The French connotations of Our Lady of Peñafrancia are deceptive, for the original image of this Virgin was discovered near Salamanca, but by a rich, conscience-ridden Frenchman. Transplanted to the southern peninsula of Luzon, the Virgin draws thousands each year to the river banks where, holding lighted tapers, they watch an immense barge bear the black image of Our Lady downstream to the accompaniment of the usual bands, fireworks and secular stage shows.

Many miracles are attributed to this image, which was carved by native craftsmen to the order of a Spanish priest in 1710. To keep Our Lady's complexion as close as possible to the original, the records state: 'dog's blood was used'. A town dog was butchered, bled and thrown into the Naga River.

Shortly afterwards, the dog returned to its master. Alive.

This was witnessed by Dominican friars, including the Bishop of Nueva Caceres. News of the miracle spread throughout the land. Soon there were countless pilgrims, especially the sick, travelling to Naga for Divine Aid. This is why Our Lady of Peñafrancia makes her annual procession a fluvial one. The dog is not remembered.

The most notable relic of Spanish times is the magnificent baroque San Ildefonso church in Tanay, Rizal, some fifty miles east of Manila. I was unable to see it, for my friends refused to drive along that highway, owing to the existence of bandits who made even day-time motoring a hazard. Experts describe it as the finest structure of its kind in the Philippines, with massive stone walls, a belltower four stories high, three main altars which have luxuriantly carved *retablos* that glitter like gold embroidery. It was built in 1784. The masterpiece of this church is the set of hand-carved Stations of the Cross, created by 'the maestro of

Tanay'. The artist was an apparently unskilled Filipino, a primitive. No one even knows his name. Describing the panels as 'the greatest art work in the country', Quijano de Manila writes: 'The figures have a Malay look, a Malay squatness, and several homely details may be clues; in the very first station, the servant boy of Pilate holds up what is unmistakably a Philippine *palayok* and a soldier brandishes a *gulok* . . . As one passes from one station to another, one begins to feel that the figures are moving, so great is the vitality of their arrested gestures, so vivid the emotion expressed in their faces.'[1]

It is reminiscent of so many churches I have seen in southern Mexico, where the artists have likewise been primitives despised by the Conquistadores.

In Tanay, too, there have been miracles. When Franciscans pacified the town in 1620, an attacking party of Aetas set the new chapel on fire with flaming arrows. The townsfolk were only able to save their image of the Immaculate Conception which, in some mysterious fashion, had been paraded by them as a pagan idol before the first Christians arrived. Perhaps it had been plundered, seized in some earlier battle. At all events, it helped to extinguish the flaming chapel. Twenty years later the town was again attacked, this time by Chinese rebels driven out of Manila. The whole town went up in flames, its people retreating to the mountains. When Chinese soldiers tried to destroy the image, two were miraculously transfixed by their own spears. A third fled in terror and hanged himself at a spot still revered as Binitinan.

Wherever you travel in the Philippines you come, sooner or later, to the recounting of such miracles. So far we have not reached beyond Luzon.

1. *Philippines Free Press*, 21 April 1962, Manila.

CHAPTER 3

Walled Cities

*Manila . . . has twelve thousand five
hundred feet of wall, seven foot thick,
and on the land side there are five
terraced bastions and two gates to go
out into the country. . . . Outside the
wall it has the suburbs of Tondo and
Minondo, and in front the Parian which
is the quarter of Chinese merchants . . .*
DON DIEGO DE PRADO, 1607

INTRAMUROS, the walled city celebrated by voyagers since the sixteenth century, is no more. Only a ruin now, it is a mile square ghost town, right in the heart of Manila. Traffic seldom passes through it, preferring the broad, newer boulevards that sweep past the City Hall, Congress or the Luneta. Few pedestrians walk its broken footpaths either, unless they have business with the one or two government offices there, the small stores, workshops or the two remaining churches in what used to be a resplendent citadel of religious faith.

The marvellously deep tones of Manila Cathedral's bells still toll across the empty allotments and shattered squares. San Augustin church, restored now, re-creates the mellow quietude it gathered over the centuries. Its broad, paved cloisters, the peaceful inner garden, the great vaulted nave have held within their silences much of the drama and steel-helmeted crusading of the New World the Spanish conquered centuries ago, a grim and sometimes spiritually rewarding pageant still depicted in huge, dark canvases on the cloister walls. The other churches have vanished in the smoke of shells and bombs.

So have the old crooked streets, the cobblestones, the mansions of the quality with their tiled roofs and frescoed balconies, the stables, wheelwrights' shops, the pavement cafés with striped awnings and a view of open squares.

Those seven-foot thick walls are here and there in evidence still, blackened with age, overgrown with lichen, breached by bomb blasts, pitted with shrapnel. There are gaunt shells of fine buildings that once housed monks and friars, the crumbling structures of schools and houses now impossible to identify. Many streets and squares are rubble only, or bare allotments where weeds and cogon grass rankly grow. Yet all this was once a stout fortress of a city behind whose embrasured walls, prickling with cannon, Spain withstood the attacks of the sixteenth century Chinese pirate Koxinga, repeated raiding by the Dutch fleet between 1600 and 1617, further attacks by the British fleet under Admiral Cornish one and a half centuries later, and innumerable revolts by Filipinos armed with little more than knives and bows. It took the war against Japan to topple what had by then become a museum piece, a picturesque backdrop for the last days of American colonial rule.

Yet it was not the Japanese who destroyed it.

Intramuros and its Romanesque churches were shattered by the pattern bombing of returning United States forces. Retreating Nipponese troops merely completed the destruction, firing churches, blowing up ammunition dumps, scorching the already scarred earth. What remains of the walled city is a symbol of that violent epoch. It separates two ages. What has come since is still violence. Despair and disillusion have followed the colonial quiet.

No one has yet attempted to rebuild Intramuros. Not even twenty years later. For more than a decade after the war, after independence, that square mile of rubble and roofless walls was crowded with squatters, thousands and thousands of them: the city's poor, derelict families, the jobless. Only in recent years has the City Hall cleared the region of its illegal occupants, finding them new settlements miles out of town. In 1964 Mayor Antonio Villegas conceived a grand project for this inner city, wanting to transform it into a cultural centre, containing an opera house, theatre, galleries and a new home for the National Library. Cynical Manileños asked where the finance was to come from. It is not so much a case, at least in Manila, as to where it comes from, but where it goes, once it has been granted. Governments are notoriously short of funds, and what is provided has the habit of disappearing.

Perhaps Manila, since the last war, has become as cynical as Warsaw or Paris. It was, as General Eisenhower pointed out, the worst damaged capital city in World War Two apart from Warsaw. Eighty per cent of the entire city was destroyed. Manila is really only beginning to recover now. Its social conscience was almost as shattered as its physical environment.

Today other walled cities have arisen in and around the capital: Forbes Park, Bel Air, Philam Village. These have arisen for reasons not too different from those actuating the early Spaniards four centuries ago: to keep the barbarian out.

Forbes Park is a showplace these days, on the tourist route. A few years ago it was an undeveloped estate, owned by the Zobel family. Now its maze of quiet, tree-lined avenues is lined with some of the most costly and expansive private homes in Asia. Many have their own high walls, or tall hedgerows, or shady trees behind which the owners of immense mansions modestly screen themselves. The electoral roll in these parts reads like a *Who's Who* of the Philippines. There is more than one street that goes by the name of millionaire's row. One mansion has more than fifty servants in livery, another has a spiral of marble steps fronting its long drive-way, sunken interior gardens, with fountains and ornamental pools. It is hard to gain admittance to a residential quarter that, with poetic justice carries the name of the most aristocratic of American colonial governors-general; for the 1909 administration formed by William Cameron Forbes has become known to history as the 'Polo Cabinet'. There is still a Polo Club in Manila, but equally prestigious is the Manila Golf Club, whose park-like expanses provide Forbes Park with its defences against an encroaching city. To play golf here requires an entrance fee alone of P10,000.

Nor is even temporary admittance to Forbes Park an easy matter. Its approaches are guarded by security posts, with barriers to be raised each time a limousine comes home. It is like passing the police and customs posts that divide one European country from another. Each visitor must be checked in and out, every taxi or delivery truck. Uniformed security guards carry rifles and revolvers.

The same precautions apply in other well-to-do suburbs. They also have their armed guards, their swinging barriers and stone walls, topped with barbed wire and jagged glass.

There is no questioning their necessity. Not in post-war Manila. Its people breathe a climate of fear.

This reached us even in our high-walled garden off Highway 54, which links Manila with Quezon City, the political capital-to-be. It was an immense garden, a compound really, for it contained a large, thriving private school as well as our solitary bungalow at the far end. On one side, beyond a stormwater channel, was a twenty-foot wall protecting the backyards of Philam Village, a planned suburb of vaguely Spanish-style villas for approved middle class commuters to Manila's business sector. The other side was waste land, guarded by a high barbed-wire fence, apparently awaiting one of those ambitious building schemes that Filipinos plan eternally without ever disturbing the waist-high cogon grass. *Ningas cogon* is a notable Tagalog phrase. It means, literally, grass fire. But the cogon grass flares and burns out quickly; Filipino enthusiasms soon wane. The drive in from this highway had double iron gates, always padlocked at nightfall, with the inevitable security guards patrolling the grounds until dawn. Allegedly so. It was always a hard job locating one of them when we drove home late at night. My wife and I joked about it; clearly these guards must have had girl friends hidden away in the school restrooms somewhere.

By day it was a pleasant place to live, for the uproar of traffic along the highway hardly reached us here. It was open to the sun, and flowering trees were everywhere: hibiscus, poinciana, poinsettia, pink as well as cream frangipani, the large, white-petalled sampanguita and the sweet-scented ilang-ilang, a green flower with an exquisite perfume I have never known elsewhere. In the Wet Season everything sprouted, blossomed and spread in fantastic fashion, fungus and weeds as well as flowers. And almost daily massive thunderclouds glowered above the distant Sierra Madre, assaulting the quiet garden with lightning bolts and torrential rain.

Our bungalow, almost hidden from the school playgrounds by a croton hedge, was my one refuge from the most restless, disorientated city in which I have ever lived. Besides, there was life enough here. Close to six hundred boys and girls came daily to JASMS, most of them arriving in chauffeur-driven cars. I found it odd, in the context of Manila's prevailing poverty, to see even tiny children coming like this to kindergarten, often sitting alone on the back seat of a large limousine. But the Jose Abad Santos Memorial School is no ordinary establishment. It is unique in the Philippines, the only experimental school in an education system otherwise dominated by Catholicism. Coeducational, catering for the wealthier middle class, it relies less on normal disciplines than on free expression and a critical outlook, which includes criticism of teachers as well. I discussed its principles frequently with the American-born headmistress, who was a dedicated woman with an understanding of modern educational methods in other countries. It seemed to me, as an outsider, to work neither worse nor better than normal schools. They were mostly bright young people to begin with, accustomed to no more discipline at home, which in itself was a new development in the Philippines, whose tradition has always been a rigid one. My own experience — I took a number of classes in English literature — was inconclusive, for this new generation of telewatchers appeared to have little interest beyond Westerns, Tagalog melodramas and comic books. My literary seeds, I felt, fell on somewhat barren ground. What I did discover was an almost complete lack of any critical impulses. Perhaps it would take generations of such schools to alter this, given the present lack of outside stimulus. Or perhaps the attitude of drift and play merely reflected parental background, for which many revealing case histories were forthcoming.

The middle-class Filipino is of comparatively recent emergence. Hitherto there had only been landowners and a peasantry, both variably influenced by paternal governments, which discouraged initiative and social demands. The post-war drive for industrialization, frustrated though it is still, has created a new high-income group whose ambitions are first realized in status-seeking, cocktail lounges, servants, cars. Their Cadillacs are not gold-plated, but they tend to come in two-tone models.

It was an outlook that contradicted this idealistic school.

An adjunct of the intelligently-run Philippine Women's University, whose founder Dr Francesca Benitez had lent us the bungalow while my wife's broken ankle mended, JASMS was built as a memorial to the pre-war Chief Justice whom President Quezon had left to represent the country, just captured by the Japanese, while he went with General MacArthur to form a government-in-exile. A man of ideals and stubborn pride, Santos refused — unlike many of his fellows — to collaborate with the conquerors. While trying to organize resistance, he was arrested in the Visayas, and executed by a firing squad. A stark painting in the teachers' common room commemorates the outrage.

Jose Abad Santos is a man in the tradition of Filipino patriots of an earlier age, Rizal and others. But his is the more poignant image today, because the wreckage of the occupation period, as well as the bitter memories of its survivors, remains part of everyday experience. The scars have burnt in very deep indeed.

Privilege of all kinds has become suspect in today's Manila. The seeds of cynicism began with the collaborators, increased with the post-war black market, the massive inflation, and the gangsterism, gained further strength with the political opportunism of modern times, the falling living standards and the struggle for economic status known, in true Filipino fashion, as 'the rice ladder'. Confronted with a soaring birth rate, the Philippines sits astride a tiger instead of its carabao.

It is not an unique situation in modern Asia. But the climate is different here; the Filipino temperament is different, too. There is an explosive quality to this humid, overcrowded city. An almost desperate unease.

I sensed it most fully on one particular week-end. On the Saturday there had been an elegant reception in Forbes Park: superb food, white-coated waiters serving drinks, traditional Filipino music, a moonlit garden with fountains cooling the hot night. There were handsome, sleek-skinned women in finely embroidered *ternos* and *Maria Claras*, their menfolk wearing their formal *barong tagalogs*, those beautifully-made, embroidered shirts of pineapple fibre. There are few places in the world where one can live in such style. The next morning I went to Tondo.

There are few places in the world like Tondo, either.

I thought I had seen slums before. I was totally wrong. It was a region I would not have dared to enter alone. Nor would I have been allowed to. A Filipino friend drove me to this dockside quarter. He had arranged for a local city councillor to meet us, a man whose ward leaders would ensure safe passage. My instructions were simple. 'Don't look as if you're staring. Don't show fear. Don't stop long anywhere. Keep on the move.' It was advice I hardly needed. I have been through some of Panama City's worst areas, down the back lanes of Hong Kong and Macao, felt the resentment of unemployed Jamaicans in depressed Kingston, but Tondo's atmosphere has no comparison.

In one area a half-mile of single railway track ran down towards the docks. Squatters, unable to find vacant land or houses, if they could have afforded to, had built flimsy plywood or caseboard shanties each side of the line. They had left just enough room for goods wagons to pass without scraping the walls. The racket when trains passed must have been unendurable. While the track was clear, an endless stream of people walked along the sleepers, the only road they had. When we turned into one especially notorious area, my friend advised me to keep the car windows closed.

'If they don't like your face, they'll chuck anything. Steel darts, too, sometimes.'

We had at that moment come to a dead end, the narrow street blocked by railway tracks. About a dozen jeepneys were lined up there, their drivers in sweat shirts and jeans lounging outside a barber's shop. A huge, negroid figure strolled among them. They watched us with sullen curiosity. A new model car in this region stuck out like a spaceship among headhunters. My friend told me not to look. It was stifling with the windows closed. Even then the stench of the *esteros* came in. He backed, turned, drove on to wider streets.

In downtown Manila I have always found jeepney drivers to be cheerful, friendly men. I cannot imagine how the chaotic transport system would survive without these ingenious vehicles. It was a touch of Filipino genius to transform, during the early post-war years, the abandoned US army jeeps and weapon carriers into minature buses. The modern jeepney is a gay affair, painted in garish colours, decorated with bright curtains, nickel and chrome accessories, images of the Virgin or patron saints, and fanciful names ranging from Tagalog or biblical titles to girl friends. They speed like racing cars through Manila's traffic, often three or four abreast, zig-zag perilously, pick up and drop passengers where they please. They have also become a profitable source of revenue for traffic police and Tondo gangsters, both of whom practice extortion on their drivers. My friend told me the Negro we had seen was the chief standover man in Tondo.

Tondo has tougher scenes than that. Police are reluctant to patrol its back streets and alleys, and they never do so alone. Tondo has no liking for policemen, either. Murder is an almost daily occurrence here, and it is immaterial whether the victim wears a uniform or not. The list of organized gangs is limitless and picturesque: Tres Cantos, Apaches, Cobras, the Chain Gang, Deadly Gang, Suicide Gang and, of more recent origin, the mutually hostile OXO and Sigue-Sigue gangs, both formed by convicted homicides in Muntinlupa jail where in July 1965 sixteen of their members were killed in a gang battle behind bars.

Tondo is Dante's Inferno, and its hot breath menaces the Philippines.

No one even knows how many people live here. Census takers are no more welcome than charity workers or the cops. There are said to be 30,000 squatters alone, that is, families squatting on any square yard or two they can find, running up their own board shacks and hovels, regardless of sanitation, health measures, rates. All told, there must be half-a-million people within less than a square mile of drained marshland, where virtually the only drainage is the esteros.

In early Spanish days these esteros were clear waters linking the Pasig river mouth with Manila Bay. Now they are open sewers, putrid, curdled with mud and waste and excrement, almost built over by squatters' shacks and hovels. There are few public latrines; and hardly any private ones at all, except portable buckets. The streets and lanes are Tondo's latrines, and one constantly passes squatting figures in the muddy roadways, adults as well as children. When it rains (and does it rain in the Wet Season!) dusty streets are churned to mud. There is no drainage, so that floods and boggy pools make walking an ordeal, and the stamped earth floor of dwellings are frequently awash. Large numbers of these have no running water, no lighting beyond oil lamps or candles. Yet I saw there neat, well-dressed girls in high-heeled shoes, smartly attired men among the flashy toughs, and once a small procession of women, like models at a mannequin parade, picking their way through slush and garbage to a wedding party. There are beauty salons even in Tondo.

In Barrio Magsaysay, its grimmest region, we went down one lane so flooded it was possible to walk only on a series of planks raised two feet above the mud. The gift of one of the ward politicians who accompanied us, these planks provided the only footpath enabling people to enter and leave their homes. A system of water pipes ran through the barrio, though public taps set at infrequent intervals meant carrying heavy buckets a considerable distance in a delicate tightrope walk. Several times I had to balance above the stinking mud below, while men, children, elderly women brushed past with water carriers on their heads. They seemed unaware of my existence.

Barrio Magsaysay alone has 15,000 people squatting on a patch of dried-out swamp, whose only entrance is a ricketty wooden bridge. The brawls, drunkenness, pandering, the pot-bellied children with twisted limbs and running sores, the arrogant young toughs and sullen, sallow adults, all of whom I made a show of not observing, produced a mood of despair that persisted for days after. How could humans inhabit such a climate and remain human? No wonder there were so many concealed guns, knives, bolos, darts, so desperate a rate of delinquency and violent crime. What could be done? What could anyone do?

And yet even here I met friendly, warm people.

We passed one windowless shack whose owner insisted that our party come in. He had some friends there drinking beer. The Malay countenance is usually more sombre than the spirit behind it. Perhaps my pale complexion was not attractive either. I hated to accept that beer, calculating its cost on a basic wage of P4 daily, if any of them worked at all. The single room had no furnishings beyond a table and two chairs, a charcoal stove at which the mother of uncounted children was grilling fish, and some shapeless bundles I presumed were bedding. In another lane I was invited to view a backyard factory, where the family of an ageing unemployed labourer was ingeniously making doormats from discarded motor tyres. I had great difficulty in refusing the gift of one of these mats, which represented sufficient rice to feed his dependents for a week.

When the well-to-do Filipino boasts, as he does frequently, of his traditional hospitality, I remember always the generous gestures of those desperately needy men of Tondo.

There are orchids as well as leeches and snakes in any jungle. But the jungle of Tondo breeds other evils besides crime. Under such sanitary conditions how could Manila ever free itself from contagious disease? Fifty per cent of the city's inhabitants are said to suffer from tuberculosis, a large proportion unquestionably in Tondo. Each year, during the Wet Season, a fresh outbreak of El Tor occurs. A particularly virulent form of cholera, it kills thousands throughout the islands every year. Barrio Magsaysay especially is a plague spot of flies, rotting foodstuffs, strewn garbage, human ordure. The four hundred tons of waste food and refuse collected daily from Manila's streets are dumped on nearby Balut Island, a maggot's paradise where children play and brawl, fishermen beach their boats and furtive lovers court.

Health services are rudimentary in other regions besides Tondo, while city hospitals cannot cope with their eternal flood of patients. Statistics published in 1964 make alarming reading. Throughout the Philippines, more than 100,000 die of controllable diseases annually; one child in ten dies before coming of age. In Manila alone the average death roll from disease is 9,000, 40 per cent of whom have not received treatment at all. Three thousand of these deaths are due to gastro-enteric and respiratory diseases. The main public hospital has to refuse from 1,000 to 2,000 sick people each month, while an estimated 150,000 are unable to secure hospital treatment annually.

Yet slum reclamation remains beyond the borders of the possible.

Political scientists usually assume that progress is determined by wealth and positions of power; from areas such as Forbes Park, not Tondo. In the Philippines the subterranean world of poverty has its decisive influences, too. No politician has yet dared to evict squatters from the railroad tracks, esteros and shoreline of Tondo. The squatter is the captive vote, and a massive one. He does not want to shift; he has grown incomprehensibly attached to his sordid environment, his suffering neighbours and even his climate of subdued terror. The unknown might be worse. That is how matters have turned out for the squatters removed from Intramuros, now resettled in a distant, semi-rural area miles from the city, with expensive bus fares to pay if any work is offering.

Barrio Magsaysay today gravely affects the development of Manila, indeed the whole national economy. These temporary shacks and lanes occupy an area long ago marked down for the extension of city docks, which are urgently needed to cope with an increasing export trade. City Hall plans also show a grand scenic road running through it, an extension of Roxas Boulevard. Drivers attempting to follow it would soon bog down in slums, mangroves and mud. It would cost any councillor his lucrative seat in the City Hall to implement this plan.

Soon after visiting Tondo, I went to a late night party on the other side of town. There must have been more than a hundred guests, a hired Filipino band, decorated tables under Chinese lanterns in the garden, formal dress, the usual crowd of waiters. The hostess was wearing an elaborate Maria Clara, designed by the celebrated **Pitoy Moreno**. She said it had cost her P2,000. At the peak of this revelry, I noticed a group of the local poor watching from the street, leaning over the garden wall. They appeared to be chatting with our security guards.

To one of the women at our table my wife said, 'How can you bear to have them watching us? I feel too ashamed to eat all this food.'

'Oh, they enjoy it,' was the answer. 'I really think they like to see how we live.'

Has no one heard of Marie Antoinette?

CHAPTER 4

Before the Europeans

> *That sea where float the islands like a*
> *set of emeralds on a paten of bright glass,*
> *that sea was everywhere traversed by junks,*
> *paraus, barangays, vintas, vessels swift as*
> *shuttles, so large that they could maintain*
> *a hundred rowers on a side; that sea bore*
> *everywhere commerce, industry, agriculture,*
> *by the force of the oars moved to the sound*
> *of warlike songs of the genealogies and*
> *achievements of the Philippine divinities . . .*
>
> JOSE RIZAL

UNTIL RECENT years it has not been fashionable to look far into the Filipino's past. The heritage of Spain lay too heavily upon him. For three and a half centuries bishop and friar had urged him to forget his pagan past, to atone for it by looking towards Madrid and Rome, to be the humble peon of a landed aristocracy, whether the lords of the manor were pure-blood grandee, creole or religious corporation.

By the seventeenth century the islanders began to lose their identity, along with their pride and craftsmanship. There grew a sense of guilt in thinking of themselves as Malay. The past was crude and barbarous. Forget the old Adam: he was a foolish, immoral creature. As for the Americans who came at the end of the nineteenth century, these were a pragmatic people, urging their reluctant subjects to learn English, to exterminate the anopheles mosquito, dig latrines and study democratic forms. There was no time for romantic studies of the past. As a result Philippine history, until lately, has been written largely in European or North American terms. It was even accepted that the islands were dis-covered by Don Miguel Lopez de Legazpi in 1521. Few statements are more offensive to the history-conscious Filipino, some of whose ancestors have been here for the best part of a hundred generations.

All this is now changing.

A resurgent nationalism has turned the historian towards a deeper penetration of his past, an inquiry that has hardly been attempted since Rizal. The new approach has been pioneered by the University of the Philippines, which is the objective, non-partisan and dynamic force in learning today. Now its Institute of Asian Studies is attempting a larger task, not only carrying out research into pre-hispanic times, but develop-ing an awareness of other Asian cultures, too. O. D. Corpuz, discussing the lack of cross-fertilization among Asian countries generally, has pointed out that 'during the period of dependency, the web of pervasive influence woven by the dominant power over and around the subject country not only tied them together in a tight and intimate relationship, but also cut off the latter from any significant associations or contacts with other countries'.[1]

The Institute of Asian Studies was founded in 1955, when the university won the sympathy of that most nationalist-minded president, the late Ramon Magsaysay. Despite the grant he secured from Congress, little initial progress was made. 'For a while no one really knew what to do with the unit,' one of its publications confessed. 'During the post-World War Two years the Philippines was unconscious of its Asian origins; no questions had been raised about commitment and identity. . . . To be blunt, scholarship about Asia was considered unnecessary, even freakish. . . . Even today it is not an exaggeration to say that Asian names and facts are better known to western than to ours.'

Ironically, one of the most influential figures in the new search for Filipino values is an American. An archeologist attached to the National Museum, Dr Robert E. Fox has spent years in remote regions, uncovering important evidence on pre-Spanish civilization. He challenged those who claimed that the art of pottery was unknown among the Malays, and duly dug up examples in Palawan. He has found many early traces of Chinese settlement, and has lately urged historians to look at their past in terms that do not attribute everything to foreign influences. He wrote, 'Despite dramatic changes which have occurred in the Filipino's way of life under the impact of Spanish and American influences [inappropriately described, I believe, as "cultural conquest"], perhaps all of the basic influences have been adapted to a social and cultural base which is uniquely Filipino — a base which developed centuries before Magellan. . . . The theory that the present character of Filipino culture and society has been due to waves of external influences is vastly overdrawn, leading students to feel that there is no Filipino culture *per se*.'[2]

Dr Fox insisted that much of what the foreigner had brought in was long ago adapted and reshaped to native tradition. The true Filipino heritage was based on ancient Malay customs. It was centred in the family, and moulded by the life of the soil and the sea.

Peasants and fishermen, after all, have hardly changed their methods for many centuries. The boats they use are of Malay origin, very close to Indonesian craft: the hand-adzed *bancas* with double outrigger canoes; heavy *kumpits* for longer voyages, and now the smuggler's friend; the flying *vintas* of Zamboanga and the Sulu archipelago, with their Arab-type curved sails. The peasant still uses his wooden plough, drawn by carabao; his womenfolk still scatter seed by hand, plant rice to the same ancient songs and rhythms, winnow it in curved wicker trays; they grind corn with stone pestles and stout wooden batons. The peasant is still

1. *Manila Times Annual*, 1958.
2. *Comment* No. 5, University of the Philippines, Manila, 1961.

largely bound to his small patch of soil, much as the feudal serfs of Europe were; and serfdom here predates the coming of Spain. Under the ancient *datus*, whose hereditary rule was over tribal groupings rather than defined areas, were three classes. These were the *maharlika*, nobles; the *timawa*, freemen or serfs, and *alipin*, slaves, most of them the result of raids on neighbouring territories. The *maharlika*, unlike the *timawa*, paid no tribute, but had to fight for the *datu*, who had absolute power. The freemen and serfs might own their own houses, though they had to give their superiors half the yield of the land they tilled. The Spanish married among the upper ranks, creating a new caste known as *caciques*. Within a few generations these were nearly all *mestizos*, no longer pure Malay. Otherwise they left the system largely unchanged. The *datus* they appointed as *cabeza de barangay* — the barrio captains of today. What they did do was to claim all the land for the crown, then set their own *encomienda* system on top of the serf structure. These were the large estates — the modern haciendas — which they gave as grants to the imported aristocracy of military officers, grandees and religious corporations. As Rizal expressed it, 'Catholicism not only did not liberate the poor class from the tyranny of the aggressive, but with its advent increased the number of tyrants'.

The descendants of these *caciques* and *encomienderos* are still men of power in the modern Philippines.

There are no records of pre-hispanic times. Spanish priests burnt everything they found. Every trace of Malay writing was destroyed, and is unknown today. In southern Luzon one priest alone burnt three hundred scrolls. Elsewhere the natives themselves were persuaded to set fire to carvings and other 'pagan idols'; the devil's works. Yet there had been a developed civilization, despite those remorseless men of God. Some of the early voyagers wrote of it in some detail, notably Morga, who published his *Sucesos de las Islas Filipinas* in Mexico. A manuscript copy, forgotten since 1609, was found by Rizal in the British Museum 280 years later. His annotated edition was not welcomed by colonial Spain, for he drew many unfavourable inferences. 'Wealth abounded in these islands,' he wrote.[3] 'All the histories of those first years abound in long accounts about the industry and agriculture of the natives; mines, gold washings, looms, farms, barter, naval construction, weaving of silk and cotton, distilleries, manufactures of arms, pearl fisheries, the civit industry, the horn and hide industry. . . . "The natives," says Morga in Chapter VII, speaking of the occupations of the Chinese, "are very far from exercising those trades and have forgotten much about farming, raising poultry, stock and cotton, and weaving cloth as they used to in their paganism and for a long time after the country was conquered." '

The true Filipino, the Malay, is believed to have reached the archipelago from the south, through Borneo, spreading gradually to Luzon, island-hopping in large canoes. His arrival was probably during the third or

3. Jose Rizal, *The Indolence of the Filipino*, op. cit.

second centuries B.C. But other, more primitive people were already in possession. These were the Negritos, a small, wiry, almost pigmy people, who were then driven into more remote regions, especially the Luzon mountains where they are found living under much the same conditions today. The theory is that these pigmy people migrated at a time when there was a continuous land bridge from the Asian mainland, which would set their coming at some 25,000 to 30,000 years ago. Until well into the twentieth century, they remained a stone age people, animists and headhunters. They resisted all efforts to tame and convert them. The rice terraces of the Ifugao seem to be the result of another migration, probably from South China or Indo-China, where cultivation of this kind was carried out. Ethnologists believe that the Ifugaos arrived somewhere between 1,500 and 1,000 B.C. It was an incredible feat of engineering three thousand years ago, for the raising and levelling of those platform-like terraces must have been carried out by hand labour alone.

But the earliest men inhabiting the Philippines were the long-vanished Australoids. These are a mystery people. One might almost say a conjectural people, except that stone implements have recently been discovered that prove their occupation. These are identical with those found alongside Java man, whose age has been estimated at 250,000 years.

Dramatic evidence, much of it still sketchy, is beginning to appear of other civilizations and empires that have flowed and ebbed across this sea-locked island chain. Manila audiences were reminded a few years ago by an Indian scholar that their true heritage has been anything but European. During a lecture on the ancient lineage of Chinese and Indian thought, Mrs Tara Ali Baig, wife of the then Indian minister, said, 'At a time when the Chinese civilization had blossomed into the doctrines of Confucius and Tao, Buddha's teachings were reaching their greatest glory under the Emperor Ashoka in the year 274 B.C., spreading their message of temperance, peace and love throughout the countries of Ceylon, Burma, India, Malaya and the Philippines to Japan and China.'

Perhaps, in 1962, the Philippines needed this unfamiliar emphasis on temperance, peace and love.

No trace of those early Buddhist influences can be found today, except those brought by more recent Chinese immigration. Yet ancient chronicles in China record a thriving commerce with the Philippines for a thousand years before the Christian era. There is also reference to the first Philippine mission reaching China with tribute in A.D. 1372. Recent Filipino scholars have also discovered that the first resident Chinese traders arrived at the start of the fourteenth century. They came into the southern islands with Islamic missionaries. It appears an odd combination: Chinese Muslims. Yet it is now believed that the introduction of Mohammedanism did not come from Arabia direct, as was hitherto supposed, but by way of China. Several temples lately discovered on Jolo reveal that Muslim Chinese became influential there, even rising to the rank of *datu*.

The Chinese have far deeper roots in the Philippines than today's nationalists will admit. They have long been an integral part of society, even of the Filipino's individual inheritance. In 1840, for instance, when the total population was only three million, official Spanish records registered 200,000 resident Chinese and Chinese mestizos. It is difficult then to understand the prevailing anti-Chinese sentiment of the present day. Yet, over the centuries, it has become almost as ingrained as anti-Semitism in certain European countries. The reasons are not dissimilar. They stem from Chinese exclusiveness, from their single-minded devotion to money and a virtual monopoly of the retail trade. The Malay generally lacks the quick, purposeful mind of the Chinese; he resents those who grasp at every advantage while he prefers to relax and play. It is a conflict that has its counterpart in both Indonesia and Malaysia, culminating in the split between Kuala Lumpur and Singapore in 1965. In Philippine politics this is frequently exploited today to divert attention from graft and financial exploitation by interests that are decidedly non-Chinese. Yet Filipinos cannot afford this xenophobia, for the Chinese strain has become an integral part of their own bloodstream. There is a greater proportion of Chinese in the Filipino than any other nationalist, including the Spanish. His typical cast of features alone makes this apparent.

Even the nationally revered Jose Rizal — the 'Great Malayan', as Carlos Quirino called him — was himself a Chinese mestizo. His paternal great-grandfather had been a Chinchow merchant who settled in Manila.

The vandalism of those early Spaniards, who burnt all Malay documents, has denied us the chance of ever knowing the great dramas that once took place here. Who today knows anything of the Sailendra Empire, also called the Sri Vijaya, that brought Hinduism to Malaya, Borneo, the Celebes, Cambodia and Formosa, making the Philippines a dependency from approximately the year 200 until 1325? Following this, for another century, came the Madjapahit Empire, based on Java, replacing Hindu teachings with Islam. Then came Chinese expansion, with the Ming Emperor Yung Lo appointing his own governor of Luzon during the fifteenth century, and forcing the people to pay tribute. Later in the same century Japanese traders arrived, though the major influence by then was Mohammedanism, creeping over this still inchoate group of islands from the south. This could well have become part of the Islamic world.

The strong influence of Islam has never been given sufficient weight in Philippine history. The assumption that this was purely Spanish territory from 1565 to 1898 overlooks one vital factor: that Mindanao and the Sulu Archipelago largely remained Muslim, hostile to Catholic Spain. It was an ancient struggle, unexpectedly revived in the New World. For centuries in Europe Spaniards had fought Moors, or Moros, as they termed them. They crossed the Pacific and found themselves in conflict with Muslims again. A new crusade. And so they called these Muslims of the southern islands Moros. It is a term these Filipino followers of Islam much resent today. Moro has connotations of contempt, second-class citizens, the lower orders despised by Christendom. Travellers in the southern regions are advised to avoid the term. Call them Muslims, yes.

But why not Filipinos?

To my mind, theirs is by far the most colourful region. It bears little relation to the westernized north, even though migration from Luzon and the Visayas has been considerable in recent times. Here you find a life that is almost undiluted Malay, the survival of ancient custom, costume and communal allegiances that have vanished long ago elsewhere. This, you feel, is truly Asia.

It is possible here to visualize the kind of world Magellan and Legazpi discovered all those centuries ago: somewhat debased now, deeper in poverty, robbed of its tribal unities, the disciplines imposed by imperious, warlike rulers of the past. But its people are still largely fishermen, sea traders, smugglers verging on piracy. They still live in their traditional villages whose crowded huts of thatch or board are built upon piles over water. They still sail the swift, graceful *vintas* of antiquity, still wear sarongs made of *batik* (smuggled these days from Indonesia), tight embroidered jackets and rich-hued, turban-like material wound about their heads. The women, too, wear these jackets, and loose, semi-transparent trousers you associate with Muslim ceremonies. By no means all of them subscribe to Islam. There are pagan groups and tribes as well, such as the Yakkans of Basilan Island, or the sea-gypsies they call Badjaos. The vital factor, however, is that all these scattered people have remained the Malays that other Filipinos might have been.

Their long antipathy to the north has created a bond of sympathy with Indonesia, as the Soekarno regime became well aware. There are strong racial as well as cultural ties, as they share from remote times a common history. On two occasions this vast wheel of islands flung out west and north from Singapore to Taiwan has been ruled by a single empire. The restoration of that forgotten Madjapahit Empire was a secret dream that Soekarno began to conjure with soon after Indonesians gained their independence. It underlies much of the friction among the Muslims of Mindanao and Sulu at the present time.

After all, it was the Indonesian islands that first nurtured the Mohammedan faith.

There exist various accounts, mostly legendary, as to who brought it to the Sulu islands and the Cotabato (Maguindanaw) region of Mindanao. One tradition claims that it was first preached by a certain Makdum, who arrived with several Chinese in Sulu aboard an 'iron tub'. These days a number of small islands each claim to possess Makdum's grave. But, after all, Makdum is simply Arabic for 'master', so that it seems likely that several masters arrived independently. Another tradition is that seven brothers made an evangelizing voyage, coming originally from Arabia, though modern authorities tend to the belief that these were not brothers in a literal sense, but a series of Islamic leaders who converted various regions at different times. More picturesque is the mysterious figure of Tuan Masha'ika who, according to the genealogy of Sulu sultans, was the son of Jamiyun Kulisa and Indira Suga, and had arrived in Sulu with Alexander the Great. But the names of his mother and father were mythological ones. They were male and female gods, related to thunderbolts and the sun. Equally mythical, no doubt, was the assertion in this same genealogy, that Masha'ika issued out of a stalk of bamboo and was hailed by his people as a prophet.

The most persuasive account was drawn by Najeeb M. Saleeby from the genealogy then in the possession of Hadji Butu Abdul Bagi, prime minister to the Sultan of Sulu at the beginning of this century. This declared that the sultan's ancestry went back to one Mantiri Asip, one of the ministers of Raja Baginda, the Sumatran prince who emigrated to Sulu early in the sixteenth century. It begins:

> The writing of this book was finished at 8 o'clock, today the 28th of Thul-Qa'idat, 1285, A.H. . . .
> This is the genealogy of Mantiri Asip, the hero and learned man of Menang-kabaw. Mantiri Asip had the title of Orangkaya at the time he came to Sulu with Raja Baginda. He named a woman from Purul called Sandayli and begot Orangkaya Sumendak. Sumendak begot Orangkaya Manuk and Orangkaya Hamba. Manuk begot Orangkaya Buddiman and Orangkaya Akal and Orang-kaya Layu and Satya Akum. His daughters were Santan, Satan, Ambang, Duwi, Siti and Tamwan. . . .[4]

There is much more of it, very much more. It is important to remember that such parchments, laboriously written in Arabic script, remain the only written sources of history. This one confirms the hereditary nature of Muslim sultanates in the southern Philippines which continue, in less influential form, to the present time. But Mantiri Asip was by no means the first Mohammedan. Saleeby asserts that it was introduced at some time during the reign of Abu Bakr, who reached Sulu in 1450. Abu Bakr then assumed the grand title of Paduka Mahasari Maulana Al-Sultan Sherif Al-Hashmi. It was he who gave the religion its political shape and influence, though the official date ascribed to its introduction as a religion is 1380.

To complicate matters more the ancient grave of an Arab has recently been found in a former *tambat* (sacred grove) on the island of Bud Dato. The date on that grave is 1311.

In general terms it seems clear that Islam reached the Philippines three centuries before Legazpi arrived with his Christian warriors and priests. It was an ironic turn of history that, in this peaceably remote corner of the vast Pacific, the two bitterly opposed creeds should entrench themselves beneath the coconut palms, each unaware of the other's presence. Immense quantities of blood were to be shed before the centuries-long battle ended.

4. Najeeb M. Saleeby, *The History of Sulu*, Manila, 1908.

The further irony was that Ferdinand Magellan, making his first landing on the small Visayan island of Limasawa, should have observed the correct Malay ritual designed to make peace. The great navigator sat down with Raja Kolambu, made a blood pact and signed a declaration of friendship in their own blood. It is a story worth remembering in some detail.

The Portuguese seaman, who had already fought in India, voyaged to Malacca and campaigned against the Moors in Africa, had finally realized his dream in 1519 by persuading Charles I of Spain to send him on the quest for an eastward route to Asia, since Portugal then monopolized trade routes around the Cape of Good Hope. Making the longest voyage in history, Magellan discovered the strait that now carries his name, named the Pacific Ocean and sailed westward across its immense blue waters, becoming the first European to do so. It was a voyage of terrible hardships as well as triumph. His crew ate rats, leather and sawdust; they were desperately short of water; nineteen died of scurvy. After two years they found relief on Guam, then sailed past Samar and Leyte to Limasawa, where Magellan's chaplain said the first mass in the Philippines on Easter Sunday, 1521. To celebrate its conclusion, Spanish soldiery on shore fired their muskets, and three ships at anchor responded with their cannon.

Those cannon shots were to be symbolic.

One month later, after baptizing Raja Humabon in Cebu and raising the immense wooden cross that stands there still, the navigator crossed to Mactan Island, where the warrior-chieftain Lapu-Lapu refused to allow his men ashore. 'We are a free race,' the legendary Lapu-Lapu cried. 'If the white people invade my land, we will fight.'

The chieftain himself killed Magellan with his two-handed sword.

When the Spaniards returned in panic to Cebu, the allegedly converted Humabon entertained them at a banquet. Everyone ate and drank lustily. Graceful Muslim dances were performed. The strangers in their breastplates and curved helmets were lulled into drowsiness. It was then that Humabon's men struck with their *kris* and *barong*, murdering all who failed to escape to their boats. In later Christian times men were horrified by this tale of treachery.

But was it treachery? It was not, certainly, in the tradition of European chivalry, which was not at all chivalrous when seen in terms of the carnage caused by the Crusades and other wars. Malays, like most other people, were accustomed to attacks by stealth and surprise. They were not playing at resistance, especially in view of those heavily-armed galleons. They wanted to win, to keep the foreigner from their shores. Warfare is only killing, by whatever means one can. What do degrees or methods of killing matter?

And yet the Malays could also be a kindly, gentle people. Scores of voyagers throughout the centuries have testified to that. The natives were courtly and generous, wrote Magellan's chronicler Pigafetta on that fatal voyage. They spoke in open-hearted fashion of the abundant fruits and metals of this land, and where they were to be found.

Grateful Spaniards raised a statue to the great Portuguese navigator on Mactan. The patriot Lapu-Lapu had to wait another four hundred years for his.

CHAPTER 5

The New Crusaders

*Civilization does not long survive the
loss of a nation's livelihood, nor do ambitions
and initiative survive long-continued oppres-
sion and brutality. . . . According to King Philip
II himself, the population of the Philippines
had, by a decade after Legazpi's death, been
reduced by more than one third. In their
haste to capitalize on the wealth and
resources of the islands . . . they turned a
prosperous and happy country into a poorhouse.*

CONRADO BENITEZ

THE EUROPEAN carries a curse around the world with him he rarely
recognizes. His colour prejudices, his superior assumptions make enemies
of those who would willingly have been his friends. The Spaniard was an
acute specimen of these afflictions. Not so much Legazpi, nor his immediate followers. Not even the priests that came after him. The disease grew
with the accretion of power, with security and affluence.

For all that someone had to pay.

Surely only the fanatical could attempt to force their beliefs upon a
race so brave and dignified as these Malays? But the Spanish were
fanatics. The ceremonial, the rich tapestries, jewels and elaborate costum-
ing of a raja's court would surely have impressed any but these flayed sons
of the Grand Inquisitor. Nothing impressed them. Neither Malay skills
in weaving cloth, their beating of gold and copper, their skills in hus-
bandry and fishing, nor their fashioning of cannon or superb brassware.
Their songs, legends and dances meant nothing; nor their unique, guitar-
like instrument, the *kudyapi*, which had long been the symbol of poetry
and romance as had been the lyre in ancient Greece. Not even their proud
and graceful women excited these black-garbed, gaunt visitants from
another planet, except for the common soldiery. The missions that
followed Legazpi were fanatical.

Between the despatching of Magellan and Don Miguel de Legazpi's
arrival forty-four years later, two Spanish expeditions from Mexico had
tried fruitlessly to establish a beachhead. Legazpi was a man of a different
order. He had been ordered to take possession of these alluring islands,
but King Philip had also insisted that he remain clear of the Moluccas,
which were in the domain of Portugal. It was part of the strange arrogance of the times that Spain and Portugal had decided to divide the

New World between them, and not to dispute the possessing of regions that, though they did not consider it, were already the property of their own sovereign peoples. Not until much later, when the Dutch took possession of Java, Sumatra, the Celebes, were colonial Spaniards permitted to make war on a rival power. The real director of Legazpi's expedition — he was the military commander only — was that remarkable priest, Fray Andres de Urdaneta. This Augustinian was soldier and navigator as well as monk, and believed that he was bringing enlightenment to the pagan islanders when he celebrated the first solemn High Mass beneath Magellan's mighty cross in the Cebu where they also landed. Recalled almost immediately to Mexico, he did not see the disillusion that was so soon to follow the first enthusiastic baptisms. It hardly matters now that pagan Cebuaños thought such ceremonies were merely an insurance against sickness and evil spirits.

Perhaps they were.

Legazpi, who became governor, also believed. In two worlds. He needed to believe in his own, for his first landings were challenged in savage fashion. From a beautiful Samar beach, the local chief signalled to his galleon, pointing a dagger to his chest as a sign he wished to drink a blood pact with the strangers. On other beaches warriors brandished their murderous weapons in different fashion. When his two galleons reached the even then thriving port of Cebu, Raja Tupas welcomed him ashore so long as artillery and muskets were not produced, though the landing of Legazpi's iron-s'-eathed men prompted the populace to fly into the hills, setting fire to their villages as they ran. In the fire that nearly destroyed Cebu, one of the Spanish soldiers witnessed a miracle. This was the finding of the celebrated image of the Santo Niño, the Infant Jesus which Magellan had presented to the Raja Humabon almost half a century earlier. The gold and jewel-encrusted image had been treasured as a rain god, a pagan idol placated with floral tributes and a queer hopping dance that was believed to have made rain fall in times of drought.

Many decades passed before friars and priests were able to persuade the Cebuaños that there were more mansions in the house of Christ than mere idolatry.

The tendency among modern Filipino historians is to underplay the destructive impact of Spanish evangelism among the fluid, if well integrated Malay society. One can sympathize with that most eloquent of modern writers, Nick Joaquin, when he wrote: 'To accuse the Spanish, over and over again, of having brought us all sorts of things, mostly evil, among which we can usually remember nothing very valuable "except, perhaps," religion and national unity, is equivalent to saying of a not very model mother that she has given her child nothing except life. For, in the profoundest possible sense, Spain did give birth to us — as a nation, as an historical people. . . . For three and a half centuries we lay within the womb of Spain; the Revolution was our violent birth; and in the

37

bitterness with which we have ever since regarded the great and tragic nation to whom we owe so much, Freudians may read a parallel to that obscure enmity that haunts the relations of even the most loving son with his father — an enmity that perhaps voices the resentment of matter that has been wrenched out of its sleep and hardened with consciousness.'[1]

Joaquin is a poetic and compelling writer. But who can say whether Muslims might not have united these islands, too, endowing them with a vaunted temperance and peace that Catholicism certainly did not bring. From the day of Legazpi's landing history became an endless procession of wars, rebellions, social unrest, and the groundswell of this aggressiveness has not subsided even now.

It was war from the start. Intermittent war, with periods of truce and even friendship, but fought with dedicated courage and desperation on both sides. Despite Legazpi, despite the more kindly of Urdaneta's disciples, sword and halberd accompanied the crucifix against Cebuaños, Visayans, the warriors of Panay, the Tagalogs and Pampangueños of Luzon, the Moros, Muslims and the pagan tribes. According to Madrid's instructions these invaders were not to be colonists, nor conquistadores. King Philip himself, after whom the islands were called, had forbidden the use of the word *conquista*, such were its evil connotations after the bloodshed and destruction of Mexico. Nonetheless, these men were forced into acting like conquistadores. Against the Muslims especially their plans for pacification began to take on the character of a Holy War. The fierce, kris-armed Malays of the south were prepared to say death to all Christians, even though it meant dying themselves. It was the beginning of the fearsome *juramentado*, which has only disappeared in the last generation. It was a form of madness perhaps, this working of oneself to a frenzy, shaving the eyebrows and vowing to kill all Christians in sight. But it was Islam versus the crusaders of Rome.

Nowhere else in Asia were such murderous passions stirred.

When Legazpi died in 1572, having just subdued Manila and made it the capital, a new phase began. The priest began to oust the soldier. The church militant became the real administration. That powerful cleric Domingo de Salazar, first bishop of Manila, entered a subterranean war with government officials which was to continue in exhausting fashion until Spanish rule collapsed three centuries later.

Meantime there were external wars as well: attempted conquests of Borneo, Celebes, the Moluccas; wars against the Dutch, threatened war with the Chinese pirate fleets under Li-Mahong and Koxinga, skirmishes with roving English pirates like Thomas Cavendish and Drake, who found lucrative plunder in galleons making that long trans-Pacific haul to Acapulco. At that period the only Spanish lifeline was Mexico, whose viceroy was also responsible for the Philippines. Soon came the backwash of Spain's Hundred Years' War with England, and for two years the British fleet under Admiral Cornish occupied Luzon and the Visayas. The

1. Nick Joaquin, *La Naval de Manila*, Manila, 1964.

surprising fact was that Indios fought for the Spanish against these foreign enemies. A triumphant naval action with the Dutch, against tremendous odds, is still celebrated in Luzon with an annual fiesta. From Manila's Santo Domingo church each October, accompanied by church bells, brass bands and rockets, a gold and ivory image of the Virgin is carried through the streets. The Queen of the Most Holy Rosary becomes once again the Virgin of Sea Battles, patron of naval victories. La Naval de Manila remains one of the authorized miracles on the Philippine calendar, an impressive testimony to the depths at which those early evangelists planted the Christian faith.

Many thousands of Indio converts were persuaded to campaign for their new masters, to make long, armed voyages, to fight men of their own race in other lands. Frequently, too, they had to be used to quell disturbances at home. To quote the inescapable Rizal again, 'It was necessary to subject the people either by cajolery or force . . . those who submitted peacefully seemed to repent of it; insurrections were suspected, and some occurred; naturally there were executions, and many capable labourers perished; add continual wars to which the inhabitants of the Philippines were plunged to maintain the honour of Spain, to extend the sway of her flag in Borneo, in the Moluccas and in Indo-China; costly wars, fruitless expeditions, in which each time thousands and thousands of native archers and rowers were recorded to have embarked, but whether they returned to their homes was never stated. Like the tribute that once upon a time Greece sent to the Minotaur of Crete, the Philippine youth embarked for the expedition, saying goodbye to their country forever. . . .'[2]

Drawing on Morga, San Augustin, Chirino and other Spanish chroniclers, Rizal recorded that Panay's fifty thousand families were reduced to fourteen thousand in half a century, the total population reduced by one-third within thirty years, whole settlements uprooted, destroyed, chased into the mountains, children and women slaughtered, their rice and cornfields uprooted, their forest lands torn down to build ships of war. On one expedition to Ilocos alone, during 1573, soldiers destroyed 4,000 houses and killed five hundred civilians. There was savage irony in his essay on the so-called indolent Filipinos. Why were they indolent, he asked? Was it not better to be indolent than toil as serfs for the new grandee landlords, the vast haciendas seized by the religious orders, or to pay tribute to the arrogant, ever-growing bureaucracy in Manila?

Perhaps the greatest miracle of all was that so explosive a situation should have remained under control so long. The periodic revolts and peasant insurrections offered a kind of safety valve, as did brigandage and banditry, but there was always a well-armed military with garrisons everywhere. And the priests and friars. The best lands were taken for their corporations, and local clerics were appointed as magistrates, tax collectors, chiefs of police. They demanded free gifts of all the produce

2. Jose Rizal, *The Indolence of the Filipino*, op. cit.

they wanted, had the best houses built for them, took to their beds the daughters of their parishioners whose protests could lead only to the loss of land or lives. The Jesuits did not engage in such practices. In the main they were the ones who built colleges and schools.

Sometimes the rule of the friars was challenged by the civil administration. But not often. Too much plunder ran in their direction, too. There was one governor-general, for instance — General Wegler — who returned home with a fortune estimated at between two and three million dollars.

The control of a restive population was effectively secured through the shrewd manipulation of the social order. This was not difficult, for Malay society has always been authoritarian. Even today the *tao* remains subservient to his superiors: he respects position and wealth, however it has been acquired and, where modern society becomes more fluid, desires only prestige of the same kind himself. The *caciques*, having Spanish blood as well, needed little encouragement to keep their serfs prisoners of the soil and attached themselves to the island aristocracy. The most energetic of these were the Tagalogs, who had swiftly secured titles to their land, supporting armed force against the rebellious *tao* whenever necessary. The Tagalogs, originally a cohesive tribe that spread over the provinces of central Luzon, especially around Manila, are still the most dynamic force in Philippine life, only a little less numerous than the Visayans. In Spanish times — as in modern politics — they are challenged only by the clannish, hard-working, frugal Ilocanos of the north, whose *caciques* have always had even greater dominance over their own tenant farmers.

This is not at all to imply that Philippine history under the Spanish kings was a static one. In three and a half centuries this remote, frequently turbulent dominion, so often forced to find solutions for its own problems, naturally developed a dynamic of its own. The era can be divided into three phases. The first covered the period of conquest, from Legazpi to the end of the sixteenth century, by which time most of the population had been at least nominally converted, except for the increasingly hostile Moros. The second period, up to the start of the nineteenth century, brought a new type into prominence: the native-born Spaniard, the creole. Only, unlike the habit in Mexico, he was not called that here. He had few ties with his homeland, which was almost impossible to reach on those prolonged and stormy voyages around Cape Horn. There were close links with Mexico, though creole society there, too, was beginning to loosen its home ties. The glimmerings of political and economic independence began to show. Creoles were starting to think in Philippine terms. But not yet as Filipinos, for the Indio was still the despised inferior.

Perhaps, too, the exhausting war with the Dutch turned these men's thoughts in upon themselves, gave them a feeling of the islands as home. They had to continue fighting Islam as well, for the withdrawal of galleons and garrisons from the south to strengthen Manila's defences

gave raiding Muslim fleets a virtual freedom of the seas. They held on to
Luzon and the Visayas only by a thread. To reinforce their often shattered
forces, Spaniards had to find new allies. They found them among the
chieftains of Pampanga and the Tagalog regions. In return they had to
concede to them a touch of power. These new leaders and their families
were added to the ruling class of the time. They were even addressed as
Don.

It is not too much to say that the regional feuding in modern politics
partially stems from the strife between tribes of that age. Nothing makes
the Filipino more arrogant than the arrogation of power, especially the
Pampangueños, a people noted for their pride and extravagant love of
display.

Once the Dutch threat waned—the result of long-sustained, courageous
fighting — a new mood developed among the élite. There began new
trading practices, almost independently of Spain. Shipping ports were
closed to all foreign powers; even the Chinese were excluded. A locally-
based galleon trade took to shipping China's produce across to Mexico,
bringing back silver dollars in exchange. It was a hazardous, if dramatic
form of commerce, for many ships foundered on the enormous wastes of
the Pacific. And there were always the typhoons. But there were large
profits to be made. The owners of galleons, their masters, even the crews,
were rewarded richly, though the huge expense involved in transporting
comparatively small cargoes soon caused severe inflation. What matter? It
was an age of gamblers and speculators. And the men of the galleon trade
lived high. This surely was better than toiling for a small wage, pushing a
quill for the government, supervising reluctant peasants on the land. 'Such
is the example men set to the Indians', wrote Leandro de Viana in 1765,
and they imitate us so perfectly that all desire to live as the Spaniard
does, to wear the same costly ornaments, and to be rich — but without
labour.' Or, as Wilhelm Roscher expressed it, looking back from the
twentieth century: 'All thrifty activity was regarded as despicable. This
contempt for labour produced a nation top-heavy in nobles, soldiers,
officials, lawyers, clerks, religious and students, with numerous servants
— and also the largest proportion of beggars and vagabonds on earth.'[3]

The second Archbishop of Manila complained to the King that Spaniards, apart from the few truly religious, had become more concerned with
enriching themselves than converting their people to Christianity, and
that they were ignoring all social welfare. He spoke of 'insatiable greed',
asserting that 'everyone has become a merchant and trader, starting with
the governor himself'.

Then, in 1782, came the tobacco monopoly. This was set up in an
effort to make the country less dependent on Mexico. It was seized upon
by government officials as a way of making profits for themselves. The
result was not only a decline in the quality of tobacco, but wholesale
chicanery, smuggling, evasion of taxes, bribery, corruption and banditry

3. William Roscher, *The Spanish Colonial System*, New York, 1904.

Critics of modern times in the Philippines would do well to keep those long-entrenched precedents in mind.

With the nineteenth century a third phase began. Mexico revolted, breaking away from Spain. So did the rest of Latin America. Unrest in the Philippines increased. The central government in Madrid stirred itself to retain a colony it had neglected for so long. Access was easier now. The Suez canal had been opened. Steamships could now make what used to be a six or even nine month voyage in a matter of weeks. The screws of bureaucratic control began to tighten.

But this was resented as much by the creoles, the upper ranks of mestizos, the free-living Spanish as it was by the poverty-haunted at the bottom of the scramble for a good life. True-blood Spaniards from Spain were crowding in now, letting it be clearly known they regarded the native born as of lesser breed. A schism also developed within the church. A number of Filipinos had taken orders in the nineteenth century, and these tended to take sides with their own people against the Peninsulars.

A major crisis occurred in 1872 with the arrest of three priests: two of them Filipinos, the third a creole. Under the comparatively tolerant rule of Governor Carlos Maria de la Torre (1869-71) a group of politically-alert Filipinos began to agitate for more liberal laws. Among them were the three priests. They aroused the hostility of public officials. When a more reactionary governor replaced de la Torre, there were protests against the new policy of repression. Filipino soldiers in a Cavite barracks mutinied, because they resented discrimination against them in terms of wages and conditions. Governor Rafael de Izquirrdo declared a state of rebellion. There were many arrests, including the priests. The subsequent trial, said to have been based on false evidence, found the priests guilty of plotting to create a 'Philippine Republic'.

Fathers Mariano Gomez, Jose Burgos and Jacinto Zamora were sentenced to death by garroting.

Their names subsequently became famous. They were made so by Rizal. Burgos had been a friend of the family. Rizal dedicated his second novel, *El Filibusterismo (The Reign of Greed)* to the memory of these unjustly executed priests. But it was not only this dedication that angered the regime. *Filibusterismo* was an odd word, for it had no counterpart in true Spanish. In the Philippines, however, it stood for outlaws and revolutionaries. And the theme of this passionately written novel — written in exile in Europe — was that the only hope for the oppressed Filipino was to rid himself of Spain. The Archbishop of Manila was so disturbed by rumours of this book, circulated during Rizal's absence, that he called for a report from the Dominican professors of the University of Santo Tomas, where the author had once studied. The report did not contain literary criticism, but it was much to the point. The Dominicans reported:

> We have noted with a red pencil the statements against Spain, the government and its representatives in these islands. With a blue or black pencil other statements, impious, heretical, or scandalous. All the narrative, absolutely all

taken together and in detail, is against doctrine, against the Church, against the religious orders, and against the institutions, civil, military, social and political which the government of Spain has implanted in these islands.

Today *El Filibusterismo* is regarded as one of the classics of Philippine literature. Perhaps, as a work of art, it falls a little behind Rizal's *Noli Me Tangere (The Social Cancer)*, which upset the clericals almost as much. But then the Tsars were notably short on critical values when they read Tolstoi, the Bourbons on Rousseau or Voltaire. When, in 1896, the authorities were informed that Rizal was linked with a new revolutionary movement, without any basis in fact, the writer was arrested, charged with sedition and executed.

It was the most foolish thing the Spaniards could have done. Rizal was innocent of their charges. In fact, he had opposed the firebrands of the Katipunan, urged his people not to listen to those agitating for violent action. But they shot him all the same. In doing so, the Spanish made revolution inevitable. Such was the immense popular appeal Rizal had.

But this properly belongs to the emerging age of Filipino heroes.

CHAPTER 6

Age of Heroes

The workhand, the goatherd do not
read social contracts and neither do
they know what occurs beyond their towns.
. . . It is indispensible that we avoid the
formation of liberals, because in a colony,
liberal and rebellion are synonymous terms . . .
SINIBALDO DE MAR, 1842

THERE is a tendency in recent years to romanticize Rizal.

The problem is how to avoid it. Artistically and in intellect, he stands so far above his contemporaries. He was a man who could do everything. In the biographies you begin to suspect he was too good to be true, a fiction of hero worship. This, for instance, is how Gregorio F. Zaide lists his achievements: anthropologist, botanist, businessman, cartographer, conchologist, dramatist, economist, educator, engineer, essayist, entomologist, ethnologist, farmer, folklorist, geographer, genealogist, grammarian, historian, horticulturalist, humorist, lexicographer, linguist, mathematician, musician, novelist, naturalist, painter, physician, poet, philologist, philosopher, polemist, psychologist, satirist, sculptor, sportsman, sociologist, surveyor, traveller, wood carver and zoologist.[1] Such a catechism lifts him beyond the human flesh altogether, overdoing the heroic legend Rizal has become.

There is no questioning the man's brilliance. But he was, after all, only thirty-five at his death. His contribution in many of these fields was marginal. Rizal was in some respects the eternal student. He read, studied and debated incessantly during his post-graduate years in Europe. He graduated from the University of Madrid not only in medicine, which he had begun at the University of Santo Tomas, but in philosophy and letters. He studied German, French, Italian and Greek, and was said to have become fluent in twenty-two languages. Clearly he had remarkable gifts, for, after a month's stay in Japan, he was reported to have been able to converse freely with Japanese on his America-bound ship. In Germany he gave a paper on Tagalog culture to a meeting of anthropologists in their own language. Though he spent little more than four years of his adult life in the Philippines, most of it under forced exile in Mindanao, he made a comparative study of two Filipino languages, compiled a Tagalog grammar, taught local children free, ran a clinic for the poor,

1. Gregorio F. Zaide, *Jose Rizal: Life, Works and Writings*, Manila, 1957.

built a town water supply, drained marshes to combat malaria and pioneered valuable experiments in agriculture.

He was also a skilful doctor, specializing in ophthalmic medicine, conducting clinics in Hong Kong and his native town of Calamba. On his first return from Europe at twenty-six — the governor-general 'advised' him to leave six months later, so great was the scandal raised by his novel — Rizal treated his mother for a double cataract, an operation then unknown in the islands. Its success brought peasants to his clinic from all over Luzon, for they believed a miracle had been worked.

Yet, throughout this crowded career, his major concern was for his two great novels. (His poetry, written with passion, sensibility and a fine command of musical Spanish, was more a matter of spontaneous impulse.) Those novels took him years to complete. He suffered for them, went hungry, lived in squalor, had to borrow the money to pay printers. They earned him nothing, and he could not have survived but for occasional sums his family sent him from Calamba. This rare dedication was the product of his peculiarly involved environment.

He could have lived as a rich man's son, and become a conventional *ilustrado*. But for his artistic gifts. And, of course, the Spanish. His father was the most well-to-do farmer in the Laguna de Bay region, sixty miles from Manila. He rented lands from the Calamba Corporation, owned by Dominican friars, grew sugar, rice, cotton, had his own mill, a fine house and a library of one thousand books. The enmity of the local judge and *guardia civil* officer, who believed themselves slighted by this Filipino's superior ways, led to the imprisonment of Rizal's mother on a trumped-up charge of conspiring to poison her sister-in-law. This, plus the garroting of his friend Father Burgos, plus assaults and arrogant behaviour by other Spaniards, hardened the young man's outlook and drove him overseas. *Noli Me Tangere* was the first explosive result. It is a fine novel, tender and ironic, its acid portraits of officialdom and friars only too clearly drawn from real people. The Dominicans were especially angered, both in Calamba and Santo Tomas. Its main influences are claimed to have been Dumas and Harriet Beecher Stowe, which led to the unfortunate comment that his was 'the *Uncle Tom's Cabin* of the Philippines'. It is a far greater work than that, even if it did have the same intense social impact. William Dean Howells went so far as to say it was the finest novel in any language for the past fifty years, which again was not being fair to its unique literary qualities.

The novel's main characters, the radical young creole, Ibarra, the immortalized Maria Clara, and the flamboyant Doña Victorina, a superb figure, have become as real to three generations of readers as the true-life heroes of their history.

El Filibusterismo, which followed four years later, is very much a sequel to *Noli*, using several of the same characters. But its tone is harsher, more rebellious. Threats of revolution becloud its sombre pages, which was why Dominicans and government took alarm. When Rizal came home, against the advice of family and friends, he was arrested and deported to Mindanao's lonely settlement of Dapitan. Yet he was by no means a revolutionary. In any other context he would have been termed a liberal. Here he became a liberal despairing of reform. In fact, during those last four years of freedom after his second return from Europe, he had formed the short-lived Liga Filipina, mostly a society of intellectuals, who drew up a programme of social reforms. This was at once banned and broken up. Rizal's real crime was a literary one. He had depicted the Spanish regime with such realism in his novels that literate Filipinos became openly hostile to Spain.

But it would be unfair to give Rizal alone the credit for this change of atmosphere. He was the late flowering of a movement that began in the eighteenth century and included many liberal intellectuals. This so-called 'Propaganda' movement had been much influenced by the French and American revolutions, though it did not become active until a group of exiles gathered around Marcello del Pilar, a Bulacan lawyer, who lived in Spain during the 1880s. In Barcelona, where he found the climate more liberal than Manila, del Pilar founded a political newspaper, *La Solidaridad*, with his own money, drawing in some brilliant Filipino minds as contributors, Rizal occasionally among them. Others like Apolinario Mabini remained in Manila, joined the Liga Filipina, then the Katipunan, and took a leading role in organizing the revolution. One of eight sons of a poor peasant family in Batangas, he won a free scholarship to Manila's College of San Juan, taught in provincial schools, then struggled against creeping paralysis of his limbs which, in his later triumph, did not prevent him from presiding over the Malolos Congress of 1898. Since Independence many such men — peasant leaders, generals of the Revolutionary army, teachers, artists — have been enrolled in the official calendar of the National Commission of Heroes. Few nations have honoured so many heroes and martyrs in so brief a period. Their statues look sternly down upon passers-by in town plazas and public parks, they have streets and squares named after them and their biographies appear regularly in the daily press.

I remember one visit to the tranquil little Cavite town of Imus, whose wide, sunlit plaza was dominated by a centuries-old church. Somehow this rustic place had escaped the rush and violence of the post-war world, despite bandits ranging the nearby hills as they had done for generations. What traffic there was took the pace of its leisurely pedicabs, while women in peasant shawls strolled among the flowers. Overlooking the square was the white statue of a handsome, robust Filipino. The inscription identified him as General Licenio Topacio; the rest was in Tagalog.

'Who is that?' I asked a friend.

'He fought for the Revolution. Three generals came from this town alone.'

The next town, Kawit, he told me, had been the birthplace of an even more celebrated leader, Emilio Aguinaldo, a schoolteacher who became the leader of the Revolution's army at the age of twenty-seven. General Aguinaldo's sombre career sums up the rise and decline of that violent epoch. It is a story of fierce personal ambitions, brutality and self-sacrifice, the corrosive inability of Filipinos to hold together.

The extraordinary fact about the rebellion against Spain was the way men who prepared it remained so long unsuspected. Leadership came through a secret society formed in 1892 by a young disciple of Rizal, an orphan who grew up in the slums of Tondo, taught himself to read and write, finally producing his own seditious newspaper. Andres Bonifacio called his clandestine movement the Kataastaasan Kagalang-galang Katipunan ng Mga Anak ng Bayan (The Highest and Most Respectable Association of the Sons of the People). The name, proving too long even for Tagalog speakers, was soon shortened to Katipunan. Bonifacio had initially joined the Liga Filipina, but lost faith in mere reforms, determining instead to arm and organize city labourers and peasants. Yet it was nearly four years before Spanish intelligence learned of the widespread conspiracy. Even then it was only by accident. One of its members, coming home drunk, confided plans for the revolt to his sister, who ran in terror to the parish priest. The alarm was raised.

Bonifacio at once put his clock forward. The first major uprising took place the same day, at Balintawak on the outskirts of Manila. Spanish troops had difficulty putting down the insurrection, and Bonifacio escaped to lead the *insurgentes* from the countryside. His resort to armed violence brought little support from more liberal people, some of whom took the side of Spain. But for Rizal the now celebrated Cry of Balintawak had fatal consequences. Bonifacio had proposed him, without his knowledge, as one of the Katipunan's patrons, although the writer was then exiled in Dapitan. It so happened that Rizal was then preparing to leave his home-land for ever. Despairing of reform, he had volunteered to serve as a medical officer with the Spanish army in Cuba, where yellow fever had reached plague proportions. The authorities, after a long silence, at last agreed to release him. As the ship was about to leave Manila, Bonifacio renewed an earlier appeal for him to join the Katipunan. Rizal refused. He would have nothing to do with armed force, warning that it could only worsen conditions for the people. The Spanish arrested him all the same, just as his vessel was sailing from Suez to Barcelona. Brought back to the Philippines, Rizal was tried for sedition and, despite the lack of any real evidence, taken before a firing squad. Spaniards watching among the large crowd shouted, 'Viva Espana!'

But colonial Spain did not live. Within eighteen months it had collapsed. The death of Rizal was the ultimate cause. He became a legend immediately, and even the manner of his dying was given a heroic touch. As Carlos P. Romulo wrote of it half-a-century later:

> His Spanish executioners had him stand with his back to the firing squad
> that he might be shot from the rear as a traitor, but at the last minute he

whirled to face the blast of gunfire. The medico who examined him just before had found his pulse beat normal.[2]

Within five days of his execution, eleven more men went to the firing squad. These were men who had been implicated in an actual uprising in distant Bicol. Among them were three priests, a wealthy philanthropist and several government employees. Thirteen more were shot a week later. They included a son of the aristocratic Roxas clan, a Manila lawyer, an industrialist. Clearly a new type of people were being drawn into the resistance. The proletarian Bonifacio was ousted by middle-class opponents of Spain, and Aguinaldo appointed commander-in-chief. When Bonifacio attempted to regain the leadership he was arrested and shot by a guard on Aguinaldo's orders.

Whether that independence could have been achieved without foreign intervention is still an arguable matter.

Spain, in the final paroxysms of its empire, committed every imaginable folly. Having arranged the Treaty of Biak-na-bato with Aguinaldo in December 1897, the colonial government at last promised reforms. These included the expulsion of the religious orders, representation in the Cortes, the appointing of Filipinos to government posts, freedom of assembly and the press. Madrid vetoed them all. Under the treaty terms, Aguinaldo agreed to leave the country, taking the other leaders with him. In return he was to be paid 400,000 pesetas, plus other expenses, the money to be made available through a Hong Kong bank. For the Spanish it was a happy arrangement. Much of the money was soon dissipated, while Aguinaldo and his companions quarrelled over who should spend it.

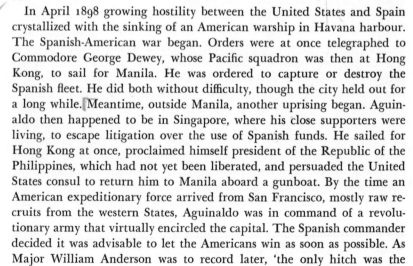

In April 1898 growing hostility between the United States and Spain crystallized with the sinking of an American warship in Havana harbour. The Spanish-American war began. Orders were at once telegraphed to Commodore George Dewey, whose Pacific squadron was then at Hong Kong, to sail for Manila. He was ordered to capture or destroy the Spanish fleet. He did both without difficulty, though the city held out for a long while. Meantime, outside Manila, another uprising began. Aguinaldo then happened to be in Singapore, where his close supporters were living, to escape litigation over the use of Spanish funds. He sailed for Hong Kong at once, proclaimed himself president of the Republic of the Philippines, which had not yet been liberated, and persuaded the United States consul to return him to Manila aboard a gunboat. By the time an American expeditionary force arrived from San Francisco, mostly raw recruits from the western States, Aguinaldo was in command of a revolutionary army that virtually encircled the capital. The Spanish commander decided it was advisable to let the Americans win as soon as possible. As Major William Anderson was to record later, 'the only hitch was the rapidity with which some of the American soldiers advanced, not allowing

2. Carlos P. Romulo, *Crusade in Asia*, New York, 1955.

e for the Spaniards to retire gracefully after fighting with honour to
mselves'.

This left American and Filipino troops confronting one another. Who
w was to control the country?

Washington was not in any doubt. Despite an incautious cable from
ewey asserting that 'these people are superior in intelligence and more
pable of self-government than the Cubans', President McKinley sent
structions that there was to be no official recognition of General
guinaldo. If his forces could help to keep order in the countryside, well
nd good. They were not to enter the city. Meantime peace delegates from
he United States and Spain met in Paris, where negotiations moved
lowly between August and February 1898, when the Treaty of Paris was
inally ratified. McKinley's government agreed to pay $20,000,000 as
indemnity, which Filipino revolutionaries declared was blood money to
purchase their country over their protesting heads.

They were not entirely without friends in the United States. The
Anti-Imperialist League, with headquarters in Boston, condemned the
McKinley administration, campaigning for Philippine independence.
Mark Twain called ironically for an assault on the brown races, flying
'our usual flag with the white stripes painted black and the stars replaced
by the skull and crossbones'.

McKinley's Republican Party had more persuasive arguments. These
ranged from the idealistic to frankly commercial. Filipinos were not ready
for freedom, he claimed, then spoke of 'the moral and political desirability of acquisition. . . . Do we need the Philippines' consent to perform
a great act of humanity?' The Methodist church supported him, because
they had heard the Igorots were pagans. Episcopalians foresaw 'lucrative'
prospects for mission work, while one Rev. J. H. Barrows, head of the
Union Theological Seminary, announced that 'wherever on pagan shores
the voice of the American missionary is heard, there is fulfilled the
manifest destiny of the Christian Republic'.

Senator Albert J. Beveridge argued with a candour that would have
appalled a modern State Department. 'We are a conquering race,' he said
in the Capitol.

> We must obey our blood and occupy new markets, and, if necessary, new
> lands. The trade of the world must and shall be ours. American law, American
> order, American civilization, and the American flag will prevail on shores
> hitherto bloody and benighted. Would not the people of the Philippines prefer
> the just, humane, civilizing movement of this Republic to the bloody rule . . .
> from which we have just rescued them? . . . The Philippines are ours forever.
> And just beyond are China's illimitable markets. We will not abandon our
> duty to the Orient. We will not remove our part in the mission of our race,
> trustee under God, of the civilization of the world . . .

The Senator from Indiana inhabited a more confident world than ours.
It was also a world beginning to grow uneasy about other commercial
rivalries. The British and French had secure positions on the Asian main-

49

land. The Dutch appeared unchallenged in the Netherlands East Indies. Germany, which had actually sent warships to 'protect its interests' in Manila Bay when Dewey appeared, was expanding its Pacific empire beyond Samoa and New Guinea. Japan, too, was starting to look south. McKinley's argument was that to support Philippine independence then would merely admit some other imperial power into the vacuum.

The awakened Filipinos were not in the least concerned about such threats. In September the revolutionary council convened a congress at Malolos, Bulacan. The Republic was officially declared, with General Aguinaldo as president. A committee, consisting mainly of lawyers and other educated Tagalogs, drafted a constitution, which was said to have been largely the work of Apolinario Mabini. This was the first democratic constitution to have been produced in Asia, and as such deserves its fame. It was an impressive document, liberal and humane. 'Sovereignty resides exclusively in the people', it began.

Here, at last, joyously endorsed by two thousand delegates from all classes and ranks of the Filipino people, was the achievement for which patriots, exiles, intellectuals, peasant leaders and rebel democrats had been striving for a century and more. The Malolos Constitution was to become an inspiration for other struggling nationalist movements in Asia, notable among them the Chinese adherents of Sun Yat Sen.

The Republic had been proclaimed. But the Americans ignored it. For them General Aguinaldo's government remained 'the insurgents'. The military governor of Manila, General Arthur MacArthur (whose son was to liberate another generation of Filipinos from Japanese occupation) kept the republican army outside the city walls. He could not do much about the countryside. There the Malolos government was in sole control, with its own supporters appointed as provincial governors, commanders, mayors and chiefs of barrios.

The deadlock was ended in February 1899. By that time the 'sovereignty' of a united people had become eroded. Exactly what happened is still a matter of fierce debate. Americans claimed that the Filipinos were too undisciplined, too jealous of individual rights, too fragmented by class and property interests to hold together, however good the constitution was as an abstract document. Aguinaldo blamed Mabini's personal ambitions; Mabini blamed Aguinaldo for his aggressive militarism; ilustrados blamed the Katipunan extremists; Katipunans said the wealthy caciques, fearing the loss of their lands, defected to their American protectors within the city. Marxist-inclined theorists of the modern age declare that it was merely a 'bourgeois' revolution, fated to split along class lines. It is unlikely that Aguinaldo had any theories about it at all, but he proceeded to act along the classic lines of the French and Russian Revolutions. He decided to save the revolution through the use of terror. And, in doing so, helped to destroy it.

At first, according to documents of the time, Aguinaldo attempted to curb the excesses of his civilian army. But he lacked the power to do so, for officers as well as men looted, raped, burnt, plundered towns, stores and private homes, while self-styled generals ranged up and down the provinces like ferocious warlords. Bandits and released prisoners joined these undisciplined, ragged armies. They shot, stabbed or hanged any Filipino who would not supply them with food and produce free, burnt their farms, terrorized women, in some cases even carried off girls from boarding schools for barrack use. Priests and friars were beaten, tortured, murdered, given the 'water cure' that *guardia civil* officers had practised for centuries. The *timbain*, or water cure, took two forms. One was to lower a man by his roped feet into a well, repeatedly plunging his head under water until he talked. The other was to pour water into his mouth and nostrils, then jump on him till his stomach burst. The water cure is still used on occasions by Philippine police, as it is by the Viet Cong and the South Vietnamese Army.

It was easy enough for the disciplined, home-bred Americans to deplore these outrages, to report that Filipinos were unfit to govern the provinces under Aguinaldo's martial law. The terror they saw was the natural outcome of the overthrow of three centuries of repressive Spanish rule. Revolutions are never pretty affairs. Besides these were a primitive people whose passions and fierce resentments had been seething underground for generations. It was, in effect, a civil war against those who had so long exploited them: Spaniards and mestizos, friars, *caciques* and petty officials who set prestige and power above national identity. The decisive factor was that the Malolos government lacked the organization to control this upsurge of barbarity. The more liberal, restraining elements began to desert the revolution.

Then, when war broke out between United States and Filipino forces, Aguinaldo as a matter of survival, fighting on two fronts, had to increase the terror. Atrocities became an accepted part of his campaign. 'Any person who fights for his country has absolute power to kill anyone not friendly to our cause', read one of Aguinaldo's orders. One of his ex-bandit commanders sent a circular to guerrilla leaders, urging them 'to learn the verb *Dukutar*', which meant in Tagalog to assassinate.

The use of this picturesque verb was what, in fact, touched off the war.

In February 1899 some thirty thousand crudely-armed irregular soldiers under General Antonio Luna occupied the hinterland around Manila, which was defended by ten thousand Americans, later reinforced to fifty thousand. Aguinaldo believed he could defeat MacArthur's forces in a quick engagement, but did not want to appear the aggressor. Captured documents later revealed the plan. Infiltrators into Manila suburbs were to take presents to American officers, some dressed as women, while others manned the tops of houses with stones, timber, red hot iron, boiling oil, and at a given signal were to assassinate unwary Americans and seize their arms.

The plan failed. But on 2 February a Filipino patrol provoked American troops to fire on them, and the spontaneous battle flared into war.

It was a desperate and savagely-fought campaign that eddied throughout Luzon and the Visayas for the best part of three years, causing ten thousand American casualties, sixteen thousand Filipinos and the death of nearly two hundred thousand civilians from hunger and disease. There were heroic episodes on both sides, astonishing acts of bravery, but appalling atrocities, too. American prisoners were boloed, mutilated, buried alive. Filipino wounded were bayoneted as they lay on the ground. Entire villages and towns were burnt, and populations driven from their smoking homes. The horrors of this unnecessary war were impartially documented, from both United States and Tagalog records, by Dean C. Worcester,[3] a zoologist who spent many years with the American administration and understood the Filipino viewpoint. Among the many documents he quoted was an appeal by one Isabelo Artacho to his people during October 1899. It was a tragic appeal, addressed largely to General Aguinaldo.

> Wherever you see an insurgent gun or bolo you will find girls and faithful wives violated, parents and sons crying for the murder of a son or brother; villages burned and plundered for the benefit of a chief or General; you will see fresh and living signs yet of those horrible crimes perpetrated with the greatest cynicism by those who call themselves your liberators. . . . Here, a *presidente* stabs a man, simply for having implored mercy for a creature arbitrarily inflicted with the *cepo* (a kind of stocks); there, a dying man, suspended by his feet in a *cepo*, charged with an unproved crime; there a poor woman driven by petty officers with their bayonets for having objected to their invasion into her house, or shop; there, generals who murder without fear, for an insignificant motive, creatures whose members are being mutilated, or their flesh cut in slices and afterwards roasted and given them to eat; there, officers braining a girl who has refused to accede to their sensual wishes, the lifeless body of the victim, pierced with shots, after having been made use of, is thrown in the river. It is not unusual to witness officers burying people alive in a tomb prepared by the victim, by order of the murderer; it is not unusual to see a Puisne-Judge pointing a revolver at a man who is about to give evidence, and threatening to brain him for having dared to ask: 'Why, and to whom am I to declare?' . . .

This open letter, written from Hong Kong, recalls a comment by a distinguished Filipino whom Worcester met at a banquet some years later. He had been giving an address on the necessity for Philippine independence. Worcester asked him what he would do if it came. The reply was succinct.

'I'd take the first steamer leaving for Hong Kong.'

With the coming of the new century — Manileños celebrated with a grand ball at the Army and Navy Club — Aguinaldo's forces were gradually shorn of their support, driven further into the country, until he was forced to lead an exhausting retreat into the Sierra Madre. The delaying battle fought by the twenty-four-year-old General Gregorio del Pilar was a heroic episode still celebrated today. It was another Thermopylae.

3. Dean C. Worcester, *The Philippines: Past and Present*, London, 1914.

Rush hour, Manila

Ancient rice terraces, Mountain Province

'They shall not pass', young del Pilar told the seventy men he posted at the entrance of Tirad Pass. They fought against nine hundred Americans. The Battle of Tirad Pass gave his supreme commander time to escape across the mountains to a secret hideout, while del Pilar and sixty of his men were killed.

This 'fugitive and outlaw', as the Americans called Aguinaldo, directed his subsequent campaign in a manner similar to that of the Viet Cong in recent years. His scattered fighters on the plains became peasants by day, unrecognized by United States patrols, then took up arms at night, raiding military posts, towns, transport lines and centres of supply. His couriers kept contact with key men in the field, set up 'shadow governments' in provincial centres, returning with sufficient information to keep guerrilla warfare going. And, like the Viet Cong, the use of terror was intensified.

All this was only to postpone the coming of defeat.

It came when the Americans captured a spy, gave him the water cure and learnt the whereabouts of Aguinaldo's mountain headquarters. It was then arranged that a party of Filipinos from Macabete, Pampanga, should guide an American patrol, which was to arrive with hands and feet bound, as though they were prisoners. The General was astonished to see them arrive, even more so when — a few hours later — the foreigners surrounded him, their firearms restored by Macabete traitors. This was virtually the end of the resistance.

Aguinaldo was taken to Manila, and kept under house arrest at Malacanang Palace, by then the official residence of the first civil governor, William H. Taft. Surprised by the unexpectedly friendly treatment he was given, Aguinaldo renounced his opposition to American rule, appealing to his countrymen to make peace. There was no explanation, least of all in his later autobiography, for this abrupt volte-face, except that Aguinaldo was allowed to go free, subsequently living the life of a leisured gentleman until his death, which to my surprise was little publicized, in 1964. Other, more ambitious, politicians passed him by.

Not until April 1902 did the last organized resistance end. The United States campaign shifted to more southerly islands, where Visayans continued to fight. The struggle became especially bitter on Samar, where American marines fought their earliest Pacific battles. It was there that General Jacob Smith tersely informed his men: 'I want no prisoners. I wish you to kill and burn. The more you burn and kill the better it will please me.'

What most impressed the Filipinos was that most American commanders fought with none of the ferocity of their opposition. Their aim was purely pacification. Having achieved it, ruthlessly if necessary, they set about helping the inhabitants to rebuild their shattered lives. Hence, as soon as gunsmoke cleared on Luzon battlefields, foreign soldiers began to fraternize, offered gifts to children, took a hand in local schools. 'It was to the credit of American military commanders,' said Sergio Osmena during a lecture to United States audiences in 1925, 'that they desired to establish, even in the midst of armed resistance, the foundation of civil institutions. The Filipinos will never forget the inspiring spectacle of American soldiers leaving their guns and, as emissaries of peace and good-will, with book in hand, repairing to the public schools to teach Filipino children the principles of free citizenship.'

This was the curious duality of American conquest. Despite Senator Beveridge, these reluctant colonials were convinced of their own propaganda, that they were occupying the Philippines for its people's good. As the twentieth century progressed, they proved this largely true.

CHAPTER 7

Reluctant Colonials

*The Commission should bear in mind that
the government they are establishing is designed
not for the expression of our theoretical views,
but for the happiness, peace and prosperity of
the Philippine Islands, and that the measures
adopted should be made to conform to their
customs, their habits and even their
prejudices . . .*

INSTRUCTIONS TO TAFT COMMISSION, 1901.

AMERICANS in Asia. . . . The very concept, at the turn of the century, had
a contradictory air. Theirs was so essentially a new civilization; a world of
carpetbaggers and thrusting commerce; of freewheeling extroverts and
innovators with little regard for tradition or the peasant ways they had
rejected along with feudal Europe. Of colonial methods they were entirely
innocent. They knew nothing of the shrewd, temporizing, sleight-of-hand
techniques that had enabled the British, French and Dutch to underpin
solid-seeming empires in Asian countries whose initial resistance had
often been no less intractable. The Americans came with one asset only:
immense goodwill.

It was inevitable that the two races should misunderstand one another.
Nor was it possible to undo three centuries and more of authoritarian
Spanish rule with a few democratic proclamations, nor by teaching
English verbs and hygiene in barrio schools. To enunciate the principles
of Jefferson was admirable, the ethics of free enterprise. But talk of
government of the people, for the people and by the people could only
be unreal in communities whose one concept of free trade was brigandage
and piracy. Even in the remote pre-hispanic past their natural order had
been an autocratic one. Certainly, once the Revolution had been crushed,
these expressions of Yankee goodwill were a potent weapon. But they
were also obstructions to progress if the United States meant to remain
and rule. In the beginning the failure of these raw colonialists was a
psychological one. It was naive to think these people were brothers under
another skin — Kipling turned upside down. They had been given a
chance, which no purely commercial empire could have achieved, to
prove that West and East could meet on equal terms, so long as uniquely
eastern points of view were understood.

The Malay outlook has sometimes devious aspects, and these, in terms
of a new experiment in colonizing, led in the long run to a disappointing

end. Materially, the American regime was a notable success. Forty years after the removal of Spain, *per capita* incomes had much increased, so had life expectancy, the literacy rate and resistance to disease. In terms of the spirit, a national ethos, it is doubtful if much advance has been made. Looking back now, which is making unfair moral judgements, one suspects that the fault lay in the reluctance of those early proconsuls to rule. It seems clear also that the Filipinos, from the early days, had made up their minds exactly what to do.

Having lost the Revolution, they determined to gain the freedom they wanted by other means. Not so much political freedom, though that was always an issue, but freedom, among a certain caste, to exploit their own country in their own free way.

Few Americans were ever aware of this. The Filipino's subtlety is what passes for Oriental in the western mind. The westerner seldom says one thing and means another. When he makes a gentleman's agreement, he breaks it only in a gentlemanly way, that is, he has attacks of conscience afterwards, and accepts legal punishment as a matter of course. The Filipino willingly adopted his legal code, but exploited the courts in other, more subtle ways. It is by no means accidental that the Philippines has become a nation of lawyers: it is difficult to get anywhere in Congress or commerce without at least a diploma in law. But in modern times it becomes increasingly difficult to separate legality from legalism.

A case in point was General Aguinaldo, a natural lawyer if there was ever one. He never studied law, but from the outset he had American officialdom in confusion. There is some doubt as to whether he was ever appointed general, except by himself. In Dewey's time, the title was always given quotation marks. He claimed to have been officially brought home on official instructions from Washington when the Commodore attacked Manila. The United States' version, endorsed by its consul in Hong Kong, was that Aguinaldo had himself requested it. He claimed that Dewey had promised the Philippines immediate independence, though no document either in American or revolutionary hands was ever found to endorse it. He accused Washington of double-dealing, first rejecting his army as an ally and thereafter imposing its own regime. These implications of dishonesty are still accepted, more than half a century later, by most Filipino historians. In one sense, it has helped to solidify nationalist sentiment. In another it has falsified the essentially honest intentions of the Taft regime.

William H. Taft was a remarkable man. Despite the conservatism of his Republican party, he was himself an aristocratic liberal, a man of considerable idealism. He disliked militarism, which led to occasional friction with General Arthur MacArthur, who favoured strong-arm methods in the new foreign possession. Taft also referred contemptuously to the 'corroded American businessman'. He was fully persuaded that the five-man Philippines Commission, of which he was chairman, should develop policies that aided Filipinos and not United States interests. The

Commission was the sole administrative body before 1907 and, in Taft's mind, its function was above all to avoid the development of an elite.

'We are not the guardians of the small portions of the educated and the wealthy,' he said. 'We are guardians especially of the poor and the weak, and we could not discharge our duty as such guardians unless we remained there long enough to give to the poor, the weak, the humble a consciousness of their rights, and a certainty that they would be preserved under any government to which they might transfer sovereign power.'[1]

The United States, he said publicly, did not own these islands, but held them in trust for a people who would eventually govern themselves. Yet his successor in 1903, Luke E. Wright, immediately announced that independence would not come within the lifetime of any of his listeners. Then came William C. Forbes, of 'Polo Cabinet' fame (the game, which he introduced, became a status symbol for the élite) and clearly stated that his support was for American free enterprise. When Woodrow Wilson brought the Democrats back to power in Washington, the administrators he sent to Manila took with them the slogan, 'The Philippines for Filipinos'.

It was all most confusing.

Yet the Taft regime began an almost irreversible trend, which could only be modified or subdued by his successors. This was especially the case in public welfare. From the beginning of the century teams of well-trained health officials ranged the islands, taking vigorous action against the cholera, typhoid, malaria and other diseases that Spanish officialdom had done little to combat. A major drive was initiated to deal with the widespread squalor and slum conditions where so much disease bred. The most graphic tribute to these achievements came from Carlos P. Romulo, who had been a major on Aguinaldo's staff in 1899. Years later he wrote:

There was no sewerage before the Americans came. Even in Manila filth ran in open drains through the streets. Epidemics wiped out thousands yearly in the city. When I was a child nearly every Filipino was pockmarked. Now such marks of disease are rarely seen. Heavy rains were prayed for, to wash filth from the streets, and bring about cessation in the recurrent epidemics of small-pox, malaria and bubonic plague. Mosquitoes bred in the swamps and rats scuttled in the towns. . . . Shortly after the American occupation the usual epidemic of smallpox and bubonic plague swept Manila. The Americans promptly stamped out both. They distributed rat poison and killed off the plague-carrying rats. A vaccine farm was established. Eighty thousand Filipinos submitted to vaccination. Hospitals were built. Schools opened. Public schools, high schools, universities, and all without cost. The new generation of Filipino youth developed not only intellectually, but in actual physical stature.[2]

The school system was itself a notable force. Education was not only free, but secular, with emphasis on the sciences, trade skills and the pro-

1. W. Cameron Forbes, *The Philippine Islands*, New York, 1945.
2. Carlos P. Romulo, *Mother America*, New York, 1943.

fessions. It brought to an end the old system Rizal had criticized so acidly in his famous letter of 1888, written at Del Pilar's suggestion, to the young Malolos women who had defied the local priest's ban on a night school to teach themselves Spanish. 'What offering will be that of a woman whose kindness of character is expressed by mumbled prayers,' he wrote; 'who knows nothing by heart but *awits, novenas* and the alleged miracles. . . . What sons will she have but acolytes, priest's servants, or cockfighters?' [3]

By the end of 1901 more than seven hundred school teachers arrived from the United States, many of them Quakers, with much the same kind of dedication that characterized a later generation of Peace Corps workers. Nor did they stay in the cities and major towns only. They went out to the barrios, lived among the people, sharing their hardships and poverty.

The influence of these enthusiastic young men and women was vital. It transformed the dependent spirit that had been generated in Spanish times and fostered a creed of equality, a belief that people could raise their own standards of living. It was at this stage that English became the common language, though the lingua franca remained Tagalog, or the native languages of other regions. The new education was also the explanation for the way Filipinos fought with the United States in World War Two, much to the amazement of the Japanese, whose propaganda slogans of 'Asia for the Asians' won small response.

Filipinos were notably the only Asians to side with the western powers in the Pacific war.

Taft's policy was all the more remarkable because it began to take effect before the country was wholly pacified. The Philippine Commission that began to reorganize public life, under his presidency, was intelligently based. Its first members were liberal American jurists. Then Taft added several leaders of the Malolos government, men who had abandoned Aguinaldo when he began to rely on the militaristic rule of terror. Another was made Chief Justice. After the revolutionary general's capture, his disorganized supporters tried to renew resistance in remote areas of Luzon and the Visayas, but they soon degenerated to banditry. This was the traditional pattern to which rebels had reverted under the ancient regime. By escaping from 'the shadow of the bell', as the old phrase put it, the dissidents banded together in the mountains of Cavite and elsewhere, indulging in highway robbery and demanding tribute from defenceless barrio folk.

In the early 1900s the Katipunan remnants became the *tulisanes*. They set themselves to make running war on American administrators, compiled a list of military officers, local governors and officials, and even their Filipino sympathizers who were to be murdered on sight. These marauding bands, some of them several hundred strong, remained a menace for some years. Some bandit chiefs developed a paranoic fervour, demanding a quasi-religious devotion from their barbarous followers. In three separate provinces bandit leaders called themselves Jesus Christ, another

3. Jose Rizal, *To The Young Women of Malolos*, Manila, 1932.

renamed himself God Almighty, and several took the names of Popes. Some even claimed to be immune from bullets, a quality they made a show of transferring to their supporters. The immunity was said to come from *anting-antings*, lucky charms hung around their necks in the form of bottles and vials filled with mystic fluids. These claims and titles have had striking parallels among the messianic leaders of disaffected 'cargo cults' in modern New Guinea.

To suppress this anarchy the United States regime formed the celebrated Philippine Constabulary, officered by Filipinos as well as Americans. It was a courageous, well-disciplined force, pacifying the countryside so effectively that its commander was able to state long before World War One that 'today banditry is practically extinguished throughout the islands'. He would have been gravely shocked had he been able to see the deterioration since the Second World War.

The Constabulary also took part in a major campaign against the Moros in southern areas: a full-scale war whose last battle was not fought until 1913. All told, the United States had a tough, often disillusioning introduction into colonial management. They arrived in light-hearted fashion, expecting to be hailed as liberators, the bearers of enlightenment, peace and democracy. Instead they were obliged to fight their way through the entire country, suppressing guerrillas and bandits right down to Mindanao, losing thousands of lives. There were bloody excesses on both sides, a desperate slaughter made inevitable by the reckless practise of *juramentado* in which Islam's warriors indulged.

The most savage battle was that fought on the fortified slopes of Bud Dajo, the grim Sulu Island volcano. There General Wood's troops killed six hundred men, women and children, and lost one-third of their own force, too. There was just no surrender. War in the south lasted another seven years, ending with General Pershing's assault on Mount Baysak, where another three hundred Muslims — again including women — were cut down with sabres, bayoneted or shot. All this violence left a bitter heritage, but it was difficult to see how it could have been avoided. The ferocious warriors of the south respected only those who proved themselves superior in battle, not men of peace. Negotiations, offers of friendship proved futile until the battlesmoke of victory cleared. At home, there was a great outcry over the alleged brutality of Americans who killed women as well as men. They had no option but to do so.

Juan Alano, who has spent a long life among these people, told me many stories of their ferocity in war, running amok with their razor-sharp, double-edged *barongs*, indifferent to pain or superior force. There were even cases where men, with bayonets in their chests, would pull the rifle closer to bring the enemy within reach of their whirling blades. As for the women, they fought with equal savagery, sometimes with a babe in one arm, a *barong* in the other. Since both dressed alike, it was seldom possible to tell male from female, except after death on the field.

Yet, once pacified, Mindanao readily supported the new regime.

Henceforth antagonism was limited to individual feuding between Muslim and Christian Filipinos, which has not wholly died out yet.

In the north, a United States administration might have been pardoned for doubting the validity of the term Christian. It had different connotations among those with whom they had most dealings; it was not of the neighbourly New England variety at all. Enquiring into the conduct of public affairs, the Taft Commission found that under Spain, 'government had been perverted into a mere instrument for the benefit of the governing class at the expense of their subjects. Revenues were swallowed up by salaries, most of which were unnecessary. The very category of public works is only another designation for salaries. There are, in reality, no public works.' Corruption, after all, had been an accepted part of government for centuries: the *padrino* system filled posts and sinecures through blood ties alone; ability, training meant nothing, while underpaid employees had to find their own ways of acquiring money, status, position as best they could. This was the accepted order of things.

In many ways it still is.

As William C. Forbes was to express it later, the commissioners, 'with their American sense of justice and dislike of delay, were turned loose upon a world of medieval mismanagement and abuses like a group of knight-errants looking for wrongs to right and abuses to end. They found plenty to do.'

They continued to find plenty.

Nonetheless, the gradual Filipinizing of the administration went on. By 1912 the proportion of Americans in the public service had been reduced from 71 per cent to 48 per cent. The date is significant, for this was the year when Woodrow Wilson became president. Among his first acts was the replacement of Republicans in the islands by his own nominees, accompanied by a new promise of eventual independence. Yet the Democratic changes were not really so radical. A legislative assembly had already been in operation since 1907, though elections were based on property rights, not universal voting. The assembly was, in fact, a lower chamber, sharing equal powers with an upper house comprising an enlarged Philippines Commission.

Worcester was almost alone in deploring the situation. Legislative power had been placed in Filipino hands far too early, he wrote subsequently. They were just not ready for it.

The main problem, as he saw it, was the assembly's social complexion. Its members were mainly the inevitable *caciques*. But where else were they to come from? Worcester himself said that headhunters from the Mountain Province could hardly be asked to take seats, nor could the still untamed Moros, while the vast mass of the peasantry were still illiterate and unorganized. Hence, it was not surprising that legislation appeared to favour a special caste. This was examined in detail by Worcester, who was not only a Commission member but Secretary for the Interior from 1900 to 1913. He listed 312 bills passed by the Assembly, but disallowed by the Commission, which in turn had 107 of its own proposed bills blocked. It was a situation that came close to fantasy: a mad hatter's democracy.

Much of the conflict between the two chambers, wrote Worcester, concerned efforts by Filipino assemblymen to abolish or reduce taxes on land holdings, though these taxes had been put forward by the Commission to finance public health measures, education and the development of roads, railways and sea transport. There were deadlocks over such questions as limiting the number of horse races per week, most of which were said to be crooked; the whittling down of health services on the ground of cost; the abolition of Spanish-style appointments to the public service by influence; the reduction of taxation on lucrative trading in liquor and tobacco, which was virtually a monopoly; measures to make the smuggling of opium more difficult; the handing over of police control to local, politically-motivated boards; and moves to make firearms more easily obtained. 'The politicians of the present day are a hungry lot,' wrote Worcester. 'The more they are fed, the more their appetites grow, and the wider their voracious maws open.'

Yet, in 1912, the incoming Governor-General, a Democrat, did not see it that way at all. Francis Burton Harrison was a staunch Wilsonian, a man who believed that doing good was its own reward. Too much should not be made of his unexpected decree that dress for all official functions was to be cutaway coats, top hats and Prince Alberts, though old hands were astounded. They were even more so when Harrison began to fraternize with Filipinos, promoting many to senior government positions. There is no record of any personal exchange of views with seasoned administrators like Worcester, but his own memoirs charged the 'Taft Dynasty' with having become prejudiced and reactionary over the years. 'A bureaucracy was built up around his policy,' he wrote, 'assuming towards the subject race all the hard and patronizing superiority typical of European colonial administrators of modern times. Distrust of the Filipino and a determination to see him kept as a dependant as long as possible were new features of the policy.'

The Filipinos were becoming restive, he added. He was also warned by General Harry H. Bandholtz in his annual report of 1912 that there was a 'probability of disturbances in the provinces'. Hence, during this term, the pace of Filipinization was sharply increased.

The new policy ignored an earlier warning by Taft, who had said that 'only about three per cent of Filipinos vote, and only five per cent are said to read the public press. To confer independence now is, therefore, to subject the great mass of these people to the dominance of an oligarchical and, possibly, exploiting minority.'

Under Harrison, with President Wilson's approval, independence was becoming a more immediate issue. The spur to Harrison's resolve was unfortunately given by what he termed the vested interests of big American trusts, whose main concern was to protect their own investments in

61

the islands. Efforts were made by lobbies in Washington to have him removed from office. He was even called 'anti-American'. In this angered clash of interests the main issue of a gradually broadening democracy was submerged.

Perhaps the Filipino attitude was best expressed by young Manuel Quezon, already becoming a political force. 'I would rather have a government run like hell by Filipinos than one run by Americans like heaven.'[4]

The next phase was the passing of the Jones Bill in Washington during 1916. Largely drawing upon Harrison's recommendations, the bill promised that the United States would withdraw 'as soon as stable government can be established', authorized a locally-elected senate and recommended placing as much control as possible in Filipino hands, including key positions in the economy. The new freedoms coincided with America's entry into the European war, which created a 'get rich quick' boom in 1917-18, with Philippine products in heavy demand, especially hemp, sugar, timber and minerals. The newly established Philippine National Bank, with local directors, began to deal out unsecured loans with the recklessness of gamblers in Nevada. First to benefit were a string of new sugar mills built by *cacique* families. Some $24,000,000 of these loans were never repaid. The directors prospered, but bank reserves that should have been retained in New York vanished in alarming fashion. The Manila Railroad Company piled up fantastic losses, further impoverishing the bank. How could it have done otherwise, when mass inefficiency, place-seeking and vanishing funds were allied to the president's handing out of 150,000 free passes for unlimited periods. The crash came in 1921.

United States experts, sent to investigate affairs, found that millions of dollars could not be accounted for, the government bank was insolvent and the general economy in a state of chaos. The only thriving sector was the landowning aristocracy. As for the administration of justice, which, apart from the Supreme Court, no longer had trained Americans on the bench, a huge backlog of cases had built up. More than 50,000 were hopelessly awaiting trial. The Court of Land Registration had been abolished by a *cacique*-dominated legislature. This meant the end of the earlier American policy of redistributing lands to give the peasants more security. 'The land-grabbers from that time took law into their own hands,' wrote Katherine Mayo, 'with bolos and crooked lawyers.'[5]

All this bore out the warning made by William Taft, as Chief Justice in Washington a decade before. 'The idea that a public office is a public trust,' he said, 'has not been planted in the Filipino mind by experience, and the conception that an officer who fails in his duty, by embezzlement and otherwise, is violating an obligation . . . is difficult to grasp.'

The 1921 mission of inquiry was thorough and idealistic. It made visits to all fifty-six provinces and eight hundred municipalities, declaring that

4. Manuel L. Quezon, *The Good Fight*, New York, 1946.
5. Katherine Mayo, *The Isles of Fear*, New York, 1924.

it wanted to hear from all ranks of society, not only those with position and wealth. Its members were sometimes surprised to find in farming areas that 'gentlemen of leisure were dressed up to resemble field labourers and stood up and said their part'. Now, it appeared, the only people who did not want the United States to leave their islands were property owners and wealthy citizens. Except, that is, for the primitive mountain tribes. In Bontoc one aged chieftain, whose tattoo marks proclaimed that he had cut off the heads of many enemies, made an appeal for the return of American provincial governors, police officers, doctors and teachers. 'When the Americans came,' he said, 'we were like wild horses that had never been trained. They taught us the way to do things. They taught us how to live. Now we are going back to our wild state.'

The mission also found that government departments had become grossly over-staffed and bureaucratic. Courts of justice were dilatory, open to political influence, and had tens of thousands of cases awaiting trial. The greatest setback of all was the abolition of the Court of Land Registration.

This had been fundamental to American rural policy.

The concentration of land in fewer and fewer hands under Spanish administration, the growth of large haciendas and religious corporations, had continually depressed living standards among the peasantry. The vast proportion were landless families known euphemistically as tenant farmers. They were really peons. They were tied helplessly to a rented patch of land, committed to giving at least half their yield to the owner, as well as meeting other charges. They were forever in debt to usurers — mostly the landlords themselves — who charged fantastic rates of interest they could never meet. They were as much prisoners of the soil as were their carabao. The United States regime passed many laws to better these conditions, to break up the largest holdings and provide new titles — much of the friar lands were bought back from the Roman Catholic Church — but somehow these never seemed to find their way to peasant owners. The *caciques* remained too strongly entrenched. It was also due to their efforts that the Land Registration Court was allowed to lapse.

The well-meaning liberal Harrison had now been replaced by General Leonard Wood, who had helped to pacify the islanders in earlier years. With the help of trained economists, he attempted a new form of pacification. He was at once accused of trying to discriminate against Filipinos, and his controls rendered more or less impotent. Quezon told a meeting of 4,000 students in the University of the Philippines that his 'ultimate aim was to make the Governor-General a mere figurehead'. This had largely been achieved by Harrison himself.

During his term he set up a three-man Board of Control, which comprised the Governor-General, the president of the Senate and the speaker of the House of Representatives. Each had equal voting powers. This meant that the United States representative was always in a minority on controversial matters. For many years the two Filipino representatives were Quezon and Manuel Roxas, both members of the land-owning aristocracy.

Quezon was to become the dynamic figure of the twenties and thirties: spectacular, eloquent and patrician, a man whose patriotism and democratic professions were allied to the good life, for these were always identified with the interests of his own caste. He began as an admirer of American ways. He fitted easily into Washington society, for he was appointed Philippine delegate to Congress there in 1911. The climate of the United States was a revelation to him and, in his autobiography, he contrasted its lack of pretensions with the earlier regime in which he grew up. 'I had seen,' he wrote, 'if only from a distance, Spanish Governors-General riding in a carriage drawn by six white horses, preceded and followed by cavalry escorts. President Theodore Roosevelt greeted me warmly and took me to his table without ceremony.' A decade later he returned in a more confident role.

He had persuaded the House of Representatives to vote P1,000,000 annually for a special fund to campaign for national independence. The United States Congress ruled that such legislation was illegal, but it made no difference. Year after year this fund was comfortably spent in prolonged visits to a sumptuous Washington office by Quezon, Roxas, Sergio Osmena, party leader of the newly-formed Nacionalista Party, and Representative Claro M. Recto, who was later to be hailed as the apostle of nationalism. In 1924 the publication of their expense accounts caused a public outcry in Manila. Each man had a monthly dress allowance of P1,800 ($900) and *per diem* of P180, as well as large but unspecified sums for travel and entertainment. The *Philippines Herald* commented:

> In the past, patriots not only fought for their country, but died for their country. Today they are paid hundreds of pesos a day and . . . P1800 given them for well-tailored suits that Beau Brummell may hide his face in shame.
> Poor Juan! It is to weep.

Yet, in Manila society, this conspicuous consumption was not considered out of place. Colonial Americans lived equally well. It was a good life, insulated from the grimmer aspects of the world outside. Even the shock of the world depression was at first muted here. There was little or no development at the peasant level, for small-scale farming was not in line with American thought. Commerce was the one reality. This was the age of laissez-faire.

During the 1920s a number of large, commercially-run plantations were formed, with overseas investment, but it was left to a few more nationally-minded Filipinos to aid the peasants. An outstanding example was a land resettlement programme initiated in 1935 by Quezon, who persuaded the administration to buy thirty-three corporation-owned estates, reselling them to tenant farmers on an instalment plan. The most successful of these was the Koronadal Valley Project in Mindanao, to which two thousand peasant families from the north were transplanted. It was a model scheme that turned these hungry, defeated people into energetic farmers.

The project was wrecked by the Japanese invasion in 1941.

The depression of the thirties had a severe impact on the Philippines, whose economy was directed almost exclusively to a hitherto profitable export in raw materials. As usual, it was the peasantry that suffered worst. Even in those fertile rice areas of Central Luzon, which had, and still has, the largest percentage of sharecroppers, the vaunted Rice Bowl of the Philippines has never meant more to its working people than a bowl of rice a day. As the depression deepened, one United States economist wrote, 'Small wonder there is serious discontent in these provinces, especially in Nueva Ecija, where many of the landless are former home-steaders who have lost their holdings through the operation of an ancient politico-socio-legal system which often makes it possible for the rich to dispossess and exploit the poor.'[6]

It was at this period that Pampanga, Tarlac, Bulacan and Nueva Ecija became the trouble centres they have been ever since. Here was the perfect seed bed for communist intrigue. There were demonstrations, riots, strikes, accompanied by violent reaction from the owners of the land. From this hostile environment grew the Marxist-led Huk movement of the post-war years.

Meantime the United States had set a definite date for granting independence. This came wtih the Tydings-McDuffie Act of 1934. The Philippines was to be given its freedom in ten years, with an additional two-year period to complete the forming of a republic. That made the final date 4 July 1946: American Independence Day. The Philippines was also raised immediately from colonial to commonwealth status, with an elected president under the American flag. It seemed only natural that the first president should be Manuel Quezon.

But leading Filipinos now took alarm. If freedom was also to mean the end of commercial protection, where would their future markets be? An additional bill was passed in Washington, providing post-independence quotas for the import of sugar, coconut oil, tobacco, embroideries and cordage. These quotas were to be on a diminishing scale of five per cent annually for twenty years.

Today these quotas have become a critical factor in the confused political scene.

Had there been no Pacific war, the bitter political wrangles of modern times could have been avoided. The gradual progression towards a free republic might have been a happier one. Bombs falling on Pearl Harbour disrupted this generous dream five years before the republic was due.

Japan was to inflict further irrevocable scars upon this nation of many faces.

6. J. Ralston Hayden, *The Philippines*, New York, 1947.

CHAPTER 8

Bataan and After

*Responsible as I was for the safety
of the lives and property of the citizens
of Manila, I faced the impending entrance
of the Japanese Imperial Forces with
uneasiness and trepidation, because
American propaganda had led us to expect
abuses and excesses . . . I believe that my
high esteem for the Japanese, which I
entertained long before the war, was
completely justified by the irreproachable
conduct of the Japanese Imperial Forces . . .*

JORGE B. VARGAS

BATAAN ranks among the most honoured names in the tormented history of the Philippines.

Like many of the world's celebrated battles it represents a defeat that has somehow become ennobled. Thermopylae, Balaclava, Gallipoli, the Battle of Tirad Pass, all these have acquired a legendary heroism that has nothing to do with lost battles. The United States has now built a massive monument on Bataan Peninsula to be seen far across Manila Bay, commemorating the fallen of two races, an idealization of the spirit of resistance. But the nationalist-minded complain that it should have been a Filipino memorial, not just another landmark on the global field of America's foreign campaigns. Filipinos who fought there see it in quite other terms, for only six per cent of its defenders were American. The humiliation of General Wainwright's surrender to the impassively victorious Homma signified the burial, without funeral honours, of a generous, largely unselfish, if confused experiment in Asian colonizing that lasted little more than forty years.

Perhaps its obituary should be that idealism is not enough.

For the modern American the more enduring disgrace remains Pearl Harbour. From the soul-searching and bewilderment that followed a naval disaster that should never have occurred has stemmed Washington's sometimes perplexing, contradictory approach to Asia today: in Formosa, Korea, Vietnam. It is difficult to offer constructive aid when you do not know who, if any, are your friends? But the Filipino has never had time to think about Pearl Harbour. The shock waves produced by the surprise bombing of the Pacific Fleet on that first Sunday in December 1941, had further repercussions throughout Asia, for three hours later bombs were falling on Manila, too. United States bombers were caught on Philippines airfields, warships were sunk in Manila Bay. Within two days Japanese troops were landing in northern Luzon, and 300,000 began a rapid drive south. General Douglas MacArthur declared Manila an open city, which did not prevent the bombing of its ancient walled city on Christmas morning. The destruction of the three-hundred-year-old Manila Cathedral and Santo Domingo Church finally shattered the old dream of Spain. On the day after New Year, 1942, the Rising Sun flew above the United States High Commissioner's residence in the former Spanish palace of Malacanang.

The suddenness of the American collapse was also a psychological disaster. It hardly mattered that three months of stubborn resistance continued in the province of Bataan, on the far side of Manila Bay. No one would ever quite be able to believe in western superiority again. The supremacy of the white man had been shattered with ease by an Asian people, once described by Americans as a second-class nation.

The Filipinos, meantime, had to find other ways to survive.

It was no use saying that the pre-war regime lacked warnings. Fears of Japanese aggression had been widespread for at least a decade. There had been a continued inflow of settlers from Japan, mainly small businessmen who challenged the Chinese monopoly of retail trade, but also farmhands and labourers. Between 1918 and 1939 these immigrants increased from 1,000 to 18,000. By 1934 Japanese owned 24,00 hectares of agricultural land. One year later this figure had more than doubled. The government became so concerned that a new law was framed to restrict land ownership to corporations that had a minimum of 60 per cent Filipino control. This troubled the Japanese little, for they simply hired Filipinos or American citizens as dummies. In cities such as Manila, Davao and Iloilo strong Japanese enclaves developed, and it was rumoured that these included a well-organized fifth column in the event of war. By the end of 1941 these rumours proved correct.

Japanese influences were also strong in Central Luzon, where a crypto-fascist Sandakalista movement had created an unsuccessful peasant rising in 1931.

In 1941 General MacArthur sent one of his aides, Colonel (later General) Carlos P. Romulo on a tour of Asian countries to learn about their attitudes towards the threat of Japanese attack. In almost every capital he found uneasiness, but a preference for Japan to their own colonial masters. The Philippines, he considered, would stand alone among its neighbours. Yet the speed and power of the long-planned invasion took MacArthur off balance. Perhaps the miracle was that resistance in Bataan continued so long, far longer than in the Netherlands East Indies or Malaya. It took General Homma's divisions three bloody months to overrun Bataan, almost a month more to force a surrender from the desperate garrison on the surf-beaten rock fortress of Corregidor. Like other allegedly impregnable fortresses, the Rock on which millions had been spent proved to be just another Maginot Line. Bataan itself, though, was less a military defeat than a failure in organization. Food supplies failed; medical aid and drugs were almost unobtainable; 20,000 civilian refugees crowded into the peninsula, hampering the defenders even more. Yet the campaign was fought with great courage and devotion.

Filipinos are frequently irked by American writers who claim this as a United States Army operation, glossing over the presence of Philippine troops. In fact, of the 50,000 who took part, 47,000 were Filipinos. Five of the eleven divisional commanders were also Filipinos. So were nearly all those forced into the terrible Death March that followed Bataan's surrender on 8 April. Thirty-six thousand men began that 150-mile trek from Mariveles, on the peninsula's southern tip, to Capas in Tarlac. They were herded like carabao, as a friend of mine who survived it said. Those who fell exhausted were clubbed, bayoneted, shot. Many were left to die of thirst or hunger. They were allowed a few hours of sleep nightly in wayside cockpits, penned there like pigs, and fed in like manner. Their guards were contemptuous of sick and wounded, flogging them with rifle butts or swords. With their arrival at Camp O'Donnell, the numbers in this concentration camp rose to 45,000. Again there were no medicines, little food. Thirty thousand men did not leave that camp alive.

Yet Jorge B. Vargas, former executive secretary to President Quezon, wrote in 1943 of 'the irreproachable conduct of the Japanese Imperial Forces'.[1] In the same Japanese newspaper article he added: 'My belief in Japanese nobility and honour has been further strengthened by the benign policies which have been followed subsequently. As I have said time and time again, the Imperial Japanese Forces came to us, not as enemies, but as a liberating army of fellow Orientals.'

I heard other versions of this 'nobility and honour' from Filipino friends after the war. They spoke of brutal bayonetings, wholesale rape, floggings for minor insults, fingers and hands cut off as punishment for theft or insubordination. Whenever Filipinos met soldiers of the occupation in the streets they were forced to bow, just as they had once been forced to do by their Spanish masters. That splendid and dignified old lady, Dr Francesca Benitez, founder of the Philippine Women's University, told me how soldiers had ejected her into the street at bayonet point. Her crime had been to smuggle girl boarders out of the University before the Japanese broke in. The magnificent library of books was bulldozed down Taft Avenue to replace a bomb-shattered bridge.

When General Homma, after the fall of Corregidor, led a triumphal march through the capital, thousands of Manileños cheered the victors as they passed. Manila is one of the world's most cynical cities, and for numbers of them there are no issues larger than a sufficiency of food. Besides, by then, the government leaders were sipping tea and whisky with the Japanese High Command. Defeated, demoralized, Filipinos had to accommodate themselves to an uncertain future as best they could. They had either to join the guerrillas and go underground, as large

1. *Osaka Mainichi*, 9 April 1943, Japan.

numbers did, or play a subtle game of follow-my-leader in the fashion of the politicos Quezon left behind. Quezon, with his vice-president Sergio Osmena, and MacArthur, had left Corregidor by submarine before Bataan collapsed, then flew from Mindanao to Australia, where the general expected to find powerful forces awaiting him for a counter-attack. Instead he found only panic and confusion. Quezon and Osmena went on by air to Washington, formed a government-in-exile and echoed Mac-Arthur's promise of 'I shall return' in short-wave broadcasts. Before the end General Roxas and Jose Abad Santos, who Quezon had made his official representative, were also smuggled out of Corregidor to the southern islands. Roxas joined a guerrilla force on Mindanao, while Santos was captured and executed for refusing to divulge the Filipino general's whereabouts.

When the Chief Justice's son broke down as he saw his father taken before a firing squad, the old man said to him calmly, 'Do not cry. Show these people that you are brave. It is an honour to die for one's country. Not everyone has that chance.'

Epic gestures of that kind were not accorded to the other leaders. While remnants of the USAAFE and independent guerrilla forces fought on in Mindanao, the Visayas and the mountains of Luzon, the rest of Quezon's former cabinet were testing the dangerous waters of Co-Prosperity. Their principals were Senator Jose P. Laurel, Senator Jose Yulo, Jorge B. Vargas, the executive secretary, and Claro M. Recto, all of them prominent members of the Nacionalista Party which had agitated for freedom for thirty years and more. Now they expressed their support for the Japanese High Command, claiming that the country would otherwise be completely destroyed. The *cacique* landlords retreated to Manila, as they had done after Malolos, leaving their haciendas in charge of overseers. Merchants and commercial leaders began to trade profitably with their conquerors. The peasants, almost alone, resisted.

In Central Luzon, especially, Juan de la Cruz went on planting and harvesting rice in stoical fashion. At least by day. By night peasants picked up their hidden guns, harried the Japanese, disrupted transport, killed collaborators and generally made it almost impossible for the invader to secure his hold on the countryside. In the Visayas and Mindanao much the same thing happened, for American and Filipino troops made common cause with the peasantry, limiting Japanese occupation to the towns. In the mountains of Mindanao, for instance, the American Colonel Wendell Fertig built up an army of 34,000, formed a civil government complete with law courts, currency, postal services and hospitals. Such organizations also supplied a vital intelligence service for MacArthur's forces. Japan had conquered the Philippines, but was unable to exploit it either as a granary, or as a secure base for its wider Pacific campaign.

In 1943 a new tactic was introduced. An autonomous Executive Commission was set up, headed by Vargas and Laurel, and all captured Filipino troops were released, as a gesture of friendship and confidence.

That, at least, was the official statement. In actual fact, these men were needed by the Imperial Army as a labour force. In July that year a Nippon-Philippines alliance was signed, and the newly appointed 'president', Jose Laurel, read his declaration of independence on the Luneta, where 45 years earlier Rizal had died for a different dream of freedom. The Japanese premier, General Tojo, flew in from Tokyo to attend the ceremony, while Laurel, Vargas and Recto were decorated for their services to the cause of the Greater East Asia War.

While President Roosevelt spoke bitterly of a 'puppet government . . . made in fraud and deceit', the new regime enunciated a policy that concentrated on economic development and cultural re-education, making no political commitment beyond vague talk of eventual independence. Claro Recto, now designated foreign secretary, made a number of eloquent speeches on the need to revise the nation's outlook along Asian lines. 'The past attempts at cultural development,' he said, 'were partial and one-sided, as they bore the exclusive imprint of occidental civilization and laid undue emphasis on its philosophy, arts and institutions which, in many of its aspects, were alien to the oriental mind and spirit. . . . It is time for them (Filipinos) to delve more in to the accumulated wisdom of the East, bring out its virile qualities and harness them to the service of the people.'[2]

It was perhaps yet another tactic in the old war of the *caciques* to free themselves from foreign domination, shrewdly emphasizing things of the mind and spirit, without touching upon Japan's physical mastery.

Was this a new mask, or a new face?

The Japanese proved themselves a subtle people, too. Baulked by the passive resistance of the people, except for the dealers in rice and army supplies, they had somehow to win support for their war effort, or at least to neutralize opposition. As Teodoro A. Agoncillo has expressed it in his two volume history of the period, 'the Japanese did not act directly in controlling the affairs of the Philippine government; they wanted to make it appear that the government was being run by Filipinos . . . collaborating with them freely and without any pressure. It was their purpose to wean the Filipinos away from the Americans.'[3]

To achieve this, Agoncillo argues, they chose Laurel to head the government, because he was known as a strong nationalist, and therefore would not appear too amenable a puppet in public eyes. At the same time, they knew him as a scholarly Orientalist who had lived in Japan and had Japanese sympathies. Agoncillo, like others since the war, does not regard him as having been a quisling. Laurel had to run affairs in the interests of Japan, he writes, because military pressures were irresistible, but his actions were also designed to protect his own people where possible. When, at the time of the Allied counter-offensive in 1944, Japan

2. *Philippine Review*, December, 1943, Manila.

3. Teodoro A. Agoncillo, *The Fateful Years: Japan's Adventure in the Philippines, 1941-45*, Manila, 1965.

wanted Laurel to declare war on the British and Americans, Laurel merely declared 'a state of war'. When Japan wanted him to mobilize Filipino troops against an impending invasion, Laurel resisted the demand for conscription and merely called for volunteers. If nothing more, it was an ingenious exercise in semantics. It did not in the least mitigate the growing hatred of the Laurel regime. It was on the home front that the conflict grew most bitter.

Here the rule of the 'Three Blind Mice', as Laurel, Vargas and Aquino were called, was almost totally ineffective. Scarcity of rice and other commodities set prices soaring, black-marketing became almost universal, crime and violence mounted, graft corroded government and business, private homes were constantly invaded by the Kempetai searching for key men of the resistance, members of prominent families were carried off as hostages. Yet the resistance continued in heroic fashion. Hundreds vanished behind the prison walls of Fort Santiago, never to be heard of again, while villages, suspected of supporting guerrillas, were burnt and destroyed. In one Pampanga stronghold of the Japanase 2,000 skulls were found after the war. Hundreds of killings were made after Filipino land-owners handed the Kempetai lists of suspected guerrilla leaders, trade unionists and peasant agitators. When the Japanese High Command insisted that Laurel take action against the guerrillas, 75 per cent of the one reliable force, the Philippine Constabulary, deserted and the remainder had to be disarmed. The breaking point came when Laurel, in June 1944, conscripted 250,000 Filipinos — including released war prisoners — for a so-called programme of public works. The principal works involved were airfields, shipping ports and Japanese army camps.

The critical point was reached, as always in the Philippines, over rice. Prices of the blackmarket rose from the normal P100 per cavan (120 lb.) to P7,500 and eventually, by the end of 1944, to P12,000. In Manila social anarchy was intensified by starvation. It was useless for the Laurel regime to say that all sections were suffering alike, for truckloads of rice and other foodstuffs were seen outside the homes of wealthy collaborators, Japanese generals golfed and dined with puppet leaders and frequent banquets were held at Malacanang Palace. On Chief Justice Jose Yulo's birthday the luncheon menu at the Palace included tenderloin steak, roast turkey, champagne and cigars.

Laurel blamed the rice shortage on the Central Luzon guerrillas. This was true enough. The great rice bowl had been almost sealed off from the outside world, and the Imperial Army was desperate for supplies. Hence the pressure put on the government to suppress the liberation forces, which had almost complete control of towns and regions in the north, even electing local commanders and mayors by popular vote. This movement had acquired the name of Hukbalahap (originally Hukbo ng Bayan Laban sa Hapon, the People's Anti-Japanese Army). It was not then a communist organization, though some of its leaders were Marxists who had been active during the depression years. In the middle of 1944

71

Laurel called the absentee landlords of the central provinces to Malacanang, telling them that 'we have to get rice. We will strengthen the
constabulary to keep peace and order, and if the constabulary cannot do
it, I will ask the Japanese to help me.'

This anti-guerrilla force, known as Ganap, was made up of former
Sandakalistas, Laurel's police and any mercenaries who could be recruited. Part of their wages were met by the landlords, while prize money
was offered for every guerrilla captured or hanged. Meantime the Huks
were clashing with another guerrilla force in the region, formed by the
remnants of the USAFFE. The Huks were said to have 5,000 well-armed
fighters, 10,000 lightly-armed reserves, and another 35,000 with no arms
but home-made guns and bolos. The situation was taking on the elements
of a civil war.

Then came MacArthur's long-promised return.

On 17 October 1944, American troops landed in the southern Visayas,
capturing several islands in the Gulf of Leyte. One of these, significantly,
was Homonhon, the scene of Magellan's first landing more than 400 years
earlier. But Filipino guerrillas, strengthened by fresh supplies of American arms, helped to immobilize the Japanese. When United States forces
reached Luzon they found the way cleared by local guerrillas, despite
GANAP efforts to destroy them. In Central Luzon Americans and Huks
fought side by side, and Manila was recaptured in far more rapid time
than would have been possible otherwise.

For the Japanese the war in these islands was over. It was only just
starting for Filipinos. The occupation years had created a new sense of
unity, mainly through the resistance, though the ancient divisions of
caste and wealth had also brought new tensions.

The *caciques* had also managed to survive. The unique genius of this
caste was summed up by a Socialist leader, Pedro Abad Santos, when a
high-ranking Japanese officer asked his opinion of the Laurel government. 'These politicos are smart,' Santos said. 'They fooled the Americans. They fooled the people. And now they're fooling you.'

Before the Americans re-entered Manila, Laurel and other cabinet
members fled to Tokyo.

CHAPTER 9

Fruits of Independence

> *I knew in that first moment when*
> *our flag stood alone against the*
> *Philippine sky that this was the beginning*
> *of freedom in all Asia. It was on its*
> *way, nothing could stop it from now on.*
> *And it was the pebble that released the*
> *avalanche; a few years later Indonesia*
> *would be set free by the Netherlands,*
> *and India by Mother England, and what*
> *can follow but Indo-China — British*
> *Malaya — Africa? It is inevitable . . .*
> CARLOS P. ROMULO

INDEPENDENCE could not have come at a more difficult time.

The Tydings-McDuffie Act of 1934 had set the date, and liberated Filipinos were in no mind to have it postponed, despite the chaos left by war. The Fourth of July 1946 it had to be: United States Independence Day. A large proportion of the people were homeless, hungry, victims of a huge blackmarket. General Eisenhower reported that Manila had suffered more devastation than any capital except Warsaw. Eighty per cent of its buildings had been destroyed; social services were non-existent; food supplies at a minimum. Elsewhere whole cities and towns were in ruins, for the cautious American system of pattern-bombing and offshore shelling before attacking had inflicted greater damage than had the Japanese. Health services had everywhere broken down, while the education system was said to have been put back a quarter century. 'A whole generation of children had never seen the inside of a schoolroom,' wrote R. A. Smith. 'Worse still, those young people — and some of their elders — had come to take it for granted that the normal mode of behaviour was to deceive, to rob, and to kill, since that was what they had been forced to do by the Japanese.'[1]

Again, thousands of guerrillas were refusing to give up their arms. Chief among these were the Huks. Their leaders had expressed surprise, somewhat naively, that the United States Army would not accept them as rulers of the central provinces. They reminded the Americans that during four years of fighting they had taken part in 1,200 engagements, killing 25,000 Japanese and collaborators. The High Command claimed that many of those dead were political enemies of the Huks rather than

1. R. A. Smith, *Philippine Freedom*, New York, 1958.

collaborators, which was probably splitting hairs. Ignoring the existence of local government bodies set up by the Huks, with elected governors, mayors and barrio captains, General MacArthur sent in troops and appointed Nacionalista supporters in their place. Many of these were suspected of collaboration, blackmarketing and terrorism. The result was to inflame peasant resentment further and lay the basis for political feuds that still poison the present-day politics in the region.

But what was the alternative?

The United States had not kept its pledge to reconquer the Philippines merely to see it threatened by a communist take-over. But to restore the status quo meant restoring the hated landlords who had fled to Manila and traded with the Japanese. The situation was made worse by the fact that President Quezon had died in exile, while Osmena returned to find himself unable to control his divided followers. To keep some continuity of government, MacArthur decided to reconvene the pre-war Congress, ignoring the fact that a majority of its members had collaborated. One of the first actions of Congress was for members to vote themselves P13,000,000 for back pay and contingent expenses, while mass meetings of the hungry sent protests to President Truman. The previous High Commissioner, Paul McNutt, was also brought back to office until the republic was declared. In January 1946 he sent Truman a revealing tele-gram. 'The situation here is critical,' he wrote. 'It does not at this moment seem possible for the Filipino people, ravaged and demoralized by the cruellest and most destructive of wars, politically split between the loyalists and enemy collaborators, with several sizeable, well-armed dissi-dent groups still at large, to cope with the coincidence of political inde-pendence and the tremendous economic demands of rehabilitation.'

Yet, under the eyes of a watchful Asia, Americans felt themselves unable to revoke their promise. The ultimate problem was to produce a strong government. Or a strong man to govern.

MacArthur's choice was General Roxas. Much mystery had attached to Manuel Roxas, following his escape from Corregidor. It was said that the Japanese wanted his head for his leadership of guerrilla forces in Min-danao. Yet he spent 1943 in a Japanese prison camp there and no one interfered with his head. The following year he was living 'in retirement' at his Manila home; at least when he was not playing golf on the private course at Malacanang, or presiding over Laurel's Economic Commission, which had been set up to stabilize production for the Japanese. Now, under MacArthur's patronage, he was being proposed for the presidency of the new republic. Vice-president Osmena protested. He had no inten-tion of giving up his leadership of the Nacionalista Party. The Solicitor-General, Senator Lorenzo Tanada, also protested. A resistance leader who joined Osmena's cabinet, he had been instructed to prepare charges against Laurel and his fellow collaborators, including Roxas. Yet he was unable to move against the general, because he could never find two American officers to sign the necessary depositions.

Frustrated by Osmena, Roxas formed a breakaway movement which he named, with unconscious irony, the Liberal Party. It had the backing of extreme right-wing landowners, including wealthy mestizo families who had helped to finance Generalissimo Franco during the Spanish Civil War, for which they were decorated by the Falange. Roxas began an election campaign which created an explosive situation in Central Luzon, where 50,000 peasants massed for a protest march on Malacanang. This was organized by the Democratic Alliance, which both Roxas and MacArthur described as communist. The leadership did include communists, but it had also socialists, agrarian leaders and middle-of-the-road democrats. A more sophisticated regime could have handled this 'united front' situation without provocation and hysteria. MacArthur, however, was in a hurry. The backers of Roxas were his pre-war friends. In addition, he was trying to deal with a critical situation in Japan, and the crumbling of Chiang Kai-shek's corrupt rule in China. The United States was also committed to preventing leftist advances across the world in post-Hitler Germany, Italy and France.

Roxas was given a free hand.

The Truman government was not happy about the situation, and the Secretary of the Interior, Harold L. Ickes, sent a mission to investigate. MacArthur sent it home again in a matter of days.

With a frankness unusual for a cabinet member, Ickes wrote a foreword to a critical book published by Hernando J. Abaya in New York that year.

'We gave the Philippines political freedom to enter the world family of nations,' he wrote, 'but did we give them internal political liberty? More important still, did we give them economic freedom? . . . The danger of continued official support in Washington of the demagogues and the grasping economic overlords in the Philippines is in disregard of every democratic principle. . . . The collaborators who held office under the Japanese during their occupation and who have ruled the Philippines in the period of a Japanese victory are in power now, despite an overwhelming American military success. . . . MacArthur promptly set free the collaborationist Roxas and proceeded to cover his collaborationist activities with a thick coat of whitewash.

'Already there is serious unrest in the Philippines with armed soldiers at the point of guns imposing both political and economic tyranny upon the people who, with the hope of liberty sustaining them, kept up the fight against the Japanese relentlessly while Roxas lived in safety and comfort under Japanese protection in Manila.'[2]

The fervour that greeted the declaration of Philippine Independence on the Fourth of July was shadowed by bitterness. When the gay flag of the Philippines replaced Old Glory on the Luneta, cynics said that it signified no more than a change of flags. MacArthur declared that the

---

2. Hernando J. Abaya, *Betrayal in The Philippines*, from the foreword by Harold L. Ickes, New York, 1946.

election of Roxas meant that the people had cleared him of his collaborationist charges. It was hardly as simple as that.

On election day, according to Abaya, 'the stern-faced Generalissimo made a round of city precincts in his car, escorted by two jeeploads of bodyguards armed with carbines and sub-machine guns. For the first time in Manila politics, city thugs armed with 45s and carbines, "patrolled" the polling places in Manila's labour districts, riding in jeeps plastered with Roxas posters. Roxas may have had no knowledge of this, but in the public mind the mere association of his name with the underworld was viewed with no little alarm.'

Many shooting incidents followed. The governor of Camarines Sur, an Osmena supporter, was ambushed and seriously wounded. In Bacolor, Pampanga, a Democratic Alliance president was machine-gunned to death. In Sulu, where Osmena carried a large majority, large numbers of voters were scared away by military police controlled by Roxas. In Manila areas other voters were blocked by army goons. In Huk country military police intimidated opposition voters and distributed Roxas pamphlets, while American fighter aircraft flew low over towns and barrios at full throttle. Many long-term criminals were also released to provide bodyguards for Roxas candidates.

Once in power, General Roxas lived up to his strong-man role. The Nacionalistas, though they included many collaborators, were outnumbered by collaborators in the Liberal Party. On the other hand, Roxas refused to allow three elected members of the Democratic Alliance to take their seats in Congress. He sent Philippine Constabulary and army units to central Luzon, where the left-wing leadership was driven underground. The result was to drive milder leftists into the hard-core communist movement, creating a dangerously unsettled climate that still remains two decades later. It ignored the reasoned warning given to a Manila Rotary Club meeting earlier that year by Paul McNutt, who said that 'a kind of feudalism has dominated the life of the average Filipino land worker for centuries. That feudalism must be progressively eradicated.'

Osmena had made a brief effort to do so in 1945, when he called a conference of peasants and landowners to work out a better system of wages and crop sharing. Under Roxas the old feudalism returned. The Nacionalistas were equally troubled by another turn in the economy.

In November 1945 the United States Congress, preparing the way for independence, had replaced the 1934 Tydings-McDuffie Act with a new one designed to help rebuild the war-shattered economy. The new treaty, signed by President Truman in May 1946 stipulated that there be eight years of free trade between the two nations, followed by twenty years of progressively decreasing quotas until the two became normal competitive traders. This seemed reasonable enough. What angered the Nacionalistas was an additional section written into the Bell Act that read:

> The disposition, exploitation, development and utilization of all agricultural, timber and mineral lands of the public domain, water, minerals, coal,

petroleum, and other mineral oils, all forces and supplies of potential energy and other natural sources of the Philippines, and the operation of public utilities, shall, if open to any person, be open to citizens of the United States and to all forms of business enterprise owned and controlled, directly or indirectly, by the United States.

In effect, practically everything.

Under the Roxas regime, resentment increased further when Liberal supporters, notably the Elizalde and Zobel concerns, were given the franchise to represent a large proportion of major American exports, including steel, motor cars, electrical and constructional machinery. Measures were taken to defeat the huge blackmarket by disposing of American war materials, mainly clothing and foodstuffs, at cheap prices. But these were sold in bulk only to the large companies. By the time they reached the poor for whom they were intended, they could again be bought only at blackmarket prices.

No wonder the 1949 elections were fought with even stronger passions.

General Roxas having died in office, the struggle became one between his former vice-president Quirino and Jose Laurel, who had never been brought to trial for collaboration. Millions were still unemployed and homeless; little reconstruction had been attempted; American dollars for rehabilitation had vanished into the pockets of government officials; while thousands of ex-guerrillas and bandits terrorized country areas with war-time arms. Hundreds died in that election. Laurel was shot at several times while speaking in Cebu City. In Negros Occidental a Nacionalista mayoral candidate, Moise Padilla, was kidnapped by policemen, tortured and killed with machine-gun bullets. Among the twenty-two men sentenced to death for this murder were the provincial governor, his police chief and a mayor.

'It was a terrible year for opposition candidates, who could hardly conduct their election campaign,' wrote C. Valmoria fifteen years later. 'They could not hold public rallies. They spent most of their time instead visiting hospitals where local opposition leaders were confined after torture and maulings in the hands of administration-hired goons. . . . The streets of Cebu were bristling with guns and the picture was practically the same in other parts of the country. Consequently, the bees, the birds and the trees voted. A province with only about 60,000 registered voters accounted for more than 150,000 votes in favour of the administration candidate. Election frauds, terrorism and other forms of abuses aroused public indignation. An attempt was made to overthrow by force the corrupt and graft-ridden administration. . . . All arsenals throughout the country were under control of the armed forces rebel group. The plan to capture Malacanang was timed so that the rebellion would be simultaneous throughout the country. Regional co-ordinators, mostly veteran guerrillas, were sent out to alert their men. After all plans were completed, Huk supremo Luis Taruc offered 20,000 fully-armed men to capture Malacanang. But no one in the group wanted a communist to join the uprising. While the group was trying to find a way to execute the original plan without Taruc, Francisco Medrano rose up in arms in Batangas, ransacked the armoury there and went into hiding in the mountains.'[3]

Valmoria then described a plot to assassinate President Quirino. This was rejected as 'inhuman'. Instead, a wartime pilot volunteered to crash a suicide plane into the President's oath-taking ceremony, firing its guns. This, too, was opposed because it might create an international incident since ambassadors and other foreign representatives were also to be in the grandstand.

Quirino survived. At the end of his four year term he was able to claim that he had restored such industries as timber, sugar, hemp and food production almost to pre-war levels. His critics said they would have recovered in any case. The terrorism associated with his regime created a strong reaction and a mid-term Senate election lost him most of his upper house support. The absence of violence at the polling booths was due entirely to his able Secretary of Defence, Ramon Magsaysay, who called out the entire army to police them. Then, disenchanted with an administration 'full of crooks and grafters', Magsaysay defected to the Nacionalistas, who nominated him their presidential candidate.

This time there was only one issue. Corruption. The forty-seven year old son of a Zambales peasant, Magsaysay was a resistance hero: a man of the people. He was widely admired for the way he had overcome his poor beginnings, put himself through school and college and then, in the devious politics of the day, shown himself incorruptible. Opposition threats to disrupt the poll won him more support. In many provinces there were shootings, gangsters patrolling with tommyguns and ballot boxes stolen, but he was elected with a record majority. In the end it proved to be a moderately peaceful election. The final score was ten dead, twenty-six wounded.

Magsaysay won because he spoke the language of the common man. For the first time a leader had emerged who looked beyond a special clique or class. He became almost at once a legend. No other Filipino has ever achieved such fame at home or abroad. He advocated giving autonomy to the barrios, setting up co-operatives and rural banks, and reforming land tenure laws. But three years and four months after taking office, before he could achieve any of this, he was dead.

The aircraft that crashed in the mountains behind Cebu in March 1957 killed more than a president and many of his advisers. It killed the hopes of millions who believed that at last a more peaceable, constructive life was possible. It was remarkable how much he achieved in so short a time. The rule of graft had been whittled down, employment rose, new industries were opened, thousands of homeless were housed and a programme for peasant resettlement put under way. His greatest achievement was the quelling of revolutionary unrest in Central Luzon, where the Huk

3. *Manila Bulletin*, 18 September 1964.

movement had again become dangerously active under Quirino. As Defence Secretary, Magsaysay built up an efficient intelligence network, then arrested the entire leadership in one swift raid. The public was shocked to find they had been meeting, not in remote mountain areas, but in Manila itself. Energetic police action then broke the backbone of the movement in the provinces. But Magsaysay did not leave it at that. He understood the peasant problem. It was his own world. He knew that communism could not be eradicated so long as millions owned no land, but were merely peons tied to the master's soil. Eighty per cent of rice farming families were in the hands of usurers from birth to death. They were drawn to revolution, because they had nothing to lose but their debts.

Instead of leaving the army as an idle peacetime force, with little to do but intimidate the peasants, Magsaysay formed several units into an Economic Development Corps, whose job was to take over unoccupied lands. He borrowed the communist cry of 'Land for the Landless', and made it a government slogan. Any captured Huk who recanted was given a land grant. By the time of his death a thousand families had been resettled under better conditions than they had ever known. Only 246 of these were actually former Huks, but the propaganda value of these contented settlers was immense.

Under his successor, President Garcia, the scheme was allowed to lapse, but Magsaysay's memory has remained an inspirational one.

American recognition of his achievements came with the sponsoring of annual Ramon Magsaysay Memorial Awards by the Rockefeller Foundation. Each year a committee of prominent Filipinos makes six awards to men and women of various Asian countries who have distinguished themselves in public service, international goodwill, community leadership, literature and journalism. This has come to be known as Asia's equivalent of the Nobel Prize. In 1964 I saw one of these awards being given to a Chinese-born Roman Catholic priest, who had spent fourteen years organizing peasant communities in South China, Cambodia and Vietnam, where he had often been under communist fire. The tribute paid to Magsaysay by Father Augustine Nguyen Lac Hoa was a significant one, for it voiced criticism of the negative methods being used by the United States in its efforts to defeat the Viet Cong.

'Theirs is a reversal of the Magsaysay principles,' he told a gathering that included President Macapagal, government leaders and the diplomatic corps. 'There were two orders to his plan. First to win the people. And only then to win the war. In South Vietnam these have been reversed. That is why we are not winning.'

CHAPTER 10

The Silent Tao

Planting rice is never fun,
Bent from morn till set of sun,
Cannot stand and cannot sit,
Cannot even rest a bit.
TAGALOG SONG

THERE are regions of these islands that can be classed among the beautiful places of the earth. In the provinces of Central Luzon, in Zamboanga del Sur, in Batangas, or beneath that immaculate cone of Mayon volcano in Bicolandia the ricefields spread their flawless beauty across eternal landscapes. The brilliance of the sun is astonishing; the luminous blue mountains at a distance, the emerald of ripening rice; sky-washed water in irrigation dykes and pools; and the angled roofs of *nipa* huts perched quaintly on stilts beneath palms or flowering poinciana trees. Somewhere at a distance there is always a carabao, motionless, as if weighted to the earth, its long curved horns like some black wood-carving from the mountain Igorots. And the bent figures under broad bamboo hats; men and women indistinguishable from one another as they work the common earth; planting, reaping, seeding behind their wooden ploughs, winnowing the *palay* in split bamboo trays.

This is not only timeless. This is Asia.

'They put a basketful of rice in the river to soak,' wrote Francisco de Sande to King Phillip II of Spain in 1576. 'After a few days they take it from the water; what is bad and has not sprouted is thrown away. The rest is put on a bamboo mat and covered with earth, and placed where it is kept moist by the water.'

Things are still not so different today. A little mechanization has come in, but not much. Some irrigation. The early friars showed the peasants how to tame the once wild carabao, introduced the plough; they brought to the islands sugar, maize, cotton, peanuts, tobacco, coffee and many kinds of fruits; but rice is still the crop that shapes and determines the existence of the common *tao*. Rice is the index of prosperity, the life-giver, the taskmaster and release from famine. The *tao* measures his days and years in terms of the yield from his infinitesimal *padi*, clothes and feeds his family from it, makes his small offering to barrio church or wayside chapel, and dreams one day of paying off the usurer from his sale of *palay*.

A whole folk lore has grown up around his planting and winnowing of the unhusked rice called *palay*: legend, superstition, dances and song. He still plants in the sodden *padi* fields to the songs his people have sung for centuries, sometimes to the gentle rhythm of guitars, whose music carries through to the barrio fiestas that celebrate harvest time or the saints imported by his unforgotten Spanish overlords.

All this is more truly the Philippines than crowded Rizal Avenue with its Chinese stores and beggars, or the shadowy night bars of Mabini where congressmen entertain till Matins. For all his stolid resistance to modern pressures, the *tao* is the man who most completely influences the nation's ideology.

Though rice is almost universal, it is by no means the only crop. There are indeed regions where no rice grows. In certain Visayan areas, where corn is the staple produce or in the indelibly green island of Negros, the astonishingly wealthy — for the *haciendero* — sugar belt. There is the broad spiny *abaca* for making hemp; camotes, cacao, pineapples, gourds, guava, yams, papaya, bananas, oranges, mangoes, avocados and all the spices; all manner of vegetable produce that should make for rich living on these fertile, volcanic soils. Above all, there is the universal coconut palm, the most graceful of all trees that transforms valleys, debris-strewn beaches, cogon-grassed hillsides to an almost idyllic re-creation of the more remote South Seas. Throughout these massive, typhoon-swept, over-populated islands copra has become the king of growing things. Seventy per cent of the world's copra comes from the Philippines, much of it of the finest quality.

Again there is the harvest from the seas. The waters of this sprawling archipelago yield an immense variety of fish: most of the world's species, from game fish like shark, marlin, sailfish, barracuda down to the much sought *bangus, lapu-lapu, dilis, talilong* and *dapa*.

Fishing, too, has hardly changed since the ancient Malays fashioned their first *praus* and *bancas* from the adzed trunks of island trees. These narrow-gutted, long canoes with their double outriggers of stout bamboo stand upon almost every expanse of shoreline and mud flat from the bleak Batanes islands to the Sulus of the far south. All day they drift upon the transparent blue ocean, many miles from villages on shore. At night their crude fishing lamps glitter on black water like reflected stars in surreptitious motion.

I shall always remember my first sight of the Philippines, coming in from the vast emptiness of the Pacific. Our dawn landfall was the rough-cast eastern slopes of Samar, a little to the north of that immense chasm in the ocean's floor, the Mindanao Deep, which plunges 42,000 feet below the surface. We had steamed for six days from New Guinea in the wake of a typhoon, and the utterly calm sea here was beyond belief. Its blue was paler, more serene than the madonna sky, though the sun soon began to heat up the windless air. We turned west into San Bernadino Strait, through which the galleons had passed on the long trans-Pacific haul to Acapulco two and three centuries ago. Here and there were smaller, vividly green islands, then, through the heat haze, the distant mountain mass of Luzon, gathering huge towers of cumulus about its serrated volcanic peaks, as if to recapitulate the turbulence and smoke of bygone eruptions. The great Mayon remained invisible, but Juban and Bulusan raised the menace of their broken crowns to starboard as we steamed between Ticao Island and the stolid peninsula of Sorsogon.

It was like entering an inland sea. As it was, in fact; for among this maze of islands are broad deep sounds and straits leading to the wide Sibuyan and Visayan Seas, which make for smooth sailing between the occasional days of terror called typhoons. Everywhere, on this hot, still day, *bancas* drifted. There were never more than two figures crouched motionless in these slender craft; more often only one. They took no notice of our vessel steaming at full speed past; seldom looked up even. Among the closer ones there was never a response to call or wave. We were not of their world. We were intruders, monsters of some foreign sort, especially when a broad-hatted fisherman with bent back was forced to paddle from the spreading furrows of our bow wave. Some of these craft had women, even children aboard; others had small canopies with plaited fronds amidships to ward off the savagery of a sun almost directly overhead. Now and again we sighted some primitive craft with mixed cargoes, making for one of the small ports of Leyte, Masbate or Panay, quaint, blunt-bowed craft, heaped with bamboo or sawn tree trunks, and driven by matting sails of an incredibly tattered nature. The emphasis here was on ancient ways, the primitive.

Later, I came to know more of Samar.

It is a sad island, a place of potential fertility gone to seed, of poor soils and narrow, patchy plains. The third largest of all the islands, it exists in a state of perpetual depression, and wages are seldom more than fifty centavos a day. Absentee landlords own the plantations, copra-making is the only employment, apart from sharecropping corn or rice, and, of course, fishing. But markets are far away and the only fish-canning factory has long been closed, while illegal dynamiting has reduced the normal haul to almost uneconomic levels. In the fishing villages especially crime with violence is an everyday event. Its causes? Either boredom, or the fierce spirit called *tuba* they brew from the coconut palm.

Too often this is a land of the *amok*. Nothing is more designed to create an *amok*, with stabbings or a swinging bolo, than *tuba*. Life here is restricted to the monotony of narrow muddy streets, whose only dwellings are the flimsy *barong-barongs*: whole shanty towns of three-ply board and packing cases. What hope is there for the young here, when few remain at school beyond the age of eight. Toiling for the family pittance must come before education.

This is only one aspect of almost universal poverty. Elsewhere, in other islands, are different aspects. Sometimes disguised, more picturesquely set in green landscapes, under someone else's trees, on another's rented land. The reasons for such a climate were set out by the Bell mission of inquiry sent by President Truman in 1948.

'The Filipino farmer is between two grindstones,' stated the report. 'On top is the landlord, who often exacts an unjust share of the crop in spite of ineffective legal restrictions to the contrary. Beneath is the deplorably low productivity of the land he works. The farmer cannot see any avenue of escape. He has no credit except at usurer's rates. . . . He is resistant to change for fear of losing the meagre livelihood he and his family possess. The incentive to greater production dies aborning when what he regards as an unjust share of the harvest of his work goes to the landlord.'

No one appears able to break the tyrannous system that binds peasant and landlord. Not that many have seriously tried. The Americans made a small-scale attempt in their early years, until the *caciques* engineered the collapse of land registration courts, taking over the disputed titles themselves.

Quezon achieved something in 1935 by splitting up a number of estates. Twenty years later Magsaysay's Land for the Landless policy began to gain results. After his death landowners were able to reinforce their influence over his successor.

Juan de la Cruz is still little removed from slavery. In theory, he has the choice of working for one landowner or another. In practice, he is chained to one master by almost insoluble links of debt and interest.

Before World War Two tenants and landlords were legally required to split the harvest between them. But from the cropper's share had to come half the cost of seed, implements, the maintenance of carabao. Nor did this include food and clothing for a family that might mean anything up to a dozen mouths to feed, perhaps more. A small plot of land might yield sixty cavans (120 lb.) of *palay*, giving a total price of P150. And out of it had to come threshing, harvesting, seedlings. In the end he might be left with P50 or a little more to live on for the year. It could only be done, of course, by borrowing, usually from the owner of the land himself. If he needed *palay* for the next year's seeding, he could pay back two cavans for every one borrowed. If he failed to do so after the first harvest, the interest doubled: from 50 to 100 per cent. As for cash advances, the legal maximum was twelve per cent, though most landlords or outside usurers charged much higher rates.

Even two decades after independence the situation is little changed, except that most — by no means all — tenants are permitted to retain 60 per cent of the crop, while the owner pays for implements and seed. But again there are many underhand arrangements, by which the tenant is forced to pay more.

It is a system that not only stultifies the existence of millions at subsistence level, but discourages productivity and leads to dangerous discontents. 'The problems of land tenure become serious,' writes the American geographer, Professor Robert E. Huke, 'whenever significant numbers of agricultural workers do not own the land they till.'[1]

1. Robert E. Huke, *Shadows On The Land: An Economic Geography of The Philippines*, Manila, 1963.

Writing in 1963, Huke noted that the percentage of tenant farmers had actually increased in recent years. Of nearly two million farmers, 58 per cent were sharecroppers. The worst areas were the three central Luzon provinces of Pampanga (88·2%), Nueva Ecija (75·4) and Bulacan (66%), followed by Negros Occidental (66%) and the traditional bandit region of Cavite (64·2%).

As he saw the problem, there were only three solutions possible. To open up public lands for resettlement, to redistribute large holdings and to introduce a progressive system of land taxation that would force owners to develop their holdings more intensively, since existing productivity was so low. How could it be anything else, when working tenants could not afford fertilizers or anything beyond a hand plough, had no irrigation facilities and no encouragement to toil harder.

Nor does this mean the *tao* is in any sense lazy. Few people anywhere are driven to live harder. He rises long before the sun, walks barefoot to his landlord's hacienda or the tiny strip of land he crops. He toils under the sun's heat until noon, taking his first meal of the day, which will probably be a little rice or, if he is in funds, a scrap of dried fish. Afterwards he takes a siesta under a tree. Is this luxury? Not when a man works ten or more hours a day, when the tropic sun burns through the early afternoon and even the carabao lie in the shade. At three he begins work again, takes supper as the sun goes down and toils once more.

By the time he carries his bolo home, his family will probably be in bed. Unless his wife has also been in the fields with him. His tattered *nipa* hut is all the shelter he needs, though the heavy rains of the Wet Season will give him many uncomfortable nights. His only light is kerosene; his cooking is done on charcoal; he has no privy but the open bush. In the 30,000 barrios of the Philippines, where 80 per cent of its people live, poverty almost ceases to be hardship. It is the expected manner of life.

Perhaps he expects no more.

Even change to him is suspect. The clever young agronomists who visit him, the government experts, those who want him to change the ancient methods his father taught him, these are seldom welcome. Who knows whether their book-learning will really work? Who knows whether they really know? At least he can live by the old ways. The peasant is a natural-born conservative. And he tends to vote in the same fashion. He votes too often as his betters tell him to: the landlord, the usurer, the local store-keeper whose credits are seldom paid. Only in the dangerous country of the Huks is he encouraged to vote otherwise.

In 1962, after the ineffectual Garcia regime was ousted by Diosdado Macapagal, the new Liberal president had a new land code passed by Congress. Its aim was eventually to convert all sharecropping relations into leaseholds, giving tenant farmers the chance to own their own land. However, Congress emasculated the Agricultural Land Reform Act by deleting a vital clause. This was to impose taxation on unused land as a means of persuading owners to throw more open for settlement. Other

Children of Tondo

Mayon Volcano, Southern Luzon

more acceptable clauses were designed to make government loans available so that yields could be improved, fertilizers and more modern equipment bought and the purchase price gradually paid off. Trained field officers were also to help the inexperienced sharecropper to reach his independence.

The scheme began well. Then, as under previous administrations, bureaucracy or behind-the-scenes persuaders abused it. The president, who was busy campaigning for re-election for at least half his term, lost interest. By the time of his defeat in 1965, only a handful of farms had been turned into leaseholds, while government funds allocated to field teams mysteriously vanished and trained officers were replaced by the proteges and relatives of politicians.

Among those who knew the land, however, there were doubts as to whether the Macapagal plan would really work. How were peasants on subsistence level to pay off the purchase price and interest on their farms? How could such small plots ever maintain a family less meagrely than they had done before? Huke, for instance, wrote: 'To merely abolish tenancy by purchase and redistribution of the landed estates is to attack only one phase of the problem. It would create a vast number of private farms mostly too small to satisfy rising expectancy of today's farmer. It is not an answer if farm units are to be so small as to provide only a bare existence.'

There has been only one other movement designed in good faith to aid those without capital. This is the Philippine Rural Reconstruction Movement, backed by United States finance. It has so far sponsored some fifty credit unions in Luzon barrios, but its influence has been little more than a fall of passing rain upon an ocean of salt.

The *tao* appears to be trapped within the ever-recurring cycle of his traditions. There is always interest to be paid back, more interest than he can afford, and when the chance comes to buy the land his father and his father's father have worked as though it were their own — more interest, more usurers, more debt.

In the Luzon provinces there are additional hazards. During each harvest season at least two battalions of troops and Philippine Constabulary arrive in Pampanga, Bulacan, Nueva Ecija and Tarlac. Their presence is supposed to prevent the Huk practice of extorting money from landowners and peasants, though this protection is seldom successful. In 1964, according to one newspaper correspondent, Filemon V. Tutay, landlords and hacienda overseers were forced to pay between 20 to 100 cavans of *palay* each to Huk agents, while tenant farmers paid one cavan. Anyone who refused to pay was threatened with 'liquidation'.[2] The agents are never known Huks, but otherwise respected individuals forced to act as go-betweens, usually barrio captains. It is impossible to estimate the size of this annual levy, though Tutay reported that 5,000 to 7,000 cavans of rice were collected from one Pampanga town alone. At P10 per cavan,

2. *Philippines Free Press*, 15 September 1964, Manila.

this would have amounted to P50,000 to P70,000. Businessmen in the region were also forced to 'donate' sums of up to P1,000, while municipal mayors had to organize large fund-raising activities. The Huk movement had become so prosperous that it owned tractors, threshing machinery and even fleets of jeepneys which made further profits from a helpless population. Terrorism had become so widespread that local government officials were obliged to appoint leading Huks to municipal posts, even to local police forces. The frequent murders in the region, including the machine gunning of town mayors and prominent officials, were acts of terror against those who resisted. Tutay asked one farmer why his people went on paying tribute, seeing that the whole of central Luzon was then under military protection.

'The soldiers come and go,' the farmer said. 'But the Huks are always with us. Maybe we can afford to be brave while the soldiers are with us. But what will happen when the soldiers are gone?'

No one since Magsaysay has attempted to answer that question. Perhaps no one dares. It calls for a drastic revision of land-owning rights, a more equable share for the tenants. It is the same dilemma that faces the Americans in South Vietnam, and Asian regimes elsewhere. It is clear that without considerable support from peasants, willing as well as unwilling, the Huks could not continue to exist. Their strength has its roots in mass poverty. Even worse than poverty, there is disillusion. The texture of life here is poisoned by bad faith, graft, crooked practices, commercial robbery, vice. There is the story of one former Huk commander who, given a grant of land under the Magsaysay scheme, deposited 100 cavans of *palay* in a government warehouse as collateral for a loan. A year later he found that neither his name nor the *palay* were listed. The warehouse later went bankrupt; the men running it did not. There are stories of children virtually sold into slavery, of juvenile gangs driven to living by crime; of daughters recruited as hostesses in tawdry nightclubs and bars, the alluring road to prostitution. Wrote Rodolfo G. Tupas in a survey of provincial life, 'Poverty and misery in the barrios — the barren fields, the hollow-cheeked men and women moving about like restless ghosts — they point out a dangerous condition and the need for immediate and sustained attention. Barrio folk have not quite entered the twentieth century.'[3]

Nor, it might be said, have those who determine how they live.

3. 'The Forgotten Frontier', *Sunday Times*, 11 October 1964, Manila.

CHAPTER 11

The Rice Ladder

> *Our people are now matured enough to realize what is good for them and their children, which includes a reasonable measure of self-denial and sacrifice to promote the nation's fight against poverty. Progress cannot be achieved by conflict but by cooperation among their leaders whom they have invested with their sovereign mandate . . .*
>
> DIOSADO MACAPAGAL

THE PHILIPPINES is one of those rare societies that has yet to develop a national ethos. There has been so constant a veering from one set of values to another: from the medieval attitudes of Spain, the friars and anti-friars, the explosive and thwarted pride of the Revolution, the anarchic materialism of Americans and the sudden realization that, after all, this was not freedom. None of these allowed an awareness of Filipinos as a single people to coalesce. They have remained two nations, locked in a silent struggle with each other for the possession of insufficient wealth. There is no unity of purpose, no shared identity. Perhaps, in the history of nations, this is not unique. Yet other societies have evolved a common outlook, a personality that can be described as national. As a rule this has been fashioned by their leaders, an elite. One thinks of the French aristocratic view, which somehow survived even the Revolution; of British middle-class morality seeping down from the rising industrial classes of Victorian times; or the commercial adventurers of nineteenth century America who left their imprint on all ranks of society, convincing them that a belief in free enterprise was a surer form of liberty than a more collectivized democracy such as, say, Australia, would tolerate.

In the Philippines there is a small, strongly-entrenched élite. But this does not determine social attitudes, which are moulded more decisively by the great, inchoate mass at the bottom. The élite, at least at the level of the *ilustrado*, is sophisticated, intelligent, cosmopolitan; yet its influence appears to extend little further than its own special caste. These are the Brahmins of Filipino life. Today their prestige is waning. They are being pushed into the shadows by a brasher, more determined class of *nouveaux riches*, which include not only native industrialists, but the politicians. And the politicians, through their curiously undemocratic control of Congress, are becoming the major force. By annually voting themselves astronomical expense allowances, with which to buy mass

87

votes, they have created a kind of Chinese-style secret society that holds the Republic to ransom.

The source of their power is not the élite, often cynical of such opportunism, but the indifferent and uninformed masses, who remain imprisoned in their age-old complex of traditional illiteracy and blind acceptance of paternal attitudes.

To a large extent the political leaders they haplessly elect have themselves climbed out of the dark pit. To those who have escaped its bottom rungs, the open pit below is like a remembered vision of hell. One must scramble out of it at all costs, escape the annihilating poverty, the half-life at subsistence level: the daily rice bowl. But one has to be tough and ruthless to climb that rice ladder up to safety.

The rice ladder almost wholly determines Filipino patterns of life today. It excuses all actions and ambitions, explains socially accepted practices in business, politics and public intercourse. This is the new morality.

'You've got to be smart to get somewhere nowadays,' said a Tondo slum-dweller when interviewed by *Philippines Free Press* recently. 'I'm not a thief. I am only taking back what society has deprived me of. If I do not take care of myself, who will? I want to get out of the slums. I will not hesitate to steal, or even kill if that's the way to do it.'[1]

The statement was published in a survey of modern living conditions throughout the islands. Six million Filipinos, the survey reported, are doomed to an animal-like existence for the rest of their lives. Another 14,000,000 are destined to live in sub-standard homes. More than 20,000,000 have houses that lack proper protection against the weather. In thousands of barrios it is commonplace to find people living with pigs, chickens, carabao and horses. Most of them have only one room, which has to make do for cooking, eating and sleeping. Of 5,000,000 families covered by the 1960 census only 17 per cent had electricity, most of these living in urban areas. Rural folk mostly light their homes with oil, kerosene or tallow; nor do they often possess beds, chairs or tables, so that they must eat and sleep on bare floors. 'It is easier for a camel to pass through a needle's eye,' concluded the reporter, 'than for a lower middle-class family to buy a house in urban centres during its lifetime. While the minimum wage is P6 per day, food consumption alone is as high as P14 a day per family.'

The raising of this minimum wage from P4 to P6 a day was one of the few achievements made by ex-President Macapagal, and even this measure was long resisted by Congress, which made it law only a few months before the 1965 elections. Nor is it yet by any means universally accepted. Agricultural workers, for instance, still receive an average of P2.50 daily. In depressed regions such as Samar or Leyte the current rate is still as low as 50 centavos: either that, or no work at all.

1. 'Wanted: 600,000 Houses a Year', *Philippines Free Press*, 7 August 1965, Manila.

It was by stressing such common realities that Macapagal won the presidency in 1961, defeating President Garcia whose family background associated him easily with wealth and corruption. Styling himself 'the poor boy from Lubao', Macapagal stirred enthusiastic support by stressing his peasant background in Pampanga. He spoke of growing up in a small *nipa* shack, running barefoot after his grandfather's carabao, toiling as the son of a tenant farmer. Mass audiences applauded him when he told them of his childhood hardships, of having to shift his sleeping mat from one part of the floor to another trying to escape leaks as monsoonal rains poured down.

One million of the voters who sent him to Malacanang Palace still live in these flimsy, unprotected *barong-barongs*. They projected their own dreams into his struggle and successes, his efforts to educate himself, the way he paid his way through university law school, set himself up in practice, climbed through the foreign service to Congress and then the vice-presidency. And in 1965, after he had failed to keep his almost unrealizable promises, they voted him out again. The big majority for the new president, former Senate leader Ferdinand E. Marcos, was largely a vote against Macapagal. Foremost on the list of projects for Macapagal's 'New Era' was the solving of the Republic's post-war housing problems.

'To remain apathetic to this,' he announced soon after his accession, 'is to encourage the creation of a social ferment which, bottled into violence, can blow up bomb-like and rock the very foundations of the free institutions of this Republic.'

Nothing was done.

His five-year Socio-Economic Plan degenerated to a mere slogan. Enormous billboards were set up along highways, announcing that such-and-such a project would begin shortly, while the boldly-lettered credits to the president merely provided free propaganda for his next election campaign. Elsewhere, during 1965, ten thousand huge portraits of the president accompanied roadside promises for even bigger and better plans if he were returned for a second term. According to the Nacionalista opposition, these coloured ikons cost the government more than P11,000,000. The votes went to President Marcos.

The top rungs of the rice ladder can be treacherous ones.

The inaction of the Macapagal regime is incomprehensible to anyone who has seen the energetic social welfare programmes of Singapore and Hong Kong, where community housing schemes have created cheap accommodation for many thousands during the same period. The annual reports of ECAFE (Economic Commission for Asia and the Far East) are also revealing.

The Philippines, which is one of twenty member countries, spends least of them all on housing. Statistics reveal that eight out of every ten Filipinos now lack decent shelter. Almost 50 per cent of the inhabitants of major cities live in squalor and filth. The 1960 census found that only 600,000 out of 5,000,000 houses were built of strong, weatherproof materials. Since that year large, insanitary, unserviced shack-dwelling areas have grown haphazardly all over Manila. Shanties have been built alongside the stinking, excreta-fouled esteros, while dockside regions have been transformed to shanty towns. These are the desperate families of squatters, who have no titles to the patches of land on which they run up their pathetic dwellings. In metropolitan Manila alone there are now at least 100,000 squatter and slum families. Yet their arrival in the capital does little but swell the numbers of unemployed, increase crime, vice and prostitution. Only 2,000 of these squatters were reported to be able to pay monthly rents ranging between P15 and P25.

Similar conditions exist in other islands and provinces, where a further 300,000 families live in extremes of poverty. In Samar, alone, 35,890 families were living in crude shanties, according to the 1960 census, in Leyte 33,114, while 33,277 families in Cotabato had only damp hovels. In many Visayan regions their plight is worsened by recurrent typhoons and floods, which force them to rebuild almost every year with whatever discarded materials they can find.

In 1964 the Joint Legislative-Executive Tax Commission published a report based on comparative incomes in 1960. This divided families into two main groups. Those earning more than P5,000 a year totalled 3·9 per cent. Of the remainder 32·1 per cent earned less than P624. In 1964 a correspondent in the *Philippines Herald* appealed to Congress to increase its allocations for social welfare which, he said, amounted to a mere P7,000,000, or, as he put it, ·465 per cent of the annual budget. He listed the needy as follows:

3,600,000 unemployed youths; 3,000,000 unable to meet minimum costs of food, clothing, shelter; 2,000,000 physically disabled; 1,700,000 abandoned or indigent children; 18,000 teenage hooligans in gaol; 10,500 prostitutes; 1,000 beggars. (The last two classifications, which lack official figures, were grossly understated.) [2]

During the same period another newspaper — the Filipino press must be the world's most candid and self-critical — referred to a second government study made in 1961. This stated, among other things, that 4,037 criminals had been imprisoned in Manila alone during the year for 'crimes against poverty', while thousands died of hunger or diseases contracted through malnutrition. 'Acute want and beggary had already twisted some minds into fearful criminal perversion,' the report said. 'Since the head of an average Filipino family has from five to ten mouths to feed daily, he needs a miracle to survive. He becomes one of more than three million voices clamouring for work, wanting to live.'[3]

The spectre of disease especially haunts the Filipino.

Infant mortality rates are of serious concern to the Department of Health, whose Disease Intelligence Sector announced in 1965 that, of

2. *Philippines Herald*, 24 September 1964, Manila.
3. *Sunday Times Magazine*, 13 September 1964, Manila.

2,280 babies born daily, 1,544 die before they are one year old. That is 563,560 annually. A percentage figure of 67·7. On the one hand, an ever-increasing population is imposing impossible strains on social services; on the other, half-a-million infants are dying in misery.

In several under-privileged areas medical officers of the Nutrition Foundation of the Philippines, supported largely by American funds, are working hard to reduce these mortality figures. But promised help from the government seldom materializes. The building of the Foundation's national headquarters in Quezon City, with a public clinic, was abandoned in 1965 after a customary government explanation had been made: 'No funds.'

Year after year many hundreds die from cholera, tuberculosis, gastroenteric diseases that sweep through Manila and other cities in near-plague proportions. Contagious diseases such as El Tor, a type of cholera, and H-fever increased considerably year by year. It is difficult to find reliable figures, for only hospital admissions are classified. Few public hospitals exist, while private ones are beyond most people's reach.

The area most affected by contagious diseases is, naturally, Tondo. At least 30,000 squatters live in the dank, insanitary streets crowded behind the docks. Nearby is Balut Island, upon which 400 tons of city garbage are dumped daily, and left rotting under a tropic sun. Few houses have their own toilets, having to depend on public ones built by the Manila Council. Large numbers habitually use the open streets and lanes. Official figures published in 1964 estimated that more than 2,000,000 homes throughout the Philippines had no toilet facilities at all. In Cebu alone 50 per cent of its 243,942 houses did not even have washrooms. Supplies of pure water were equally rare, more than two million homes depend on open wells or contaminated springs and creeks.

The same report added that it had proved impossible to gain popular support for improved hygiene while the mass of the people remained apathetic. There was a close relation between apathy and illiteracy, it noted. The overall literacy rate stands at 67 per cent, but this drops sharply in more remote areas: notably in the Sulu Archipelago (28·2 per cent), Zamboanga del Sur (53 per cent) or Cotabato, Negros Oriental and Lanao del Sur, where school attendances range from a mere 10 to 15·6 per cent of those eligible.

In the context of such universal poverty it is difficult to know where progress can begin. Much easier to make your own personal bid to climb the rice ladder.

Yet even those at the top seldom appear contented or secure. Instability is, perhaps, in the nature of these volcanic islands. The soil shifts, walls crack, the house timbers groan in the night. Forty years ago Katherine Mayo called her study of this country *The Isles of Fear*. Fear is everywhere; in the upper echelons of society, as well as in its substructure. Wherever he goes today the Filipino inhabits a climate of fear.

It's drawn, anxious face is everywhere. In the armed security guards posted night and day outside banks, stores, government buildings and the mansions of the wealthy; in the barbed wire and brick walls topped with broken glass that surround prestige suburbs like Forbes Park or Philamlife; in the warnings against walking the city streets alone by night, or hiring any but recommended taxicabs; in press advertisements for pistols, carbines and gas-charged pens in the name of self-defence ('Just-rite-softness of trigger when fired: wood penetration 5 inches'); in the spiralling crime rate, the mistrust of police, the ritual crusading of politicians against 'graft and corruption' which, once in power, they never mention again.

It is possible to trace such influences even in the febrile, neon-lit excitements of Manila's night life, the 'conspicuous consumption' of official receptions, private parties, banquets and discreet downtown gambling rooms which police are normally persuaded not to raid. Nor is Manila by any means the only city that has made a thriving industry of night clubs, expense vouchers, whisky, cabaret hostesses and no-questions-asked-motels.

No one but a Filipino can express the full disenchantment of this life, where soft lighting, plush decor and the sophisticated combo band black out the dawn realities of Tondo or Mandaluyong, the spectral rice ladder, the drawn faces of the poor, the fear.

This is how Wilfrido D. Nolledo, poet and short story writer, has seen it all:

> Highballs, possession of firearms, temptresses in backless sheaths plus the night make heady companions. Perfume, mascara, rouge, bouncers and floor managers, the decorative chantreuse, the flock of hostesses to choose from and to 'table', ice cubes in tumblers, slow drag, tips — these are the feathers of the raven that taps, taps, taps gently on the glass door of night club or cocktail lounge, saying 'evermore'. The unhappily married, the unhappily unmarried, the unhappily separated, the unhappily alone and the happily alone, the blooming bachelor, the searching spinster, the novitiate of the night, the one who carries a night monkey on his back, the other who cannot sleep — these are legion and they meet in the night spots, blind to each other. . . .
>
> In a second-storey cocktail lounge, five uniformed policemen are passing a gun around in a game of Russian roulette. In a car just come from an assignation, a prostitute rages against her pimp, screaming to be taken back home so she could pick up her veil to hear the first mass. On the other hand, most husbands are in by that time. They can be comfortably faithless in the daytime, during office hours, as long as there are motels and massage clinics. *La noche vida* goes on and on as the lost dancers dance to the music, while singers cry out their blues to decrepit Don Juans who have nothing to hold up their spines but their wallets. Here in this speck of a country, where a fairly grave dawn could kill our economy, many a Manilan waits in abject patience to be destroyed, to be deformed by his nights. But a playwright once wrote in anguish and hope over the maimed creatures of the dark: Oh, you weak beautiful people who give up with such grace. What you need is someone to take hold of you — gently, with love, and hand your life back to you, like something gold you let go of . . .[4]

4. Wilfrido D. Nolledo, 'La Noche Vida', *Philippines Free Press*, 11 July 1964, Manila.

Filipino writers are among the most sensitive and agonized in modern literature. Such a climate could scarcely fail to produce them; Dostoievski, Lorca, Camus do not come from comfortable, welfare societies. Though the modern Philippines may inhabit a purgatory such as its early conquistadores never dreamed of, it is also fashioning a literature of conscience and sensibility that the bourgeois do not know.

This, too, belongs to the rice ladder.

CHAPTER 12

Cross of Magellan

*The Santo Niño makes so perfect a
symbol of Philippine Christianity because
it came with Magellan, became a pagan
idol, was re-established by Legazpi, and
has become so native that native legends
annul its European origin by declaring
it to have arisen in this land. The
Cebuaños sent to Legazpi to ransom the
image, offering any amount of gold,
declared that it had been their god from
time immemorial . . .*

QUIJANO DE MANILA

To FIND the conscience of the Philippines, if not its soul, you must travel to the Visayas.

Manila carries too heavily the stamp of materialism. Despite the pent emotionalism greeting the annual parade of Quiapo's miraculous Black Nazarene through crowded streets, the mass visitations by candlelight to elaborate cemeteries on All Soul's Day, the cathedral bells that spread their mellow boom across the ruins of Intramuros and the socially-conscious intellectuals of the Ateneo de Manila, you feel sometimes that the capital's conscience is as readily for sale as the trinkets and smuggled cigarettes peddled in the aisles of churches during Sunday mass. Cebu City appears to have more moral fibre. Provincial, stained with poverty, confused by tense rivalries in politics and real estate development, it has preserved a more Asian character. It is also a rare community in which you feel that the West has left some creative impression: an ideology. The last time I went there its half-million people were preparing for its most important festival in modern times. Within a month the four hundredth anniversary of the coming of Christianity was to be celebrated.

Just before dawn the inter-island ship passed through the narrow strait between Cebu and Mactan Island, where Magellan was killed. From my porthole I saw the Southern Cross resting upon the skyline: a magnificent, jewelled crucifix that stood right side up for the first time in my experience. Only then did I remember that Magellan had been its discoverer. The Santa Cruz de la Maio was first seen by him in exactly this region of the Pacific.

We berthed just as the rising sun lit up the twin octagonal towers of Cebu Cathedral. Already there were people moving about the stone quay;

dock labourers, hawkers, vendors of *balut*, ice-cream and hot corn, and the drivers of waiting jeepneys and *tartanillas*, whose quaint, high-wheeled cabs looked too cumbersome for the small, thin-legged horses between their shafts. One leisurely, middle-aged character in frayed jeans and white pandanus hat was laying out guitars on the wharf. A whole row of them. Clearly this was his enjoyment as well as trade.

He sat on a bollard, strumming.

For the first time I sensed something of the more lyrical, easy-going atmosphere these islands must have had before the war. There is little enough to recall Cebu's more ancient character. Pigafetta, Magellan's chronicler, noted that its inhabitants not only dressed themselves in silks and gold, had their own laws, religion and handicrafts, but were devoted to music and the dance. During early Spanish times, Morga described the port as a 'somnolent little town of cobbled streets and massive, tiled-roof stone buildings in the shadow of whose walls the Spanish masters drank wine and made love to pretty native women. The Cebuaños themselves lived in simple *nipa* houses, tilled the land, fished in the sea, paid the impossible taxes and took turns at the quarry, cutting the stones to build the stately mansions and churches under threat of the lash.' Very little of the Spanish past remains today, due to pattern bombing and the spread of squatters' hovels.

Yet this is very much Magellan's city. You are reminded of him by the great column in Magellan Park, overlooking the strait that led him to his death on Mactan; in the broad Magellanes Street where the wooden cross he planted four-and-a-half centuries ago still stands; by the image of the Santo Niño, which he brought to the island on his two-year voyage out from Spain. The image of the Infant Jesus is kept in the beautiful church of Santo Niño, second oldest in south-east Asia. Bejewelled, dressed like a feudal prince in cloth of gold, this carved wooden figurine has become a national symbol.

Equally impressive, to my mind, is the immense wooden cross Magellan planted to commemorate the first Christian mass. Scholars still argue whether or not Legazpi shifted it to another site, but it is the original cross. It has been sheathed within a second timber casing to preserve it.

Enclosed in a small, octagonal building with a tiled, temple-style roof, it has barred gates at its eight archways to prevent the faithful from chipping away fragments for holy relics. The devotion it arouses is remarkable. I have seen peasant women dragging themselves on their knees to those gates, lost there in prayer as trucks, cars, jeepneys race past on either side.

Significantly, it is only a few yards from the statue of another revered figure in the tree-shadowed public plaza: the free-thinking Jose Rizal whose death sentence touched off the revolution against Spain.

Opposite are the tall, wrought-iron gates that lead you to the Santo Niño church. You reach it along a quiet, paved walk past a two-storey, half-timbered former convent that looks like a piece of medieval Spain.

The main facade of the church is magnificently carved in the florid Chirruginesque style of the period, with massive oaken doors, also carved with Augustinian figures. Above is the tall, hexagonal bell tower, a miniature replica of the Vatican's.

The interior has a rich and soaring quality you would hardly expect of builders in such primitive times. The transept is spanned by four immense archways, elaborately decorated in brilliant designs, while fine-spun chandeliers hang from the high, painted ceilings. There is a patina of age about it, a spaciousness heightened by those flying arches and breadth of nave.

The high altar is quite overpowering in the beauty of its detail. Three-columned tiers of stone niches rise almost to the domed roof, each niche containing the wonderfully carved and painted wooden images of saints. For centrepiece this richly coloured wall has the Santo Niño. The golden, jewelled crown, the flesh tints of the rounded infant face, the outspread, cloth-of-gold cape and wide jewels flashing create a glow that seems to suffuse the entire church. No wonder pre-Christian Malays were as moved by its chiarisma as modern Cebuaños are, that the miracles attributed to this golden image seem more than an act of faith.

I tried to picture the awe it must have had for the superstitious people of Magellan's day.

The arrival of these gaunt, white-fleshed strangers with their helmets, plated armour and powerful cannon must have created awe enough, for they had voyaged two years since King Charles V commissioned Magellan to find the legendary Spice Islands, fed on leather and sawdust and rats, suffered scurvy and thirst to cross the Pacific for the first time. Yet Raja Humabon had welcomed them peaceably enough, allowed 800 people to be baptized, and feasted these dour-spoken Christians. Then the Santo Niño was produced. Pigafetta, Italian chronicler of the expedition, described the event like this:

> After dinner, the chaplain, with many of us, went ashore to baptize the native queen. While the priest got ready for the ceremony I showed her an image of Our Lord, a little statue of the Infant Jesus. . . . When she saw it she was deeply touched, and, crying, asked to be baptized. The queen wanted the image to take the place of her dolls, so I gave it to her . . .

Having likewise made her husband, Humabon, a Christian, Magellan overreached himself. He tried to force the raja on the people of Mactan Island nearby. This was too much for the islanders' own proud chief, Lapu Lapu.

Magellan's belief in his muskets and cannon was misplaced. His armoured fighters were routed by bows and arrows and several killed. Among them was Magellan himself.

In early Spanish times a monument was built where he fell. It stands near the modern jet airport on Mactan. But the heroic Lapu Lapu had to wait for his monument nearby until the Filipino revolution of 1898.

When Magellan's soldiers retreated to Cebu, they were given another feast by Humabon, despite his clear knowledge that they were no longer invincible. Then, as they feasted and drank, his retinue fell on the Spaniards with kris and sword, murdering another twenty. The rest left in panic flight for the true Spice Islands — the Moluccas — and eventually completed their encirclement of the globe, for which the slain Magellan deserved much of the credit.

According to later evidence, the Santo Niño with which the raja's wife had replaced her dolls soon became an idol for local worship. Sacrifices were offered to it. The Infant Jesus became a pagan rain-god, carried in procession to the sea and plunged into it, the focal point for rituals in which drummers and wildly hopping dancers invoked the skies to drop rain.

The rediscovery of this image by Legazpi's expedition is another remarkable story. Perhaps another miracle.

When the galleons from Mexico sailed down the long, emerald-hued strait between the mountains of Negros Occidental and Cebu, they were thought to presage a vengeance raid for Magellan's death. Legazpi's peaceful overtures failed, and he opened fire on the hostile town. The Cebuaños ran for the hills, setting the town alight. A company of soldiers was sent ashore to put out the flames, whereupon one house was found to have been miraculously spared. This was Legazpi's account:

> A soldier went into the large and well-built home, where he found an image of the Infant Jesus. . . . This had been kept in its cradle, all gilded, just as it was brought from Spain; and only the little cross which usually tops the globe in its hand was lacking. The image was well-kept, and many flowers were found before it, for what object or purpose no one knows . . .

Fray Urdaneta ordered a chapel to be built for the recovered image, which was transferred to the Augustinian church of Santo Niño on its completion in 1602. Twenty years later the church was destroyed by fire All but the Santo Niño. This was the second miracle.

The present church, built in 1740, has been its permanent home, for it is never allowed to leave, except for the kind of fluvial procession that took place during this week's festival. Yet its permanence there was never intended by the Spanish colonial rulers, and thereby arose more legends of its miraculous powers.

In Legazpi's time the centre of government was moved from Cebu to Manila, by then freed of piratical Chinese junks from the mainland. The authorities decreed that the Santo Niño must also travel north, as the symbol of religious power. The Augustinian friars resented this. However, they crated the image and shipped it to Manila.

On arrival the crate was empty. The Santo Niño was back in its Cebu shrine.

Again orders went south. Again the image was crated; and the crate set within a second crate for safety. In Manila the crate was once more found empty. Next time three crates were set one inside another, but the Santo Niño reappeared in Cebu once more. For the last time, in desperation, the shippers devised a system of Chinese boxes, with the innermost, seventh box containing the image. Yet it still persisted in returning to Cebu.

As a last resort, the friars decided to cut off the Santo Niño's legs, so that it could no longer escape. This, too, was in vain.

The legs have since been restored, though devout Visayans say you can still see where they were amputated, symbol of the Santo Niño's devotion to its original home.

But who can speak of an original home? No one even knows who made it, or where it came from, before Magellan's expedition brought it from Spain. It is believed to be at least five hundred years old, possibly more. Urdaneta was convinced that it came from Flanders, perhaps taken to Spain by soldiers returning from the Low Country wars. What its true value is no one can even guess. It is beyond any worldly value, so intimately has it become a part of Cebuano fiestas and devotions.

This is why, once again, it was prevented from travelling around the Philippines during a campaign to centre attention on the Fourth Centennial celebrations. When Cardinal Santos carried the Santo Niño through Manila airport, it was a craftsmanlike replica he carried. Not the previous original which, as in Legazpi's time, still rested with the Augustinians in Cebu City.

The 400th anniversary celebrations in May 1965 drew nearly a million people to the city. They came by every conceivable form of transport, from turbo-jets and light charter aircraft to rust-stained island steamers, lateen-rigged fishing craft, *kumpits*, sampans, scimitar-sailed *vintas* and the sea-worn little gunboats of the Philippine navy, which had spent the past year or two fruitlessly chasing pirates and smugglers in the Visayan Sea. Everyone of any importance in the Republic was there: the President, his cabinet, ambassadors, the cardinals, bishops, senators, industrialists and the leaders of wealthy families. There were more than fifty archbishops from other lands, official representatives of foreign states, including, of course, Spain. Pilgrims, tourists, Catholics and Muslims jostled with the remnants of pagan hill tribes in the city's narrow thoroughfares, flooding by thousands into the huge celebration arena looking out to sea in the direction from which the Santo Niño came. On the last day of a Christian festival unprecedented in Asia pilgrims marched in a procession five kilometres long, while tossed flowers, fireworks, excited cries curved and rang through the humid air.

In several of his sermons during the festival the Papal legate spoke of the need for closing the ranks between poor and rich. He called on the national leaders to work for 'the just emancipation of the poorer classes of people . . . and to uphold fidelity to the social doctrine of the Church'. He reminded them of the terms of Pope Paul's decree when appointing him his representative at the fourth centennial:

We are not unaware of the social difficulties which our beloved Filipino people, ever increasing in numbers, have to confront today. Let then, the sons of the Church, particularly those in high office, give their assistance and provide such aid as the Church's teaching has frequently demanded. Let special care be taken to see that the character of the young, while they are in school, be formed according to proper discipline so that later on they may make their contribution in public life.

It was a dramatic setting for such a message, for the grandstand was occupied by President Macapagal, his advisors and administration chiefs who were even then campaigning against election charges of corruption and indifference to public welfare. The princes of the church were there, the great landowners, the prestige names in commerce, politics, education. Massing about them, in the fierce glare of the sun, was a vast crowd of peasants, fishermen and the unemployed, wearing — in the words of one observer — 'the pinched look of poverty'.

Another wrote of the legends attributing miraculous powers to the Santo Niño, centre of all that huge throng. For the Cebuaños, he said, he had always been their saviour and protector and had delivered them from plagues, fires, sickness and the marauding infidel. He was said to have been used by their grandparents to break long droughts, by making pilgrimages into the nearby sea. They had only to dip the image in this ocean for the rains to pour down, it was said. Now the survival of Christianity in this sector of south-east Asia was attributed to his powers, and the pagan *Pit Senyor* was danced once again in the presence of prelates and cardinals.

'To the unbelievers who sneer at religious phenomena,' he concluded, 'it might be pointed out that Cebu, during the whole post-war era, was a sinking, squalid little city where one choked on pulverized horse-droppings, the stench of garbage at every corner and the stink of slums. There were no roads, only strings of holes connected by small patches of level ground. It was the Philippines' dirtiest little city, on its way to becoming a third-rate town. In the past twenty years not a single politician or city administration has managed to tidy up the pre-war Queen of the South-turned-tramp. Two months ago the whole city was transfigured because of the festival for the Santo Niño. Broad, paved, lighted avenues now stretch where before there was only dirt road or slum area. Every single street in Cebu is now clean and paved. It is now, by unanimous verdict, the cleanest city in the country. The Santo Niño achieved in two months what all the politicians in Cebu province and in Manila could not do in the last twenty years.

'If that is no miracle, it's something close to it.'[1]

1. Napoleon G. Rama, 'Cebu's Biggest Celebration', *Philippines Free Press*, 8 May, 1965, Manila.

CHAPTER 13

Typhoons and Travellers

*They boldly crossed the seas from
the south in various fleets of sailboats
called* barangays, *and reached Philippine
shores in several waves of immigration,
beginning at about 200 B.C. and continuing
downwards to 1500 A.D. They were good
mariners and warriors . . .*

GREGORIO F. ZAIDE

FILIPINOS are experienced sailors. They need to be. They voyage in all
manner of craft whose owners clearly subscribe to the famous dictum that
it is more blessed to travel than to arrive. There are many such vessels in
Philippine waters. For the adventurous voyager typhoons, reefs, shoals,
pirates, overloaded or unseaworthy craft add a certain zest to travel even
in the calmest of waters. The virtually land-locked Visayan Sea is a case
in point. The beauty of islands, sounds and straits lulls the passenger into
a belief that he has left all hazards behind on the sidewalks or dockside
lanes of Manila. That depends largely on the time of year.

My last arrival in Cebu coincided with Typhoon Louise, which swept
in from a south-easterly direction across Leyte and Bohol, raising storm
warnings from Palawan up to Romblon and southern Luzon. Once sluggish rivers began to flood, inundating farms and roads throughout the
Visayas. Airline flights were cancelled and ships took what shelter they
could across the China Sea. It was not one of the worst typhoons. Winds
at its centre reached no more than 260 kilometres an hour. A 162·5 mile
an hour wind is not to be taken lightly, yet such velocities are normal
enough when the customary four or five storms boil up each year during
the typhoon season. The danger period lasts from July to November. In
September 1964 one of the most ferocious on record was Typhoon Sally
which was reported to have reached 335 kilometres an hour over Samar.
It seems incredible that any building on land or vessel at sea could with-
stand blasts of 210 miles an hour.

Many of them, of course, do not. But the most severe damage is done
by floods, which leave thousands homeless, disrupt communications,
destroy crops and tear the topsoil off once fertile hillsides. In July 1964
Typhoon Dading killed forty people and injured 300, made 400,000
homeless on Luzon alone and destroyed property worth ₱10,000,000. For
several days Manila was almost entirely without light, power or water,
while a naval destroyer capsized off Bataan and freighters went ashore in

Manila Bay. Typhoon Louise, four months later, was even more destructive. At least 750 people were killed, 600,000 lost their homes, and one 300 ton vessel sank with all twelve passengers. More than 300,000 homeless victims were given aid by the Philippine National Red Cross. Outbreaks of El Tor were reported in Cebu, Surigao, Negros Occidental, while hunger and disease spread through the flooded Cagayan Valley in northern Luzon. Official reports put the total destruction of property at some P100,000,000. Ninety per cent of the houses in Surigao province, north-eastern Mindanao, collapsed; 1,200 schoolhouses and other public buildings vanished; landslides blocked roads; seawalls, dykes, dams and irrigation controls were washed away; ten small ships were lost, and more than 10,000 coconut trees demolished, putting the local copra industry back at least eight years.

Yet our 9,000 ton passenger vessel, coming down the exposed east coast of Cebu, rode out this typhoon without apparent difficulty. I was not even aware of wind and high seas (having selfishly, my wife complained, slept through it all). So it seemed had our radio officer. We heard later, in Cebu, that we had been reported missing, because no radio contact could be made.

In spite of their destructiveness, typhoons have a certain creative value too, for they bring about one-third of the rainfall. They are, in fact, simply huge and violent depressions that originate mainly in the area of the Caroline and Marshall Islands, spinning westward and north-west across the Visayas and Luzon towards the Asian mainland. They keep to a clearly defined belt, seldom reaching as far south as Mindanao, except for the north-eastern coastline of Surigao. The rains they bring are essential to fertility, though it is characteristic of these wild latitudes that they never know when to stop. I remember some bleak, humid, sodden weeks in Manila when you felt the sun would never shine again. A typhoon in 1911 gave Baguio its world rainfall record, 49·99 inches falling within twenty-four hours. Perhaps it is no coincidence that the Tagalog word for typhoon is *baguio*.

Fatalism is said to be a normal attribute of Asian society, but surely it has been fashioned mostly by the catastrophes of nature: typhoons, volcanoes, floods and dangerous seas. I am not nearly so inured to the casual travelling of Philippine waters, where fear of death becomes a disadvantage. Manileños always suggested that we choose shipping companies and their vessels with more care than the thousands who set out so blithely on any kind of inter-island ship. The one we travelled on to the Visayas and Mindanao was modern and well-designed. There was even air-conditioning in the first-class cabins, though what was described as a spacious passenger lounge had every foot of floor space covered by sleeping people night and day, some of whom had even hired folding beds. Not even the juke box blaring at all hours disturbed them. Nor was it possible, as advertised, to walk on deck: hundreds slept there as well. Second and third-class sections were as crowded as Manila side streets. There must have been at least a thousand passengers on board. The six lifeboats had accommodation for sixty in each. Still it was re-assuring to read, alongside instructions on how to use a life jacket, this advice: 'In case of emergency, do not panic. Proceed in an orderly manner to lifeboat number three.'

But what happened if you found that lifeboat already crowded to the gunwales, its occupants in Filipino fashion wearing revolvers, bolos, daggers? That is, if you could even reach it through the crush of those for whom there was no escape at all. Did you simply smile and say, 'Excuse me, I think that's my seat. Do you mind?'

At that time I had not read the 1964 report of a government Committee on Transportation and Communications. Many vessels it inspected in Manila and Cebu were described as 'floating coffins'. Their lifeboats, rafts and jackets were totally unusable. Firefighting equipment on board was frequently said to be for 'decoration only'. Fire extinguishers were either empty or filled with some harmless liquid or other. In 1946 alone, the Cebu customs had issued 6,694 special, though illegal, permits to carry inflammable liquids, without any check as to whether fire-fighting equipment was in order. Radio instruments on most ships were inadequate, often with a range of less than twenty-five miles. Ineffective radios were blamed for at least two shipping tragedies in recent months. The most dangerous factor of all was the habitual overcrowding of passenger vessels, which neither shipping companies nor the authorities policed.

According to Congressman Abrigo in January 1965, strong action was to be taken to end this perilous state of affairs. Recommendations were sent to administration officials at Malacanang. Nothing more was heard of them. Twelve months later further action did come. It took the form of an announcement by the Bureau of Customs that a new round of inspections had shown 90 per cent of ships to be 'unfit as passenger carriers'. No remedies were proposed.

In the meantime there had been three major disasters. Corpses from one of these were washed ashore near the house we occupied on the Zamboanga waterfront. Another one, some miles up the coast, reported seventy drowned when a motor vessel changed course too rapidly in heavy seas. In Catbalogan harbour, Samar, most of the 150 passengers on a launch licensed to carry forty ended in the sea. Many of these were children. The official report said that the vessel had been about to dock when everyone rushed to one side, scrambling to set ashore first. The rows of dead photographed by one Manila newspaper made a horrifying picture. It was not hard to visualize how such fatalities occurred. We made one crossing of the calm Sulu Sea between Zamboanga and Basilan Island. A sudden windstorm set the ferry plunging and rolling in short, steep seas. There was immediate panic on the lower deck: people ran from one side to the other; others rushed for the stairs to our upper deck. The panic was skilfully controlled by the chief engineer, who checked the rush with his revolver cocked.

The most chilling eye-witness account I have read came from a young man who joined a party travelling from Zumarraga, Samar, to a fiesta in Tacoblan. Near the Leyte coast they sighted a capsized launch, and threw ropes and life jackets to men, women and children struggling in the water.

> It was then that I saw a pregnant woman. She was struggling to save the lives of her two children she was holding close to her body. Every now and then she and the children would go under. One of the men in the sea shoved one child toward me. Then I proceeded to rescue the other child and the mother. Presently I saw a man looking for his wife. Failing to find her, he dived back into the angry sea. Some of the men decided to refloat the capsized motor boat. Once we had done so, we saw the body of a little girl emerge from below the boat. It was the missing daughter of the pregnant woman who had then broken into doleful weeping.
>
> We looked out of our boat toward the man looking for his missing wife. He was still there struggling among the mocking waves. Sometimes he sank. But every time his head popped out of the swirling waters, he would look around hopefully. We called for him to climb back into the boat. But he would not listen to us.
>
> We left him there still looking for his wife.[1]

Fatalism supreme.

Sometimes what the ocean casts up is of less natural origin. Less than a month after its mass homage to Christianity, Cebu City was shocked by news that pirates had raided a small passenger ship twenty miles along the coast. I had seen the Chinese-owned *Dona Pacita* a number of times in the Visayan Sea, and thought her a reasonably safe vessel to travel on, if clumsily built and comfortless. The cramped space afforded its deck passengers might have complicated the raiders' plans. That, no doubt, was why four men went aboard her in Cebu as paying passengers, giving it out that they were professional gamblers returning home. When the pirates' launch drew alongside after dark, these four pulled out their guns, ordering those around them to lie face down on the deck. The raiders had also taken the precaution of wearing P.C. uniforms, as if they were just making some routine search for contraband cigarettes. No one was killed in the gun fight that took place, but P100,000 had been taken from the safe by the time the ship was allowed to go on. This was the third time that vessels owned by the Go Thong Shipping Company had been plundered in the same area in recent years.

Such events are not unusual in an archipelago where piracy has existed for centuries. Malays were plundering one another here long before the Spaniards came, ranging the seas from Leyte, Mindanao and the Sulu islands, through the Netherlands East Indies to Malacca and Singapore. Action by the British Navy in the nineteenth century drove them back to Borneo and the Philippines, where even today they are little hampered by a government with too much other crime on its hands to trouble much about small ships at sea. By 1964 the situation had deteriorated so

1. *Philippines Free Press*, 19 December 1964, Manila.

much that piracy was actually being practised in Manila Bay, within a few miles of the capital.

'I never bring my ship in before daylight,' said the captain of a Norwegian freighter on which I made one voyage from Hong Kong. 'I keep always the other side of Corregidor till the sun comes up.'

The night before we arrived, a Korean ship in Manila Bay had been obliged to raise anchor three times in one night. Three times its crew had to fight boarders off the decks. Each time the captain blew his siren, but no assistance came. There appeared to be no harbour patrols at all. The raiders usually arrived in fast, high-powered *bancas*, which are long, heavily-built outrigger canoes normally used by fishermen, but equipped with outboard motors. It was no longer possible to distinguish between genuine fisherfolk and pirates, most of whom made their living from smuggling.

'Sometimes they blacken their faces,' the Norwegian skipper told me. 'Sometimes they even wear black-coloured pyjamas, and you just can't see them in the dark. They carry 45s or rifles, and long-bladed knives. Machine guns sometimes. They come aboard with ropes and grappling hooks, or climb through a porthole someone has been stupid enough to leave open. Before you know what's happening, they've ransacked the ship's stores, or one of the holds, and they're gone. If you try to grab them on deck, they'll kill you.'

That first night in Manila harbour, I heard what sounded like machine gun fire out in the Bay. It was approaching Chinese New Year, so I thought at first it could have been fireworks. The next morning the chief officer told me that a Customs patrol had chased an unidentified launch. As usual, the patrol boat had broken down at the crucial moment. The pirates had made their escape in the direction of Cavite.

During the Christmas period the mayor of San Nicolas, Cavite, called a meeting of town and barrio officials along the coast. The Philippines Constabulary attended. The only discussion was to decide what could be done about piracy. From many remote beaches fishermen reported the consistent loss of nets, *banca* motors and valuable equipment. Before 1964 these sea-borne bandits were small-time operators, working in isolation. Now they were using high-powered *kumpits*, those clumsy, but fast-travelling launches used by organized smugglers between Borneo and the southern Philippines. They had been grouped into syndicates, used modern weapons and even diving gear of an advanced pattern made in the United States.

The situation became really out of hand in January 1965 when an Australian passenger liner, *Francis Drake*, was invaded by these pirates. This was the captain's report:

We dropped anchor inside the breakwater at 0909 hours and were immediately surrounded by a number of launches crowded with prospective purchasers of contraband. In view of this, one deck officer remained on duty on the gangway, and two apprentices maintained a constant patrol using a walkie-talkie for communication.

Illegal boarders still managed to get on board, particularly over the stern, and some through a porthole. During this time no assistance whatever was received from the guards who merely stood by and watched.

Eventually, on the insistence of the ship's officers, they half-heartedly assisted in rounding up some of the boarders. By this time there were so many that the job became almost impossible. Authority was then given to the guards, and the confidential agents, to use whatever force was necessary to arrest illegal boarders, and any member of the crew found having any dealings with them. This proved to be of no avail.

Two hours later the so-called *cumbancheros* were all over the ship. An apprentice was ordered to evict them from the crew's quarters. When he implemented the order, he was threatened with guns. He asked for assistance from the chief officer, who sent four men to help him evict the *cumbancheros*.

Things quietened down somewhat in the afternoon, though a few 'unauthorised persons' remained on board. The watchmen could do nothing to stop them from moving freely about the ship. By then many of the *cumbancheros* were armed with high-powered guns.

During the evening things warmed up again. At about 2100 hours the chief officer was called by one of the crew, who told him there were more armed men aboard. Many crew members said they had been intimidated. The ship was then put under a 24-hour watch to see that nothing serious happened.

Half-an-hour after midnight on the 9th, with the chief officer, I saw several packages being lowered over the stern. No crew members were involved in this, though the packages, presumably cigarettes, had obviously been bought from them. It was decided that it would not be prudent to interfere – a decision that was amply proved right a few minutes later when, on my own, I was told at gunpoint to keep well away.

Later it was also reported to me that *cumbancheros* had broken into the cabins of a hairdresser and the nursing sister. I have been deeply concerned about the safety of my passengers, some of whom have been terrorized in the passageways and on deck. The situation is an intolerable one, especially as similar occurrences have already taken place on other ships in this port . . .[2]

The Association of International Shipping Lines asked the Customs Commissioner, Alberto de Joya, to take action. Its American president, E. H. Bosch, informed him that officers on other ships had also been threatened with violence, even death and that several shipping lines were proposing to by-pass Manila in favour of other Asian ports.

One week later a conference was held in the sombre Customs building overlooking South Pier, where uniformed guards patrolled gun on hip, steel-helmeted soldiers with rifles lounged about smoking contraband cigarettes, and Filipino wharf labourers leisurely handled a confused mass of cargo, some of which had been lying under the hot sun for weeks. Among those attending the conference were naval officers, constabulary, Manila Police, officers and members of the Presidential Anti-Smuggling Co-ordinating Committee, for no one doubted that influential smugglers were also involved. The Commissioner for Customs shocked shipowners by declaring that, 'It's you who are to blame for piracy. Stop your crews

2. *Manila Times*, 17 January 1965, Manila.

selling them blackmarket cigarettes. Why do you declare so many cargoes in transit for other ports, then smuggle them ashore here? This is the honey attracting the pirates. Our men are exposing their lives to stop pirates boarding your ships. Your officers and crews must also help to fight off pirates and *cumbancheros*.'

However, what really shocked this conference was the Commissioner's admission that his department had only three slow launches to patrol hundreds of square miles of open water. Two of them were usually under repair. Requests for more modern, faster craft had been rejected for the usual reason: 'No funds.'

During a press conference that followed some days later, the Commissioner was candid enough to state other reasons why his officers had failed to stop this piracy. He referred to intelligence reports from his own department that linked his customs men with smugglers. The accepted 'pay-off', he said, was 50 pesos for each case of contraband cigarettes bought by *cumbancheros* from foreign ships.

'All they are expected to do,' he said, 'is see nothing and report nothing. The *modus operandi* is well known on the waterfront. At a given signal, the customs boat veers away from the path of a *banca* approaching or leaving an anchored ship. When the customs boat reappears, the *cumbanchero* will already be on his way to an appointed spot to meet buyers of contraband goods ashore.'

Yet the operational base of these *cumbancheros* (the phrase, significantly, has a Spanish origin) was known to everybody. They docked their *bancas* beside a shanty town known as Puting Bato. This squalid collection of caseboard shanties and iron huts had been built, illegally, on a breakwater off Roxas Boulevard, where Manila's leading hotels, night clubs and restaurants look out at the Bay. The curious factor was that Puting Bato had been built on Philippine Navy property.

The Commissioner, who was transferred to another department soon afterwards, met his final frustration when postal officials complained of the amount of overseas mail, including valuable packets, that never reached the shore. He rejected their appeal for a special, police-guarded launch taking consignments direct from ships at anchor, because the only boat available had already had its motors stolen on two occasions from the customs zone. He said he feared that any new boat might itself be hi-jacked. As a Manila columnist expressed it: 'Foreign vessels will soon be posting up warnings before entering Philippine waters: "All hands at battle stations. Prepare to repel boarders." '[3]

Public order had reached a desperately low level by 1965.

3. *Manila Times*, 1 June 1965, Manila.

CHAPTER 14

Forgotten Frontier

*In describing the immense group, the
old chief conveyed to Magellan in
pantomime that they had once been part of
a single piece of inhabited land which a
kindly giant had carried upon his
shoulders. This patient giant finally
grew indignant at the constant
quarrelling of the ungrateful men he was
serving, so he flung his burden into the
sea. It broke into thousands of
fragments which became islands . . .*

FR. BRAGANZA

IT IS STRANGE how little the great island of Mindanao occurs in the
thinking of most Filipinos. The administration seldom concerns itself
with anything beyond Luzon and the more developed of the Visayas.
Despite its largely agricultural economy, the Philippines has acquired an
urban outlook, strongly centralized. Power tends to concentrate in the
president's office, so that almost every policy decision must be decided
along the labyrinthian corridors of Malacanang. Seldom does the fresh air
of a potentially fertile countryside blow through them. This is especially
so in the case of Mindanao.

For half a century this rugged, mountainous, heavily-forested island
at the meeting of the Sulu and Celebes Seas has been proclaimed the
'promised land'. In the early American period, enthusiasts urged northern
Filipinos to 'Go South'. It was to be the new frontier, the land of wealth
and opportunity.

Few people went.

Some United States capital did flow in that direction, invested in large
scale cattle ranches and timber concessions. In 1934 Quezon began his
notable Koronadal resettlement scheme for landless peasants, and leased
large areas to several United States concerns. After the war Hawaiian
pineapple growers saw the possibilities of Mindanao and transferred their
operations to the Philippines. Filipinos with or without capital remained
nervous of the region. Old memories of Moro intransigence were too
much for them. The island remained very much an isolated kingdom of
the Muslims, who still resented intrusions from the north. Sometimes
they reacted violently, though the *juramentados* that once so intimidated
Christian settlers have now receded into a sullen acceptance or frontier
banditry.

107

Nonetheless, the past decade has brought a considerable increase in settlement. The population has doubled, and this is by no means through natural increase alone. There has been a steady influx from the Visayas, where low wages and unemployment continually force large numbers to migrate. But the old faith in Mindanao as the fabled land of opportunity is fading. No longer do many see it as the safety valve for an exploding population, or virgin terrain awaiting only tractor and plough to unlock its riches. This myth was further deflated recently by the American geographer, Robert E. Huke. The Philippines, he claimed, has a far greater population pressure on its cultivatible areas than Burma or India, though not yet as desperate a situation as China and Vietnam. The population of Mindanao has risen by less than 100,000 between 1913 and 1939, when it passed the million mark. This allowed an average of 10 hectares per head. By 1948 it had increased to 1,216,348, presumably from natural births only, then leapt to 5,090,433 at the last census in 1960. Hence there were less than two hectares for every settler. But, he added, much of the land in this mountainous country was too steep for effective farming; rice, in particular, needed fairly flat areas for flooding or irrigation. Some soils were also poor, giving low yields, while considerable areas were swamps that would be costly to drain. In fact, of that original estimate of 9,500,000 hectares, only 4,400,000 was really suitable for cultivation. Meantime the demand for land in the post-war years had been so heavy that only 2,100,000 remained to be opened up. Government policy also insisted that sixteen hectares were needed to settle each new family.[1]

It appeared as if Mindanao's 'vast empty areas' were vanishing more quickly than theoreticians could parcel it out. Yet where else was the Republic's alarming increase of one million a year to be accommodated?

The answer could only be to find other forms of production beyond subsistence farming. Although no proper survey of Mindanao's resources has yet been made, it is known that considerable deposits of iron ore, copper and other minerals exist and that the Sulu and Celebes Seas are extremely rich in fisheries, which no one has attempted to process; that more use could be made of cattlelands on the central plateau and of large timber resources. Plans have long been under way for a steel works in Iligan, which has iron ore nearby, but the project remains in the clouds because no one knows what happened to the money.

'Mindanao is still the Land of Promise,' wrote one disenchanted correspondent to a Manila newspaper in 1965. 'Thousands of them are made by politicians, who never keep promises.' The land of broken promises, Ferdinand Marcos termed it while campaigning for the presidency in October 1965, and at once made a further promise: he undertook, if elected, to restore life to the Mindanao Development Authority, a government agency set up in June 1961 with a guarantee of P300,000,000 to be advanced progressively over a ten year period. So far the Authority

---

1. Robert E. Huke, *Shadows on The Land: An Economic Geography of The Philippines*, op. cit.

has achieved no development. It has been given none of the promised government finance, because President Macapagal regarded the M.D.A. as a Nacionalista creation. Four years after its establishment, the general manager said that the only money he had received was just sufficient to pay his office staff.[2] President Marcos has so far done nothing either.

Such is politics.

Yet the Authority did manage, between 1963 and 1965, to carry out twenty-two 'feasibility studies' in such areas as secondary industry, cattle-breeding, the growing of cacao, coffee, rice and corn, vegetable farming, deep-sea fishing, canneries, mining, timber, road-building, and cottage industries. However, no further action was possible because the president failed to give his approval. The only development such politics appeared to encourage was the kind of story I read in the *Western Mindanao Chronicle*:

> ILIGAN CITY, Nov. 27 — Camilo P. Cabili conferred today with Police Chief Jose Orbe for the acquisition of high-powered firearms for the city police department.
>
> Cabili expressed concern over the increasing incidence of cattle-rustling at the city outskirts by heavily armed cattle thieves.
>
> The police, he said, were totally helpless to combat rustling under the present conditions because they had nothing but 45 and 38 calibre sidearms.

This, at least, was in keeping with the frontier character of Mindanao. Its occupations are, in the main, frontier ones. Despite the indifference of governments, progress is being made by private enterprises. Cattle ranches are prospering in the uplands of Bukidnon; experimental dairying has begun near Davao; logging mills and plyboard factories are exporting from several coastal areas; high-grade copra, abaca and tropical fruits go north by a dozen shipping services. Cities like Davao, Zamboanga, Cotabato, Dadiangas are increasing once stagnant populations. 'You can't fail here,' one corporation manager told me in Davao with rather dogged optimism. 'Only men can fail. There is nothing wrong with the land.'

He might have added, as others did, that the real failure was in the supply of capital, the willingness to take risks, the absence of administration aid. Curiously, the fact that several American plantations were really moving ahead appeared only to discourage smaller enterprises, especially when neither government nor private banks were prepared to make loans. On a lower scale, widespread unemployment and poor wages were also causing discontent.

This frustration came to a head in 1964, when rumours of the sale of a model and highly-productive government undertaking began to circulate. This was the Davao Penal Colony, which had been in existence for thirty-four years. The 15,000 hectare settlement, designed to regenerate long-term prisoners through paid labour, had achieved a good deal of fame throughout the Philippines and abroad. The colony had far more than experimental value, for it was well-established agriculturally, and

2. *Manila Times*, 11 June 1965, Manila.

was actually making a profit. It was also a valuable producer of coffee, cacao, coconuts, abaca, rice, corn and rubber. Suddenly President Maca-pagal decided to uproot it. It was an affront to Mindanao pride: a betrayal.

In October 1964, Senator Lorenzo Tanada flew from Manila to investi-gate and wrote an open letter to the president. This, in part, was what he had to say:

Dear Mr. President:

I take the liberty of writing you, so shortly upon your return from the United States, to bring to your attention a matter of the gravest urgency. I refer to the projected Agreement between the Philippines Government and the United Fruit Company involving the lease and delivery of the Davao Penal Colony reservation for a banana plantation. When the nature of this Agree-ment was first revealed to me, I could not believe it. I could not believe that an administration of this Republic would consciously and cavalierly sign away an entire operational penal colony to an alien corporation. I could not believe that an administration in office would reach such cynical straits and that it is now ready to barter away not simply vital natural resources of the country but the appurtenances of Government itself.

The Davao Penal Colony reservation is to be transferred ostensibly to the Mindanao Development Authority, which will in turn deliver the same to the United Fruit Company by an Agreement scheduled to be signed not later than April 1st, 1965.

Ceding a penal colony reservation to an alien corporation is shocking enough; but what makes the deal more shocking is the kind of reservation that is here being surrendered in the guise of 'benefiting the national economy' a well developed agricultural 10,000-hectare estate with a present annual income of over P800,000, which is expected to increase to more than P1,000,000 yearly within the next two years as its rubber and coconut plantations begin to yield their produce.

The Davao Colony is today the most successful penal experiment in the country. The reservation boasts of the largest abaca plantation in the Philip-pines, said to be worth P4,150,000. It has 40,542 coffee trees and 4,230 cacao trees valued at P193,000, 39,720 coconut trees worth P198,600, 46,747 rubber trees worth P785,035. All told, the agricultural improvements, some rice and corn lands, are worth P5,339,324. Moreover, it has set up a P1,550,000 abaca decorticating plant, and buildings and other fixed assets with an estimated value of P1,128,800. All of these highly productive assets, the products of so many years of patient labour, are now apparently to be destroyed or removed so that an alien company could grow bananas!

What is to be done to the rubber and coconut trees, the coffee and cacao, the abaca plantation? Are these to be destroyed and substituted with bananas by the United Fruit Company? And if they are to be turned over to this alien company, are the rentals contemplated in the Agreement proportionate to the value of these improvements? Will they match the P800,000 yearly income actually realized by the colony at present, or the P1,000,000 expected income yearly by 1966-67? Will there be compensation for the fantastic expense of transferring an entire, fully operational penal colony with 3,800 prisoners to another site, an expense estimated at P13,145,000?

What does the government propose to do with the million and a half peso decorticating plant?

What will happen to the 387 employees whose salaries are paid out of the income of the colony?

Who will pay for the cost of operating the new colony which necessarily will be unproductive and fund-draining for the next five or ten years?

Where are the 3,800 prisoners now living in the colony to be transferred? Will these prisoners be required to begin over again the back-breaking task of opening forests and new land? What effect would such a cynical alienation have on men being painstakingly weaned away from a criminal past?

One might understand, though not sanction or condone, the alienation of large tracts of virgin land to foreign entities for the latter to pioneer and develop. But it is incomprehensible why a fully operational and agricultural estate — a penal colony at that — should be offered on a veritable silver platter to aliens.

Mr. President, in the name of our people, I appeal to you to desist from this act of wanton folly . . . this betrayal of our national patrimony.[3]

Senator Tanada's letter touched off widespread protest. The issue made newspaper headlines for days. 'The Banana Deal', they termed it; or *Silang Macaw*, that is, Monkey Business. The president at first denied all knowledge of the plan, though he was known also to have described it in private as one of his major achievements. Local banana growers declared that competition from a powerful overseas corporation would ruin them, or at least destroy their price structure. Nacionalistas threatened to impeach the president for defying the Constitution, which forbade the granting of leases beyond a certain size to foreign interests. Besides, the proposed seventy-five year lease contravened the Laurel-Langley Agreement as well. They expanded their attack to a general one on Liberal policies, which were said to include further 'sell-outs' to United States interests for personal gain, or, as one newspaper expressed it, to ensure that the president had enough funds to buy his re-election. Before long the issue began to take on anti-American overtones.

'United Fruit,' wrote I. P. Soliongco in the *Manila Chronicle*, a Nacionalista organ, 'has had the evil reputation of instituting a policy of political corruption and of inspiring minority coups in at least nine Latin American countries. . . . But it was these less politically sophisticated, less alert and possibly less honest Latin Americans who imposed as a first requirement that it establish itself in the wilderness, which it must hack away, criss-cross with roads and railroads and otherwise render habitable. In the vast uncultivated space of the Latin American lands discovered by United Fruit, modern towns and seaports arose from the wild and almost impenetrable jungle. . . . Nevertheless, like Frankenstein, they are helpless before the commanding presence of a giant American corporation for which the Marines had landed and for which the quiet and unquiet Americans in the State Department have sharpened their intriguing minds, perfected the art of coups and popularized the use of the endless struggle against communism as a noble and holy cloak for a multitude of political and economic crimes against the despised Latin Americans.'[4]

3. *Zamboanga Times*, 14 November 1964.
4. *Manila Chronicle*, 2-3 November 1964, Manila.

Within a matter of days the president announced that he had decided to 'reject the offer'. It was an embarrassing situation for the United Fruit Company's agricultural experts, who had already established themselves in the colony, assured of an early start. Perhaps they found it even more like Latin America than they had supposed. This was only one of several major scandals that disrupted Macapagal's bid for re-election. With the accession of Nacionalistas to power, the Davao Penal Colony remains. However, southerners have not yet recovered their confidence, for a Senate Committee of Inquiry accused the outgoing administration of having planned 'a systematic scheme to carve up Mindanao into pockets of alien-controlled plantations'. It will require large subsidies to the Development Authority before morale can be restored.

Finance for transport and communications is desperately needed. It is now almost impossible to open up the country. Roads and highways, so-called, are in a worse condition than during the war against Japan. Before the Americans left motorists could drive from Davao, through Cotabato, to Iligan in eight hours; a distance of more than 300 miles. Today it is hardly possible to do so at all.

This was a journey I had planned to make, using public transport. Friends urged me on no account to do so. The alleged highway, sections of which are marked on maps as 'first class', now consist largely of pot-holes, dust traps and broken causeways. The only form of transport are lumbering, uncomfortable, broken-down buses. There are worse hazards.

I was in Zamboanga when news came through of the Bukidnon bus hold-up which had been ambushed by bandits between Cotabato and Davao. The inspector and one passenger were killed, and everyone else robbed at gunpoint. Next day the same gang held up an entire barrio, escaped with money, jewels and three high-powered rifles belonging to an army officer. The bandit leader, Boy Antonio, was later killed by a Philippine Constabulary unit in a roadside gun battle.

Still why go that far for adventure? One month earlier an American truck driver, having broken through a bandit ambush fifty miles from Zamboanga, managed to reach the city with three bullets in his chest. He died there at the wheel. A few miles inland, during the same week, the Constabulary fought another pitched battle with an outlaw band led by the chieftain, Omang. The bandits, who had been sacking farms and barrios for months, left four dead and two wounded behind. The same month forty armed men attacked a crowd gathered in the market place of a town three miles from Jolo, fired indiscriminately at whoever happened to be standing around fires where stolen beef was being roasted, took over the entire barrio until the Philippine Constabulary drove them off. You could make a long catalogue of such incidents, especially in the lawless Sulu Archipelago. Those small scattered islands frequently contribute such headings to the Manila press as BATTLE AGAINST BANDITS IN SULU: EIGHT KILLED IN GUN BATTLE: MASSACRE BY ARMED BANDITS: ROBBERS SLAY TWO IN CAGAYAN SULU. Or else picturesque news items of this kind:

December 8. — Eight wanted murderers surrendered to the 113th P.C. company at Buntod, Sulu. Another outlaw, Nurol Alib Matagong, surrendered the same day, wanted for forcible abduction and double homicide. Also captured was Bendicio Iscala, alias Bening, on charges of robbery and large-scale theft of cattle. But there are still many at large.

In January 1965 Lieut. Tarciano M. Martinez published in the Manila press a dramatic account of a four-month running war against the famous Namla Mangkabong's outlaw band on Sulu Island. 'On the afternoon of October 25,' he wrote at one point of a battle that numbered twenty known casualties, 'I was informed that close to a hundred armed men were massing at Lantung to ambush government vehicles on the national road. The armed band, I was later to learn, was led by Manjodan Jalissan, alias Uddah, who had killed a woman and burned houses two weeks earlier in another *sitio*.' This ferocious Muslim gang was finally driven off by the 27-strong Ranger detachment, when Lieut. Martinez sent for a 60-mm. mortar from a nearby Army camp.

The Sulu islands are a law to themselves. By comparison Mindanao is a land of peace — with the exception of Cotabato province. I spent only one day on Cotabato City, because the shipping agent there was anxious to have the ship's passengers returned safely down the Rio Grande before dark. The dusty, western-style city is a place where even the locals do not walk the streets after dark, or only certain well-known ones who parade with revolvers ostentatiously strapped to their belts. Political feuds, Muslim-Christian antagonisms and naked gangsterism created a continually explosive situation, while mountain regions nearby hide bandit and rustler gangs that scarcely encourage travel. In certain town markets there you find machine gun parts laid out for sale alongside meats, dried fish and vegetables. At the mouth of the Cotabato river is a long, steep, scrub-dark island that does not encourage visitors either.

During the war guerrillas used this island as a secret cache for ammunition. No Japanese troops could ever land there, so efficient was the warning system of flashlights, smoke signals and hidden gongs. These days the Constabulary is equally unable to make surprise searches, though it is a known centre for smuggling arms, contraband and illegal immigrants from Indonesia.

I was in Mindanao when the first alarm was raised over Indonesian infiltration. They were reported to be arriving in hundreds. The revelation followed the arrest of Dr Jesus Lava, a long-sought leader of the Huks in Central Luzon. This was in September 1964. Military intelligence informed a Senate committee on national defence that Lava had revealed long-term Indonesian plans for annexing Mindanao.[5] The target date was 1970. Meanwhile some fifty agents of the P.K.I. (Partai Kommunis Indonesia) were said to be active among the Muslims, who were expected to be more sympathetic to their Indonesian brothers than to

5. *Manila Bulletin*, 29 August 1964, Manila.

the Christians of the north. Chinese Communist agents were also reported to be active, distributing propaganda for the Soekarno brand of socialism. Political schools had been established on Karakelang and Isang islands in the Sulu Sea, within easy reach of Mindanao. Indonesians had also settled illegally on Baluta and Sarangani Islands, which rise dramatically from the blue ocean on the shipping route to Davao.

Subsequent investigations found that the majority of lease-holders on those islands, as well as mainland areas nearby, were Indonesians. One congressman reported indignantly that the only way for Filipinos to acquire land on Balut was to go first to the Indonesian consulate in Davao. Later intelligence reports spoke of Indonesian army officers settling on the coast, where they were said to retain authority over the fellow migrants. Others had found acceptance by marrying the daughters of influential Muslim leaders. Others again formed poverty-ridden communities of squatters.

There were also reports of unidentified submarines, and of aircraft landing unannounced in Mindanao from Indonesian Borneo, ostensibly en route to Manila for engine overhauls. One of these, a C-47, had its cabin door missing and wire cables fitted inside, as if for parachute drops. Civil aeronautic officials found it difficult to protest against these intrusians, for they had been caught before, owing to Soekarno's habit of occasionally appearing in his private Jetstar over Manila, where his favourite Filipino film star had an apartment. The most puzzling factor, however, was the discovery that Indonesians had been entering Mindanao in large numbers for many years. Intelligence estimates gave widely varying numbers: anything from 6,000 to 20,000.

It may seem reasonable to assume that immigration authorities were not altogether unaware of their existence. Everyone else in Mindanao knew about them. Even I was told in Zamboanga and Davao of the way Chinese were smuggled ashore in fishing boats, disguised as Muslims in turbans and *patadyongs*. The landing price, I was informed, was P1,500. Yet there were only the sparsest of records in official files. I recalled the same kind of official surprise in Manila when, earlier that year, the files of 8,000 Chinese on short-term visas were found to be 'missing'. *Tong*, after all, was originally a Chinese word.

To claim that the settlement of all those Indonesians was a sinister move by Soekarno was, of course, unreal. But Filipinos remembered the large pre-war enclaves of Japanese, especially in Davao. Most of the Indonesians were refugees from the economic chaos of their own islands. They had come mainly from central Sumatra and Java, where living conditions were much worse than in Mindanao. Moreover they had been surreptitiously welcomed by their employers, especially in remote country areas, because they were willing to work for far lower wages than Filipinos. Others, growing coconuts, were also smuggling in lower-grade copra from the Celebes and elsewhere, mixing it illegally with the Filipino product to gain higher export prices. Since confrontation began with Malaysia,

114

Indonesian growers had been denied their traditional outlets through Singapore. Others again were suspected of aiding military infiltration of Sarawak and Sabah, which could be reached more easily from the Philippines, due to British and Australian naval patrols operating in areas further west.

The situation revived Philippine fears of Soekarno's well-known ambition to re-create the thirteenth century Majapahit Empire based on Java. They recalled President Quirino's shock when, back in 1952, he visited Soekarno in his summer palace at Bogor. There he had seen a prominently displayed map on which Indonesia and its Malay neighbours, including the Philippines, were uniformly painted in gold. Soekarno assured him that the colour had no political significance, though the map was again noted by Filipinos at the time of the Asian Games ten years later. One Manila newspaper then asked whether it reflected Indonesia's imperialist desires, drawing a wrathful denial from Djakarta. A mass demonstration was then held outside the Philippines Embassy, forcing the Foreign Affairs Department in Manila to disown the newspaper's 'unfriendly' attitude. In recent years relations between the two countries have been more cordial, though Soekarno had not forgotten that Mindanao and the Tawi-Tawi group were used to channel American arms to Sumatra and the Celebes during the 1958 rebellion against his regime. Nor that certain high-ranking Filipino officers had passed on the rebels' army equipment, flown from the United States to modernize their own defences. In October 1965, after hundreds of these Indonesians had been repatriated. Soekarno claimed that C.I.A. agents sent in with them had a hand in fomenting the rebellion against his regime.

Back in April 1965 the National Defence Committee's chairman, Senator Rodolfo Ganzon, stated his belief that Indonesian activity was designed to give tactical aid to Communist China, and urged the building up of southern defences. The army sent 150,000 troops to Mindanao, while requests were made to the United States to subsidize a new naval base near Cotabato. These moves were probably made unnecessary by the events of October 1965 in Indonesia, when the P.K.I. ceased to be a political force. However, the Manila commentator, Napoleon G. Rama, believed that there was never any necessity for an army build up in Mindanao. He suggested that it was merely a manoeuvre by the high command to gain a bigger budget for its own purposes and added prestige. 'What faces the government in Mindanao,' he wrote, 'is a police or constabulary problem, not a military one.'[6]

It was, nonetheless, a warning that some day these southern islands might become another cockpit for conflicting national ambitions in south-east Asia. The time had come to secure the allegiance of the long-neglected 1,500,000 Muslims in Mindanao by giving some attention to their social and economic plight. Unless some action is soon taken, the inter-island smuggling, already ruining the national economy, could well

6. *Philippines Free Press*, 10 April 1965, Manila.

lead to more serious types of contraband, notably smuggled arms and foreign agents.

As things are, the Philippines Navy is totally unable to cope with these smugglers, let alone infiltrators of a more politically dangerous kind. According to Senator Ganzon, the naval might of the Philippines in this maze of islands consists of two slow and obsolete gunboats, hardly a force to command great respect.

Manila Times

Men of the barrio

Philippine Travel and Tourist Association

Magellan's Santa Niño, Cebu

The well-loved carabao

Philippine Travel and Tourist Association

CHAPTER 15

Muslims and Moros

*In time, many of the beautiful
elements in the culture of the Muslims
in the south, will be considered common
property by the majority of Filipinos.
Communication between peoples which
have been separated by colonial
dominance will be re-established,
mutual tolerance will flourish, and the
Muslims will find it easier to serve
their country, the Philippines.*

CESAR ADIB MAJUL

WHATEVER course Indonesia takes in the future, it is clear that Muslims in the Philippines will assert themselves more and more. They are no longer in a mood to be regarded as second-class citizens. The spirit of Islam has had a remarkable resurgence in the past two decades. A new sense of unity has grown among the various groupings of the south: they have gained more independence, new pride.

The operative term is pride.

These were always a proud people. Often too much so for the peace of mind of northerners, who related it to arrogance and aggression. This question of pride among Christian Filipinos is always a touchy question, for often it becomes confused with vanity, *amor propria*, a painful sensitivity that takes offence at the least imagined slight. It stems, perhaps, from a sense of inferiority, the colonial's reaction to many generations of foreign domination: Australia's notorious 'cultural cringe'. The Muslim attitude is different, for they never really knew this dominance. Their own proud responses come from centuries of resistance, an awareness of their own racial strength. The ancient preoccupation with *maratabat*, face, often had ferocious results; in the *juramentado*, the tendency to run amok, and spontaneous killings due to nothing more than offended pride. There remains, even today, a touch of contempt in their acceptance of outsiders, as though these were of a lesser breed.

The so-called Moro stare is a discomforting thing. You come across it almost everywhere: in villages, the town markets, on the wharves. The impassive face, the fixed, unblinking eyes; the bold inspection of the stranger that, if you return it, sometimes retreats into shyness, sometimes derisive laughter. After a while, you come to accept it as a matter of course. You find other qualities to admire: the dignity of gait and manner, even among the poorest, the smooth, dark, sea-tanned complexions, the aquiline noses that reveal a blending of Arab with Malay, their flamboyant costume. In some regions, notably Cotabato, the habit of chewing betel nut gives a startling brilliance to their lips, while the shaving off of eyebrows and filing of teeth to shark-like points creates a frightening appearance that is not in the least mitigated by friendly smiles. Today dress is becoming more westernised, at least among the younger people; that is, western in the Filipino fashion, which leans towards gaudily striped shirts, pictorially-embossed singlets, jeans. Yet even the young men retain a taste for round black fezzes, or silk and cotton squares wound turban-like about their heads. Among their elders are many who wear the skull-tight white caps that denote having made a pilgrimage to Mecca. In Zamboanga or Marawi City, from Cotabato to Basilan and the Sulu islands more traditional dress is still commonplace. Sarongs and loose-cut shirts of *batik*, baggy cotton trousers known as *sauvals*, coloured and braided vests like medieval jerkins, cummerbunds into which are sometimes thrust daggers with gilt scabbards, sometimes brass boxes containing betel nut. Muslims have a flair for strong colours, which in native materials blend in striking fashion: red, orange, yellow are the dominant tones, with purple and green to enrich them in un-expected harmony. Women's dress, too, gives them extraordinary poise. The rich dyes of ankle-length sarongs, their blouses of coloured silks with gold thread and buttons of gold coins, the *patadeyongs* loosely worn like togas and open veils over their heads. There is a rare grace to these women that does not come from their Arabian Nights costume alone. Their erect carriage, with almost a sway back, the slow, long, flat-soled stride, the full stretch of arm with fingers out-curving to the last silver-pale flash of long nails. All this, even at village level, creates the grave delicacy of a ritual Muslim dance. However, they lack the boldness of their males. These creatures are as feminine as their ankle bells, shy as their deer-like eyes. Yet you dare not look at them. Not for long. Jealousy is also a Muslim attribute. Chastity, before marriage, is almost obligatory, as it is in all communities where a costly bride price is expected from the male. Adultery, at least on the female's part, brings brutal punishment. I recall a Filipino priest telling me how be came upon a Muslim girl bathing herself at a roadside creek; a not uncommon practice even today. 'Ah,' he said, 'to stop is dangerous. One can look only, keep walking — and pray.'

The joys of Mohammed are for initiates only. Perhaps this is why Muslims are still allowed several wives.

I attended a wedding once on the small island of Gaunan, two hours cruising from Pangasahan, Basilan. It was a poor community living in a huddle of *barong-barongs*, with thatched houses built upon stilts over a tidal estuary. Its people had only two ways of living: by fishing or smug-gling. Few of them, by their reactions, had seen a European before. They treated us with immense courtesy, though conversation was impossible in any but the local Malay dialect. Many of the guests had journeyed a long way, coming from as far as Jolo and Zamboanga. I have rarely seen such richness of costume, so many jewels, so much gold displayed. A four-piece orchestra played on a canopied platform outside the home of the bride: two men with ancestral versions of the violin, one girl singing Muslim love ballads and another gently playing the *gambong*, a kind of melodious xylophone which is common throughout the Indonesian islands. The most impressively dressed of all were the Yakkan people, who belong to the rough jungle country of Basilan. The men had almost the appearance of toreadors, wearing many-hued jackets and trousers that were skin-tight from the knees down, and massive lengths of brightly coloured striped cloth wound around their stomachs. These six-metre lengths of hand-woven cotton have more than decorative value, for they serve as blankets and as protection against bolo or kris. The Yakkans, who are related to the Dyaks of Borneo, have a centuries-old reputation for fine horsemanship. Hence their tight trousers, which they are unable to take off until the material rots with years of use. In earlier days they were also the most bloodthirsty of enemies. Theirs, in fact, is still bandit country, through which my friends would not drive me during a recent outbreak of raiding in the hills. Just before I left Zamboanga for Basilan two young men, for no known motive, were found decapitated in a mountain areas behind the Yakkan capital of Lamitan. On my only visit to the picturesque little market town, it seemed a friendly enough place, despite the fearsome display of daggers, long knives, and finely-wrought kris on public sale. Yet, as recently as August 1965, a Basilan correspondent for the Manila press could write: 'In the hinterlands: robbery, killings. Kidnappings in town. Pirates and smugglers at sea. Rustlers in the hills. This is Basilan Island, as notorious today as it was ten years ago, when it became known as The Island of Sudden Death.'[1] He wrote of stolen livestock shipped aboard motorized *kumpits* for Sulu, teachers threatened with stabbings unless they gave protection money, buses in remote areas ambushed, and of two families beheaded by outlaws.

It recalled several occasions of unexplained tension we had experienced while staying on Don Juan Alano's coconut plantation, some miles inland from Pangasahan. An uproar of dogs barking and human cries in the compound at night; our host's uneasiness when his jeep broke down in a lonely area, obliging us to send an armed runner six miles for assistance; the anxiety of Mrs Alano and her driver when another jeep became bogged after heavy rain on a cross-country journey back to the port of Isabella. The Filipino planter had made no secret of the fact that bandits sometimes rode into his property, that he had even made a pact with them, undertaking not to appeal for police or army action if they left his Muslim employees alone.

Yet the modern atmosphere is comparatively tame. You have only to read the description General George Davis left of the Moro world, when he was military governor at the turn of the century.

1. *Philippines Free Press*, 21 August 1965, Manila.

With a people who have no conception of government that is not arbitrary and absolute; who hold human life as no more sacred than the life of an animal; who have become accustomed to acts of violence; who are constrained by fear from containing the practice of piracy; who still carry on slave trade; who habitually raid the homes of mountain natives and enslave them; who habitually make slaves of their captives in war — even when of their own race; who habitually observe the precepts of the Koran, which declares that female slaves must submit to their masters — it is useless to declare a plan of government that is not based on physical fact, might and powers.[2]

It was hardly the Gettysburg code.

At that stage, however, no one had made any attempt to understand these people. How could they? First the Spanish, then Americans, had been trapped in a bitter war of attrition. It was impossible then to make studies in history or anthropology. The term Moro was then a convenient generalization for a wide variety of tribes and cultures. Some were Muslims, some pagan. There are now known to be twenty-three different tribal groupings, only six of which were strongly influenced by Islam. The rest were pagans, living at a more primitive level: the superb horsemen of the Cotabato hinterland, the Bilaans; the fishing Samals with their *vintas*; the sea-gipsy Badjaos and other smaller tribes. The principal Muslims were the Maranaws, who had settled centuries ago on the north coast of Mindanao and developed agriculture around the magnificent Lake Lanao, where Marawi City stands today; the Maguindanaws, conquerors of the Cotabato Valley, from which they drove the original inhabitants to set up their own wet-rice culture; and the Tau-sugs of the Sulu archipelago. Each group had one or more sultanates, whose rule was not so much over specific regions as over people. The boundaries shifted; they counted their strength and influence by the number of their followers. And beneath each sultan was a descending pyramid of lesser rulers and nobles: the *datus, maharajas, panglimas* and others. The *agama*, the sultan's court, imposed tithes collected from a peasantry which had to pay set fees for a variety of services. There were fees to be collected on births, deaths and marriages, divorce, harvesting and religious festivals, as well as fines for breaches of Islamic and civil law. The principal source of a sultan's wealth in earlier times was through the plunder of neighbouring tribes, while his prestige was measured by the number of his male slaves and concubines. In this fashion were local aristocracies built, creating an elaborate court life, with titles and privileges that have little meaning today. Some of the prestige remains. So does the old caste system and a reluctance to allow the daughters of sultans and *datus* to marry beneath their class. It is not a heritage easily convertible to the needs of a democracy. But it does give insight into political influences, nepotism and an acceptance of paternalism that retain almost universal currency in the modern Philippines, whether the environment is Christian or Muslim.

Here is the explanation of the habit of modern congressmen to make

2. *Daily Mirror*, 1 June 1957, Manila.

their public appearances surrounded by bodyguards and hangers-on, nowadays armed with revolvers and automatic weapons instead of brass-hilted swords. At election times, especially, their followers carry guns and are often known by the grimmer American term of goons. Whether or not these courtiers in modern dress succeed in gaining votes, they remain important symbols of prestige.

In recent years Islamic leaders have done a great deal to change the image of anarchy and violence. The troubled areas these days, especially at election time, are in Christian provinces — among the Ilocanos, in Pampanga and Nueva Ecija. The new mood was expressed a few years ago by a noted scholar in Sulu, Nooh H. Indin, who declared that 'the root cause of the unsettled peace and order situation in the Muslim region is the people's lack of knowledge about their own religion. A man who knows and practises his way of religion is at peace with God and His followers.'[3]

Islam may be the only faith at present able to bring about a more peaceable atmosphere. The work of its priests and missionaries is having a widespread effect that was inconceivable two decades ago, when the religion of Mohammed was little observed. There were then few mosques: few went to them to pray. The *imams* (priests) themselves knew little of the faith they preached. Nor were the educated much concerned, so long as they held on to what remained of their ancient power. The moral principles of Islam went unobserved, and it was a rare man who could recite verses from the Koran. The changed mood has been due to a postwar resurgence throughout the Islamic world, strongly influenced by a general advance of nationalism in the Arab bloc countries: in Indonesia and Pakistan especially. There is a constant stream of Muslims from Egypt, Arabia, Pakistan, Malaysia and Indonesia, while considerable numbers make the pilgrimage to Mecca, often at almost ruinous personal cost.

In one mosque near Zamboanga, I found an Egyptian teacher running a school for sixty children, as well as instructing parents in the faith. The mosque was a new one, elaborately tiled, with a high tower and imported paintings of Mecca. It had been built, at considerable cost for so small a community, by its one wealthy inhabitant. As elsewhere along the Sulu Sea, you heard hints of how certain leaders gained their wealth from smuggling. Almost every sizeable house of any size in the city of Zamboanga, it appeared, had similar origins.

Why not? The smuggler's art is numbered among the socially acceptable professions these days. There are precedents enough in Manila. Besides, the central government has left these southern communities little other way to raise themselves from almost universal poverty.

The really impressive fact is the modern drive for education, which has had small support from the north. The *madrasa*, the religious schools, built without government aid, have become prominent in many areas,

3. Najeeb M. Saleeby, *The History of Sulu*, Manila, 1908.

teaching the Koran, the Arabic language and principles of Islamic morality and law. The oustanding example has been in Marawi City, capital of the Maguindanaws, where a Muslim school has been raised to the status of a university, with government aid, providing secular as well as religious training at primary, high school and college levels. More and more students are going to Islamic universities overseas, assisted by several newly-formed associations and societies, chief among which is the Muslim Association of the Philippines. Its founder is an influential Muslim, Damacao Alonto, a former senator who has become the most successful planter and cattle-raiser in the province of Lanao del Sur. His wife, Princess Tarhata Kiram, is a daughter of the last Sultan of Sulu, and can trace her ancestry back through twenty-five sultans to the first Islamic missionaries to reach the southern Philippines.

Jolo, where the sultan had his palace (actually a small palm-thatched hut) was once the great centre of Muslim influence. It was a seaport centuries before Cebu, hub of extensive trade with other lands. The strategic position of this one large island in an archipelago of drowned mountain peaks, atolls, reefs and coral islets once brought great wealth to Jolo. The close resemblance of these two names is confusing. The island was originally called Sulug, or Sug, meaning sea current, but the early Spanish transcribed it as Xolo, after which the island became known as Sulu, and its capital Jolo.

In pre-hispanic times large vessels came from all points of the compass, when the Chinese dominated trade. The Sulus, who had been seafarers since antiquity, brought in silks, silver, amber, porcelain from China and Japan, gold dust, dyes, foodstuffs and wax from Luzon, cannon, gunpowder, brass, copper, iron from Malacca and Brunei, pepper and spices from the Celebes, Java and the Moluccas. Jolo was also by tradition the great market for pirates, while the slave trade brought wealth to the early sultans. Within a century of the Spaniards' arrival, these were almost the only commodities left, for legitimate trade with other nations was prohibited. In their early efforts to crush Tau-sug resistance, the Spanish occupied Jolo, built a fort there, surrounded the town with a high wall and laid out broad, clean streets lined with *arbol de fuego* (fire trees), acacias and sweet-smelling *ilang-ilang*. The Moro population was kept outside this wall, one of whose five iron gates — known as the Busbus Gate, opened directly into the clustered *nipa* huts of the old settlement.

The name Busbus had a grim meaning. In the local dialect it meant to chop up, as with firewood or coconuts. The gate led to the place where Tau-sug criminals were customarily tied to trees and chopped to death. It was this kind of ferocious outlook that later forced the Spaniards to retreat to a region of Mindanao they thought they could defend more easily. Zamboanga, on the south-eastern tip of a peninsula, seemed an ideal point to dominate the Sulu Sea. Yet they had to surrender that, too, when a Chinese pirate fleet besieging Manila forced them to withdraw the garrison. It is a story you can still read on the thick, moss-covered walls of Fort Pilar. This ancient fort is now used as an annexe for the Zamboanga High School. At the main entrance a bronze plaque recalls the gunsmoke and triumphs of its history:

> Founded as southern outpost of Spanish domain under the supervision of Melchor de Vera, 1645: attacked by the Dutch, 1646: deserted when troops concentrated in Manila to drive away Chinese pirates, 1663; reconstructed by the Society of Jesus, 1666: rebuilt under the management of Juan Sicarra, 1719: stormed by Dalasig, King of Butig, with 3,000 Moros, 1720: cannonaded by the British, 1798: witnessed the mutiny of seventy prisoners, 1872: abandoned by the Spaniards, 1898: occupied by the Americans under General J. C. Bates, 1899: seized by the Japanese, 1942: taken over by the Republic of the Philippines, 1946.

On the eastern wall, facing the rising sun, is the Shrine of Our Lady of Pilar. Hundreds of Zamboanguenos come here every Sunday, light candles to the Virgin (even the Muslims are shrewd enough to sell candles to Christians here) and pray in concrete pews before an altar that has been standing for more than two centuries. The painted backdrop of this altar depicts the Virgin Mary appearing to James the Apostle on the banks of the Ebro in Zaragosa, Spain. There she was said to have left her image on a pillar. The Spaniards, believing that Our Lady of Pilar would protect them against their new southern enemies, imported her spirit into Zamboanga. And protect them she did.

There is no exact record of when her image was miraculously translated into stone in Zamboanga. It was said to have happened during an early eighteenth century year of violence, when a religious procession carried another wooden image of the Virgin to the fortress. The main entrance was then where the shrine is now. Suddenly the alarm sounded. A Moro war fleet swept in to attack Zamboanga. Everyone fled to safety inside the fort. Even the image was abandoned. Then the entrance was mysteriously closed, sealed up with stones. When the attack passed, no one could find the image. Instead the populace was struck with awe at discovering a stone statue of the Virgin set in the wall above this gateway.

Another legend tells of how the Virgin materialized before a Spanish soldier guarding the entrance. He was a stolid fellow, and commanded her to halt. She reproved him gently, asked if he did not recognize her. Terrified, he asked Our Lady to forgive him, then ran to tell the officer on watch, who stubbornly insisted that he was lying. To test his truthfulness, the officer made him hold his hands over a candle flame. The story ends on a somewhat uncommitted note. 'The soldier, seeing that nothing happened, went to sleep and never woke.'

Further miracles were attributed to the shrine. The Spaniards desperately needed a miracle in 1720, when the small garrison was attacked by the King of Butig's hundred sailing ships, when 3,000 Muslims scaled the walls and fought with one company of defenders hand-to-hand. The enemy was routed. In 1798 a powerful British fleet was also driven from Zamboanga by the outnumbered Spanish. In 1872 a mass revolt by prisoners in the fort was crushed at the very moment of marching out to loot the city. Twenty-seven years later an outbreak of plague was mysteriously suppressed, while a series of earthquakes failed to damage life and buildings. These divine intercessions are still cherished in local lore. The place remains very Spanish in its attitudes.

Zamboanga is my favourite city in the Philippines. I know nowhere else that has its charm, its individual atmosphere, its sense of withdrawal from the exclusive materialization of the modern world. The crooked and narrow streets, cobblestones, wrought-iron window grilles, the great rain-trees and crowded fish market appear scarcely to have changed their character since Spanish colonial times. Life moves still at the pace of a *calesa*.

The mayor's office has diverted these flimsy, two-wheeled cabs from main thoroughfares like Governor Lim Avenue, Madrid Street or Calle Carmen, for the tiny, slender-legged Filipino horses that draw them seldom stir themselves to a trot. They were an extra hazard in crowded streets, I found, when driving Don Juan Alano's immense automobile through town. But speed limits are set at 15 kilometres an hour.

In the month or so we lived on Cawa Cawa Boulevard, where Don Juan's house faces the Sulu Sea, the prevailing sound through the upstairs shutters was the clip-clip of leisurely hooves. It was only a quarter-mile to town, but the sun's heat, only seven degrees above the equator, tempted us often to take a twenty centavo ride along that curving sea road to the market place or Plaza Pershing. The triangular, grassy plaza, with its colonnaded bandstand and turbaned Muslims dozing on stone benches, commemorates the first United States governor of Zamboanga. Soon afterwards General Pershing was transferred from campaigning against Muslim kris and sword to the leadership of American troops in France.

The locals speak a unique mixture of two Visayan languages and Castilian called *chavacano*. 'Bamboo Spanish,' the locals call it. And more melodious it is than any Malay dialect. As far as the girls go, Spanish is always a fascinating blend, but the Muslim strain has added something to their grace, femininity and upright carriage, too. And perhaps a touch of arrogance.

I was first drawn to Zamboanga by a lyrical description by a former United States judge, George Malcolm, who could hardly bring himself to leave it in the years before World War Two. He compared it with Java, Tahiti and Samoa. Such comparisons are no longer possible, because of the demoralization brought about by the Japanese occupation years, by the devastation of American forces recapturing it in 1945 and the overcrowding of recent times. Only the shattered floor of the old cathedral remains, few of the once handsome Spanish houses. What post-war Filipinos have put in their place is tawdry and commonplace. Yet, somehow, this leisurely little city of 120,000 people still has atmosphere. It also has a moral for the staid, unadventurous westerner. This is in its use of flowers.

Every house, every flimsy shanty or cottage, however poor and sub-standard (and the people are desperately poor) has a gay facade of flowers. This region of southern Mindanao is especially rich in plants and flowering trees: frangipani in many hues, white, yellow and red hibiscus, poinsettia, poinciana and the national flower of the Philippines, the white, sweet-scented sampanguita. But king of them all is the bougainvillaea.

Orchids and bougainvillaea: these are the natural decor for thousands of window boxes, doorways, garden fences, gates. The entire city seems alive with flowers.

Even the perilously stilted, crowded shacks of Muslim fishermen, built like the lake-dwellers of Europe's prehistory over tidal waters, repeat this theme of flowers. Back in suburban Australia I had the feeling of a return to desert; a wasteland of soulless cement and arid brick. Poverty is the overshadowing impression you take away from the Philippines, but I wonder if it is more corroding than the poverty of imagination displayed by the newer countries of the affluent West.

Driving out of Zamboanga to the shabby Muslim villages, the rice *padis* where women in broad bamboo hats labour under the afternoon sun, the great timber forests and dark mountains in which Filipino guerrillas bamboozled the Japanese, you see everywhere a profusion of flowers and blossoming trees. On the city's outskirts, at Pasonanca, is the only well-developed area of natural parklands I have seen in these islands. It was the conception of a former mayor, Cesar Climaco, who later went on to 'clean up' the nation's affairs as chairman of the Presidential Anti-Graft Committee in Manila.

What fascinated me above all were the fishing *vintas* on the aquamarine Sulu Sea. Hollowed by adzes out of tree trunks, buoyed by twin outriggers of bamboo, they skim over the water at fantastic speed beneath a single sail. At close view their rigging seems clumsy. Yet, more distantly, these sails, often forty or fifty upon the shimmering skyline, have the symmetry and glide of Moorish scimitars: like sharks' fins skimming upon a sea of glass. Many of these sails are coloured, striped, like irridescent fish lifted above the surface of a coral sea. The skill of these Samals is extraordinary. They sail for hundreds of miles by dead reckoning, find their way through the complex of Sulu islands, reefs, shoals and tide rips in effortless fashion, and frequently travel as far south as the Celebes or Borneo. It is said that, like the ancient Polynesians, they have acquired through centuries an intimate knowledge of the stars, fixing their positions by them without the aid of calendar or sextant. One planter on Tawi Tawi told me of the bewilderment among these seamen when the first Russian and American sputniks began to circle space. What were these mysterious, fast-moving stars? The planter found it quite impossible to convince these people that humans somewhere beyond their horizons were able to hurl live stars into the night sky.

Perhaps the most remarkable voyages made by these Samals were to the north coast of Australia when the Japanese invaded the Philippines.

During the hurried evacuation of southern islands, a number of American soldiers and Samals escaped from Zamboanga in slender *vintas* and somehow found their way across at least three thousand miles of sea. Since Indonesia was already occupied, these voyages must have been extremely hazardous, even though the vessels might easily have been mistaken for those of Indonesian fishermen.

The instincts of the Badjaos are even more remarkable. These people spend their entire lives at sea. Their shallow canoes are the only homes they know. These gypsies of the sea, skins blackened by eternal exposure to sun and wind, rarely spend any time on land, except to sell their fish. You can expect them to turn up anywhere: in Zamboanga, Basilan, the Sulus or even along the coast of Borneo. You come upon their outrigger canoes far out to sea, so low upon the water they are hard to see more than a mile or two away. Sometimes they use sail, more often they remain immobile on the ocean, difficult at times to distinguish from the small floating islands of waterlogged growth that drift from the mouths of tropical rivers. What happens when the monsoons begin blowing, or an unexpected storm blows up? Fabian Alano explained it one day on Basilan. 'They never get caught by a storm,' he said. 'They come in for shelter at least forty-eight hours beforehand. When you and I couldn't even see a sign of it. With a clear sky, no wind, and a smooth sea. How they can tell, I've no idea. I don't think even they could explain. But suddenly one day, you'll find their boats crowded into port or sheltering among the mangroves — and you know there's a big storm coming.'

The Badjao's only protection from sun or rain is the detachable roof of palm fronds he sets above the shallow craft. Beneath this the family sleeps, eats, cooks and dozes during the fierce heat of day. In the stern there is usually a small charcoal fire, which has to be kept at least smouldering in all weathers. Each small family is a lone unit eking out a lean existence, breeding and dying upon the blue wastes of sea. Children are born here, weaned and raised, and the dead return to the ocean. When a baby is born, the father takes it in his arms as soon as he cuts the umbilical cord and drops it in the sea. If it swims, it lives.

It was a tale I doubted until one day, in Zamboanga harbour, I watched a dozen of these canoes clustered around an island steamer. Women and young girls, wearing little more than rags, gestured and shouted for passengers to throw them food or coins. I saw one small boy, perhaps six months old, fall from his mother's arms into the water. At once he began to swim. One of his sisters climbed without concern across the outrigger and lifted him on board again. It was distressing to watch these people begging all day around a steamer. Subsistence living on the sea, it seemed, was even more degrading than on land. 'Drop a centavo piece into the water,' say Filipino tourist brochures, 'and watch these people dive for it.'

I preferred to give them money rather than reduce human beings to the level of performing seals.

CHAPTER 16

The Fishing Eagles

*As surely as spiders abound where
there are nooks and corners, so have pirates
sprung up wherever there is a nest of
islands. . . . The semi-barbarous inhabitant
of the Archipelago naturally becomes a
pirate. It is as natural to consider any
well-freighted, ill-protected boat his
property as it is for the fishing eagle
above his head to sweep down on the weaker,
but more hard-working bird and swallow
what he has not had the trouble of
catching . . .*

HENRY KEPPEL

IN PANGASAHAN I met a boy to whom pirates were not interesting. Amam
Raja was a rare lad for his age. Not for him the excitement and glamour
of meeting pirate ships in a tropic sea. For one thing he had never read
the storybooks. For another, this ten-year-old boy had seen pirates. He had
a three-inch scar above his forehead to prove it.

A month earlier he had crossed the Celebes Sea with his parents, who
had just made a trip to Jolo, presumably connected with smuggling. On
the returned journey to Basilan, his father Hadji Raja told me, they
noticed a long, lean-bowed *kumpit* on their beam. It was travelling very
fast. The vessel turned and cut across their bows, firing as it came.
Bullets began to strike the hull and decking, and everyone dived for
cover. The only one hit was his son. Amam was a lucky boy, for three
bullets from a high-powered rifle ricochetted off the engine housing and
merely grazed his skull. The doctor on Basilan had been obliged to
remove one spent bullet from his head. The boy wanted to see no more
pirates.

Hadji Raja's party might never have reached Pangasahan, but for a
second boat appearing nearby. The pirate craft vanished over the sunlit
sea. Other travellers have been less fortunate.

Just before I went to Basilan another boat was held up off Lamitan. A
group of masked men, disguised in P.C. uniforms, climbed aboard with
automatics and blade weapons. They ordered the passengers to jump into
the sea, took P750,000 from one man and, though their leader was recognized, were never seen again.

Further south, among the Sulu islands, such events are not infrequent.

Sometimes they are not even reported to police, who are seldom able to take effective action. It is not easy to trace or even identify vessels continually moving about the many islands, with their complex of bays, lagoons, channels and hidden mangrove reaches. Besides most of them look much alike, indistinguishable from those travelling on more legitimate affairs. There is only a fine distinction to be made between smuggling, piracy and normal trading. It has always been so in these remote seas.

Piracy goes far back into the history of the Malay Archipelago, long pre-dating the arrival of the first Europeans, even though theirs was the **major influence in** fostering it. 'It is in the Malay's nature to rove on the seas in his *prau*,' wrote Henry Keppel last century, 'as it is in that of the Arab to wander with his steed on the sands of the desert. It is as impossible to limit the adventurous life of the Malay to fishing and trading as to retain a Bedouin in a village or a habitation. . . . This is not merely their habit; it may be termed their instinct.'[1]

The Arabs, in fact, had a good deal to do with the beginnings of piracy here. It was they who brought Islam to the Malay regions, and the first Malay princelings moving into Sulu and Mindanao brought the militant faith with them, driving those who resisted into poorer, inland regions or recruiting them to fight in massive sea raids on their rivals. Raiding and trading were much the same, for it was the custom of these sultans and *datus* to buy or sell only when they had to. For the rest, they lived like the sea eagles, frigate birds and hawks that range these seas in equally predatory fashion.

'The Malays have no history beyond piracy,' wrote an English newspaper correspondent, Alex Josey, in Singapore recently. I was in Malaysia at the time and remember the excitement his statement caused. In Kuala Lumpur, Malayan members of parliament protested, demanding the journalist's expulsion. Tunku Abdul Rahman alone was amused. 'What about seventeenth century Britain?' he asked. 'Have you never heard of Drake, Hawkins and Cavendish?' The Tunku, who had read his history, knew that even in Malayan waters English privateers had not been exactly symbols of virtue. What he might also have said was that the early European colonizers were those really responsible for aggravating Malay piracy: the English along the coast of Malaya, the Portuguese and then the Dutch in the East Indies.

Their conquests had the immediate effect of destroying ancient trade routes. Chinese junks and traders were driven off, robbing the entire Malay Archipelago of the traditional sale and barter of spices, rattans, camphor, bird's nests and other rare products that had made local sultans wealthy. The result was to reduce their subjects to poverty, leaving no outlet for them except the forcible seizure of passing trade. Piracy became an essential if these island people were to survive. In the Philippines Spain played the same disruptive role. The galleons driving southward into the Sulu and Celebes Seas, the temporary seizure of the Moluccas

1. Henry Keppel, *A Visit to The Indian Archipelago*, London, 1895.

brought to an end the life-giving trade with Japan, China and Formosa. And the Muslim Malays had been the main carriers on all these routes. They had to learn to live by other means.

And that meant piracy. It came to be regarded as an honourable profession. A patriotic one. It was a god-given crusade against the 'white barbarians'.

The traditional port of Jolo became a private port. The nobles of the sultan's court set themselves up as official receivers of plunder and slaves. The Sulu Archipelago became another Caribbean. No longer was it possible for navigators to sail from Borneo or the Moluccas along the coast of Palawan to Luzon or China. There were squadrons of pirates patrolling these seas. The most powerful of these were the Ilanuns, a people related to the Badjaos. When William Dampier sailed through the Philippines to north-western Australia in 1686, he spent six months among the Ilanuns, and described them as a peaceful people. A century later they had become cut-throats and barbarians. 'Catching fish is hard,' said an Ilanun proverb, 'but it is easy to catch slaves on Brunei.'

Borneo became the principal target for their operations. The Ilanuns and the Balinini sailed down on the north-west monsoon, fleet after fleet of them, raiding villages, plundering and capturing slaves. Their vessels were double-decked *praus* up to ninety or a hundred feet long, and rowed by a hundred slaves. They returned when the trade wind changed. The north-west trade came to be known as the Pirate Wind.

During the eighteenth century the two powerful rulers of this area were the sultans of Sulu and Brunei. Then came James Brooke, the self-styled White Raja, who had once been employed by the British East India Company, before founding his own empire on Borneo. His own ambitions obliged him to undermine the prestige of the Sultan of Brunei, who was soon overshadowed by his rival on Jolo, subsequently trading on the Borneo coast — if you can give to raiding for plunder and slaves the name of trade. When Captain Blake, of H.M.S. *Larne*, called at Manila in 1820, he was told by the Spanish Governor-General that it was useless to complain of islanders breaching international peace treaties by harassing his vessel off Palawan, because not even the Sultan of Sulu had 'means, power nor influence over these Ilanuns; that they were a race purely piratical, of a distinct community of wild ranging, predatory habits, dependent on no one, and acknowledging no external authority.' They manufactured their own bronze cannon, and imported their ammunition from Borneo. Thirty years later a scheme for setting up British plantations on the coast of Borneo had to be abandoned, so ruthless and destructive had the Ilanun pirates become. Further north it was the ferocious Maguindanaus who terrorized the Philippines. From the sixteenth century they had been known to travel in fleets of up to a hundred vessels, which were so fast, so well-manned, and seaworthy that not even the larger Spanish ships could cope with them.

'The *caracao* used by the Maguindanaus on their raiding expeditions was called a *mangaio prau,*' wrote the Spanish historian, H. de la Costa, s.j. 'It averaged about three or four tons burden and carried a round or pointed sail on a tripod mast of bamboo. Beside speed, it had the advantage of extreme manoeuvrability, for being prowed at stem and stern, it could reverse direction without having to put about. . . . The *caracaos* of the more opulent *datus* mounted small bronze swivel guns called *lantakas.'²* From these developed the modern, equally speedy *vintas* that now grace Sulu seas with their scimitar-shaped sails. It took many armadas to pin back these dangerous sea rovers to the southern waters, where they defied almost every Spanish attempt to subdue them.

Though the fortress at Zamboanga did much to check Moro war fleets sailing up the west coast of Mindanao for the Visayas, Spanish commanders found themselves unable to quell pirates raiding the island's southern coastline.

In 1848 another fort was built on Basilan. From there, in the sheltered waterways around Isabela, naval vessels patrolled the Celebes Sea, though the area of protection they afforded was negligible. In 1849 Isabela was attacked by three thousand Moros, who were driven off only when troops arrived from Zamboanga to reinforce the desperate garrison. Two other major battles had to be fought in the next fifteen years before Isabela could feel in any way secure. When a fleet of French vessels arrived from Indo-China in 1844, with plans to claim Basilan for France, it was not Spanish resistance they had to contend with, but Malays. The amazing fertility of Basilan impressed the French, its forests and timbers and fruits, but piratical *caracaos* flying upon them from Maluso, further along the coast, killed their ambitions as well as members of their crew. Three French seamen were also carried away as slaves.

The first man to impose any kind of order on this island was an escaped prisoner from the San Ramon penitentiary, near Zamboanga. Pedro Cuevas had a fantastic career. A Christian, the son of well-to-do parents in Bacoor, Cavite, he lived a gay life in Manila until he killed a Spanish soldier in a duel, which led to his imprisonment. Another story claims that he was victimized for political activity. He made his escape by *vinta* in 1878, landed on the wild coast of Basilan and attached himself to a local chieftain, Panglima Atao. Though Muslims were reluctant to accept an infidel, he proved himself in a number of fierce sword fights, then fought with them to subdue their enemies, impressing Maharaja Itoy of Lamitan with his brilliant tactics in war, and married the chief's daughter. He then took more wives, until he had one in almost every barrio. If there is one thing Muslims admire more than a great fighter it is a great lover. Cuevas also found his women valuable as intelligence agents. It never occurred to Muslims resentful of his growing influence that veiled women within their own households could betray their secrets. Pedro Cuevas, or Panglima Kalung as he had then become, had a flair for pillow talk. Though his main achievement was in quelling inland

2. H. de la Costa, *A Spanish Jesuit Among The Maguinandaus,* MS., Manila, 1959.

bandits, he did a great deal to suppress piracy simply by his feud with
the Sultan of Sulu, who saw his own influence being undermined. The
former Christian defeated an invasion attempt by the Sultan, drove back
his raiding fleet and was finally rewarded by the Spanish government,
which retracted the price offered for his head, making him instead their
representative on Basilan. When an Arab *agent provocateur* was sent in
to stir rebellion and have him assassinated, Cuevas was duly warned by
one of his amours. She had heard the attempt planned in the house of a
datu and warned him that three men were to ambush him in the shadow
of a certain rock. He saddled up and rode to the rock, called on the men
by name to come out.

'Kill me if you dare,' he cried. 'I'm not afraid of you. Allah is my
protector. He has told me who you are.'

The men came out, threw their daggers on the ground and kissed his
feet. From then on he was regarded as possessing supernatural powers.

This did not prevent him dying at the age of fifty-eight. Today a statue
of him looks down with cold pride from the centre of Lamitan. The
figure wears Muslim costume, has a kris in one hand, a *barong* in the
other. He passed on his title to a nephew who tried to emulate his spectacular life, especially in the conquest of women. He succeeded all to
well, and died young.

By this time the Americans had taken over the Philippines, though it
was many years before they pacified Mindanao and points south. They
had first to capture the famous pirate, Jikiri, whose armed *vintas* sailed
out of Jolo to create havoc and fight a land and sea war against United
States forces. Several years of massacres and atrocities preceded his execution. Again, in 1919, a pirate leader on Basilan forced government troops
into a long bloody campaign, for the oratory of the Iman Hadji of
Kamangalan kept most of the population fighting on his side. His eventual defeat brought to an end the fanatical *juramentados* of his time, and
piracy dwindled to minor forays in the treacherous sea lanes of the Sulu
islands. But efforts to exterminate it grew less and less as Filipinos took
control of the administration during the 1930s.

The Pirate Wind remained a dangerous reality even after World War
Two.

These independent, free-roving, predatory seamen in their nest of
islands cared little for any post-war revisions of international boundaries.
Indonesia had its revolution: the Dutch retired. The Philippine Republic
inherited United States territories. Sandakan and Sabah became British
protectorates and then members of the Malaysian Federation. For the
Sulu people these legalistic changes were of no account. Perhaps they did
not even know of them. They went on sailing between their own homes
and Borneo or the Indonesian islands as they had always done, trading,
bartering and fraternizing with their neighbours, who were so closely
related to them by tribal or family ties they regarded them as brothers.
What did they care if different coloured flags flew above their traditional

trading grounds. International customs agreements meant nothing to them, nor tariffs and regulations about import duties. It was impossible to explain that what they had always regarded as normal trading was now termed smuggling.

The only law they lived by was the law of supply and demand. When cigarettes were short in the northern Philippines, they sailed down to Sabah or Sarawak and bought supplies; especially those popular, if prohibited American brands imported by Chinese merchants there from Hong Kong. If people wanted transistor radios, or perfumes or *batik*, the *kumpit* men were happy to take them north, too. It was not their affair if customs officers in Manila inexplicably refused their entry. They had to find ways of avoiding the customs men, which was easy enough to do along thousands of miles of seaways and deserted beaches. Before long they were finding profitable outlets through Borneo for their own products as well: copra, sugarcane, nutmegs, the fine Sulu pearls, all of which they used for barter. Chinese merchants in Sandakan or Labuan were only too happy to trade.

'We don't call it smuggling here,' one Labuan businessman told a reporter of the *Borneo Bulletin* in 1964. 'This is a free port. Anyone can bring anything in and take anything out. As far as we're concerned, this trade is absolutely legal. If the Philippines don't like it, they should stop it at the source. But it will continue as long as Filipino naval officers can be bribed, as we hope they will be for ever.'

Borneo traders had reason for these hopes. They had seen an occasional Philippine gunboat off the coast. With the best will in the world, these slow, obsolescent vessels could not match high-powered *kumpits* for speed. Besides, naval headquarters in Manila insisted on them reporting their position by radio at regular times. Needless to say, the *kumpits* had radios, too.

So did the Sulu Sea pirates.

The risks involved in this inter-island trading were discussed in the same issue of the *Borneo Bulletin*, when a reporter interviewed one English-speaking crew member of a *kumpit* from Jolo.

'Officially,' he said, 'we are not allowed to trade with Sabah. But the Jolos are a long way from Manila and everyone has to live. We give a few hundred pesos to the customs official in our home port. Usually he orders his men to carry the copra or sugar to our boat. On the way to Labuan we have to be on constant look-out for pirates and naval patrol boats. If the navy stops us, we pay another peso or so to the captain in "tax". After that, it's usually plain sailing.

'The people we dread most are pirates. The Philippines Government lends us carbines to protect ourselves. All we have to buy is the ammunition. If we meet a big pirate gang we would either run or give ourselves up. There would be no point in resisting. They would kill us all. We would fight only if we were attacked by a small band.'

The crewman was asked why Sulu vessels made such long, sometimes

The Black Nazarene, Quiapo

Children unlimited,
Mindanao

Muslim princess,
Mindanao

Philippine Travel and Tourist Association

rough voyages down to Borneo, when Philippine ports like Zamboanga were so much easier to reach.

'The export duty is so heavy,' he replied. 'The dock workers are so lazy and officials so corrupt we would hardly show a profit. We may make more from one trip to Labuan than six months of legitimate trading at home. But it is now becoming harder to leave Jolo with the necessary papers. At sea there seem to be more unfriendly patrol boats. There are one or two captains who refuse to take presents. They confiscate cargoes and arrest the crews.'

Soekarno's *konfrontasi* had also added to the hazards of trade, he said, for British, Australian and Malaysian naval ships had taken to patrolling North Borneo waters, and their commanders did not appear to understand the meaning of tong. Yet godowns in Labuan are still crammed with negotiable goods, especially contraband cigarettes manufactured in the United States and Hong Kong. The annual reports of the Sabah government make enlightening reading. According to official returns, Sabah contains, per head of population, the greatest smokers in the world. Imports of cigarettes are valued at some HK$3,000,000 annually. No export figures are shown, because officially the massive sales to owners of visiting *kumpits* are merely internal transactions.

The impetus to post-war smuggling came from government efforts to stabilize the internal economy. In 1949, when dollars were in short supply, stringent import controls were imposed on a large range of American-made products, including cigarettes. Smuggling at once became big business. When President Macapagal was elected in 1962, he set about abolishing these controls, largely because currency smuggling had become so commonplace in the government's own Central Bank. In their place he raised a tariff wall covering 700 classified items, which put them beyond the reach of most buyers. In the case of cigarettes, this was designed to protect local manufacturers, whose product dropped in quality because they were unable to import American leaf for blending. Filipinos, for whom the term 'imported' has great status value, preferred to smoke what they called 'blue seals'. (American-made packets are sealed with a blue sticker denoting excise duty paid, while those produced in the Philippines have a brown seal.) The demand became so large that Chinese in Hong Kong set up three new factories, exporting to the Philippines by way of North Borneo.

The absurdity of the situation was brought home to me while travelling on an American freighter to Hong Kong. While other cargo was unloaded in Manila, crates of cigarette cartons labelled 'Made in U.S.A.' were carried on to the British possession. They were then transhipped to Singapore and Labuan, there to be picked up by *kumpits* and smuggled past ineffective naval and police patrols back to Manila.

In a candid survey of the smuggling problem late in 1965, the managing editor of the *Philippines Herald*, M. N. Querol, summed up the effects of the presidential policy in these terms: 'Smugglers had entrenched themselves in the government — from Customs to the lower levels of the judiciary. Recently forty-one officers and men of the Constabulary and the Navy were disciplined for trafficking with smugglers. Some cases could not prosper because fiscals and judges were in the payroll of smuggling teams. Finally Mr Macapagal saw smuggling as an economic problem. He sent two bills to Congress, one reducing specific customs duties on manufacture tobacco, the other reducing taxes on cigarettes. For some reason the Liberal-dominated House of Representatives did not consider these bills.'[3]

It would have been naive to ask why.

The Manila press has spent thousands of words explaining in detail why 'blue seals' continue to flood the market, what classes of people are involved and the economic damage caused. Even the statistics of this illegal industry have been published. Congress alone has ignored the situation. In 1960, according to one survey, some 30,000 cases of cigarettes were smuggled in to the country each month. By 1963 this figure had increased to 60,000 cases monthly and two years later, to 250,000. This represented 125,000,000 packets of cigarettes, with a retail value of P600,000,000. On an average less than one per cent of these cigarettes were confiscated by the authorities.

The same newspaper then outlined what could be done, given the active support of law-enforcing agencies. It pointed out that between January and March 1964 smugglers delivered 1,500,000 cartons a month. Macapagal was forced to act. He formed a Cabinet Anti-Smuggling Committee, called service chiefs to the Palace for a conference that had all the overtones of wartime mobilization, instructed the armed forces and police to take sterner measures, the courts to impose more stringent fines and also appealed to the public not to buy smuggled goods. During the next three months 'blue seals' imported dropped to a mere 400,000 cartons a month. Then the drive lost energy. From July to December the rate of entry was averaging 1,200,000 cartons monthly. The report concluded, 'Many politicians are said to be in connivance with smugglers. Some politicians are likewise reported to be engaged in smuggling, either for purely personal motives or to raise money for election purposes. . . . A spot check on Congress on March 8 reportedly revealed that while none of the senators was found smoking "blue seal" cigarettes, the same could definitely not be said of many of our congressmen. . . . Governor Castillo of the Central Bank, on the basis of statistics on "outward invisible movements", whose purposes could not be traced, estimated that smuggling led to an outflow of $35,000,000 (P1,360,000,000) .'[4]

Four-fifths of this vanishing revenue was attributed to 'blue seals'.

Meantime the press continued to publish sensational accounts from the underworld, of smuggling. On New Year's Eve 1964, one arrested smuggler in Albay province said he had regularly paid a feet of P1,000,

3. *Philippines Herald*, 27 October 1965, Manila.
4. *Philippines Free Press*, 31 March 1965, Manila.

plus two hundred cartons of 'blue seals', to an officer of the Philippine Constabulary for every successful shipment from Sandakan. The officer was also alleged to have himself supervised the transport of contraband to his own ranch. The following March, Cesar Climaco, then chairman of the Presidential Anti-Graft Committee, said his investigators had been informed that a foreign ship was to unload 'blue seals' off Quezon Province, but that members of the Constabularly had prevented them from taking action. The same month a customs patrol boat was arrested in Manila Bay for attempted smuggling. A few days later another customs patrol tried to board a Philippine Navy cutter suspected of running contraband, but was driven off by 'a show of guns'. In April reports from Zamboanga spoke of constabulary officers driving cars and jeeps owned by smugglers, while from Batangas came an account of men in army uniforms preventing police from interfering with the unloading of an estimated P75,000 worth of 'blue seals'. These were then taken by five trucks, escorted by armed jeeps to an unknown destination. In May a press correspondent in Samar reported that a certain barrio on poverty-shadowed Samar consisted largely of modern concrete houses, equipped with electric stoves, refrigerators and radios, all owned by 'a smuggling syndicate that has apparently flourished on government tolerance'. A month later it was reported that attempts to prosecute a 'fisherman-millionaire' in Cavite had been dropped because of alleged connections with a relative of the President. The millionaire smuggler was also said to have employed two members of the Constabulary as escort drivers for his convoy of contraband and to have paid 'hush money' to three officers.

In August the manager of the government-owned Namarco (National Marketing Corporation) proposed a solution to the smuggling problem. If 'blue seals' were imported free of duty, he told the President, his corporation would distribute them and thus make a profit for the administration, end the drain on foreign currency, aid local tobacco manufacturers by putting the smugglers out of business and reduce import duties on blending tobaccos.

'The fatuous presumption is that the smugglers don't incur expenses in bringing in the goods,' he said. 'Everybody knows that the smugglers have to pay their way through. They have to pay a lot of people — the policemen, the political *padrinos*, the mayors, the governors, the constabulary, their own goons.'

Warning that influential smugglers were planning to set up their own cigarette factories in Jesselton, he said that they would then be unable to deal with an already efficient ring that had expanded to smuggling narcotics, textiles and electronic goods as well. Shortly before his election defeat in November 1965, President Macapagal made one slight concession by reducing the tariff on United States cigarettes by 50 per cent. The smugglers are still in business.

This was the first action since his widely-publicized investiture at the Manila naval base a year earlier. In December 1964 the President decorated twenty-eight officers and ratings of the gunboat *Misamis Occidental* for distinguished conduct on active service. Their Military Merit medals signified the first naval victory of the 1964 anti-smuggling campaign. 'In a four day period,' read the presidential citation, 'your gunboat has seized 2,000 cases of blue seal cigarettes worth one million pesos from *kumpits* off the shores of Palawan.'

The redoubtable gunboat had avenged an earlier engagement during which two naval ratings were wounded in action. The smuggling *kumpit* had escaped unharmed.

In the eighteenth century British and American navies were accustomed to quelling Caribbean pirates with a whiff of grapeshot. In the twentieth century Philippines a whiff of cigarette smoke has stronger repercussions.

Yet Senator Raul Manglapus, during his 1965 presidential campaign, declared that the whole question of smuggling could be resolved without difficulty. 'Smuggling in this country is controlled by only five big men,' he told an election rally in Mindanao. 'They are known to the authorities. The President could stop the nefarious activities of these five men if he wanted to.'

The climate of smuggling closely parallels the prohibition era that demoralized the United States during the 1920s. Without the massive increase in contraband cigarettes, smuggling in southern waters would be of little more than nuisance value. However, its virtual immunity from police interference has fostered more dangerous types of smuggling as well, notably drugs. In 1964 enquiries by one security agency revealed the existence of a well-established traffic in narcotics. 'Because of its key position off the Asian mainland,' the report stated, 'the Philippines has become a vital centre for the world distribution of opium, heroin and morphine shipped from Hong Kong, Macau, Bangkok and Singapore. Manila remains the seat of direction, while Sulu, Palawan and Cavite are the smuggling centres. From Borneo fast *kumpits* carry the contraband from Borneo to Balabac, Palawan, where innocent-looking fishing boats take over and relay the drugs to Manila or Cebu.' Narcotics were also said to be brought in by merchant ship and commercial aircraft. The couriers were mainly crew members, though the report referred to certain 'professional travellers' as well.

These travellers are well known to customs men — 'commuters' is the local phrase — and pass almost weekly through Manila airport. On rare occasions someone is charged with smuggling silver pesos, imported jewellery or textiles, but generally these people are too 'well-known' to customs men to be questioned at all. As the security report stressed, a few small-time peddlers of drugs have been arrested, but none of the 'rich and influential Chinese or Filipinos' who control the traffic.

'The illicit traffic in narcotics spawns not only criminals, but also prostitutes,' stated one press comment on this report. 'It is claimed that many of the call girls in Manila and suburbs were forced into their trade by their addiction to narcotics. Peddlers and their henchmen are to be found outside places like *sari-sari* stores, canteens, poolrooms and other places of recreation, where they are likely to find students and other young people. An undetermined number of these addicts are pupils in the elementary grades or students in high schools and colleges. The most pitiful, and also the most dangerous of these addicts, are those who do not have the means to satisfy their periodic craving. If they cannot raise the money, they are forced to steal, and they may even kill, if need be. Research shows that adults who become drug addicts are either psycho-pathic or suffering from some neurosis.'

Here, indeed, may be a major contributing factor to the ever-increasing crime wave of recent years. It has certainly given new life to the ancient trade of piracy.

If, in these parts, the smuggler is only an illegal trader, the pirate is only an illegal smuggler, or counter-smuggler. What the Americans of prohibition days called a hi-jacker. My ideas of making a journey by *kumpit* to Jolo and Sabah was not encouraged by friends in Zamboanga. 'You'll never get me on one of those boats,' said 'Dynamite' Ivanoff, a former resistance fighter. 'Not unless I told three separate people where I was going and by what boat. Next I'd tell the crew what I'd done. I'd say "This man knows where I am — that one knows — and that one. So! If you still want to kill me, they'll know who did it!" '

Ivanoff, with his one eye, intimidating Russian accent and fame as a guerrilla, was not a man to be scared easily. The local police captain told me Ivanoff had put so much dynamite under wartime bridges they were still dangerous today. But no *kumpits* for him! He spoke of the still unsolved mystery attached to the American, Menhart Spielman, who vanished in the Sulu Sea in April 1962. Spielman had been a key witness in the Stonehill scandals of that year, when the financier was deported for the alleged corruption of officials and congressmen in Manila. In a desperate bid to escape men attempting to kill him, Spielman had char-tered a plane for Zamboanga, then boarded a *kumpit* hoping to reach North Borneo. He was never seen again.

Sometimes complete vessels have vanished in similar fashion, their fate recorded by the simple phrase: 'lost at sea'. I recall the discovery of a crewless ketch, ironically named *Mecca*, which was sighted off the coast of Ilocos Sur in 1964. A constabulary report said that it was owned by a Captain Harry Willys, whose personal effects were still on board, though the vessel had been looted. The vessel carried New Zealand registration. It was an event that could well have thrown light on the disappearance of an Australian ketch, the *Ian Crouch*, which left Hong Kong for Adelaide in August 1958. No trace of her, nor of the eight Australian crew members was ever found. Her course would have taken her along the coast of Palawan and through the Sulu Sea. The official inquiry in Hong Kong, nearly three months after her disappearance, made an open verdict. Only two possible explanations were offered: some unreported storm in the China Sea, or piracy.

There seems little likelihood at present of ending this lawless atmosphere. In the Sulu Archipelago the smugglers' trade is at least a means of staying alive.

'*Hulas sangsah*,' wrote a Muslim correspondent in the *Philippines Free Press*. 'These are words that mean "blood and sweat" to the Tau-sug. He believes that what he earns through sweat and tears is honestly earned. He argues that smuggling is legal since he invested money, endured sleepless nights, battled waves and wind, and suffered the scorching heat of the noonday sun.'[5] The trade between Sulu and Borneo is a necessity for the Tau-sug, Sani Abing concluded, suggesting that the only solution was to relax the kind of restrictive legislation that turns traders into smugglers. If Jolo could be made a free port, he wrote, as are Sandakan and Labuan, the rest of the Philippines could cease interfering with a traditional exchange of produce that is really none of its affair. To repress it is only to give it a more devious and violent character.

5. *Philippines Free Press*, 7 November 1964, Manila.

CHAPTER 17

Discord in Maphilindo

*The struggle to stabilize the
frontiers of power along the periphery
of Communist China will be inconclusive as
long as the Maphilindo area of south-east
Asia remains in turmoil. If this vital
area becomes the cockpit of contending
powers, the struggle will almost surely
extend beyond it and engulf a much wider
area.*

NARCISO G. REYES

FEW PEOPLE had ever heard of Sabah until the Malaysian Federation was proposed in 1963. Hitherto it had been known as British North Borneo. This 30,000 square mile region of jungle, mountain and sluggish, equatorial rivers at the north-eastern tip of the world's second largest island had been noted for little more than its picturesque postage stamps, the uneasy mixture of Malays, Chinese and Dyaks, and the fact that it had been largely the private preserve of the British North Borneo Company for eighty years. It is slightly smaller than its neighbour, Sarawak, ten times the size of the oil-rich and still independent Brunei, but exists somewhat precariously along its common frontier with Indonesian Borneo, which Soekarno renamed Kalimantuan.

Then, quite suddenly, the backward, infertile Sabah became a bitterly contested international issue. Everybody seemed to want it.

All three north Borneo regions, controlled by British colonial administrations since World War Two, were given self-government in 1963. Proposals were then made that they should join with Malaya and Singapore in a single federated state. Indonesia objected. So did the Philippines. Soekarno's opposition was understandable, considering his dream of a Pan-Indonesian empire. Without accepting his unique theories of *Necolim*, one can recognize Britain's motives for encouraging a federation that would protect British investments in a region vulnerable to the spread of Asian communism. The attitude taken by the Philippines was more esoteric. It rested upon certain claims that Sabah was historically Filipino territory, claims that had first been raised in 1947 after Britain took over its administration from the British North Borneo Company.

In June 1963 the subject became a major item on the agenda of a conference between Philippine, Indonesian and Malayan foreign ministers in Manila. This was followed two months later by a meeting between the three heads of state. From this August meeting, known as the Manila Accord, came the Macapagal Plan, which proposed a close-knit confederation of the three predominately Malay countries 'working together in closest harmony, but without surrendering any portion of their sovereignty'. A statement of their common aims was issued on 5 August, and signed by President Soekarno, President Diosdado Macapagal and Tunku Abdul Rahman Putra Al-Haj. Among the most significant sections was Paragraph 12, which read: 'The Philippines made it clear that its position on the inclusion of North Borneo in the Federation of Malaysia is subject to the final outcome of the Philippine claim to North Borneo.'

It was a crucial reservation. After all, Tunku Abdul Rahman, as prime minister of Malaya, had endorsed a clause that was to prove embarrassing two months later when he became chief executive of the new Malaysian Federation, with Sabah as an important member. It was rumoured that the British protested strongly.

Yet the wording of the official Manila Declaration, made on the same day, made innocuous reading. Designed as a new charter for the Malay peoples, it spoke in grand generalities of 'the historic significance of their coming together for the first time', their 'emergence after long struggles from colonial status to independence', and the 'inspiration of the spirit of Asian-African solidarity' (phrases in which the handwriting of Soekarno was plain) , and thereupon declared that the three leaders were agreed as follows:

> First, that they reaffirm their adherence to the principle of equal rights and self-determination of peoples as enunciated in the United Nations Charter and the Bandung Declaration;
> Second, that they are determined, in the common interest of their countries, to maintain fraternal relations, to strengthen co-operation among their peoples in the economic, social and cultural fields in order to promote economic progress and social well-being in the region, and to put an end to the exploitation of man by man and of one nation by another;
> Third, that the three nations shall combine their efforts in the common struggle against colonialism and imperialism in all their forms and manifestations and for the eradication of the vestiges thereof in the region in particular and the world in general;
> Fourth, that the three nations, as new emerging forces in the region, shall co-operate in building a new and better world based on national freedom, social justice and lasting peace; and
> Fifth, that in the context of the joint endeavours of the three nations to achieve the foregoing objectives, they have agreed to take initial steps towards the establishment of Maphilindo by holding frequent and regular consultations at all levels to be known as Mushawarah Maphilindo.[1]

Maphilindo — shorthand for Malaya, the Philippines, Indonesia — made no reference to alliances already entered into by the first two countries, most of them being discreetly banished under those casual

1. *Manila Declaration*, issued by the Republic of the Philippines, 5 August 1963, Manila.

references to colonialism and imperialism. Nor was any reference made to the earlier A.S.A. alliance (Association for South-east Asia) between Malaya, Thailand and the Philippines. Soekarno, the gifted persuader, appeared to have enchanted his fellow Malays with the 'spirit of Mushawarah', meaning brotherly love.

Yet, behind that summit conference was another shadowy figure of which no one seemed aware. Shortly before Soekarno sent Dr Subandrio to that June conference of foreign ministers, the defence minister of the Chinese People's Republic, Marshal Chen-Yi, made a second visit to Djakarta. This perhaps helps to explain certain clauses proposed by the Indonesian president. In a third document issued on 5 August, Clause 11 stated that: 'The three Heads of Government further agreed that foreign bases — temporary in nature — should not be allowed to be used directly or indirectly to subvert the national independence of any of the three countries. In accordance with the principle enunciated in the Bandung Declaration, the three countries will abstain from the use of arrangements of collective defence to serve the particular interests of any of the big powers.'[2]

It would be stressing the obvious to note that the largest bases of the big powers were in Singapore, Manila Bay and Clark Air Field, Luzon.

President Macapagal's endorsement of those aims was puzzling. Hitherto he had been known as 'the American boy'. The head of a Roman Catholic state, in which communism was outlawed, he had frequently expressed his fear of Chinese subversion. Perhaps he was not a chess player. Perhaps he had been too eagerly the guest of Soekarno at the Bogor Palace, where the two had been much photographed in embraces of brotherly Mushawarah. His critics suspected that he had been given, in the Australian phrase, the 'duchess treatment'.

At all events, he supported Indonesia's criticism of the plebiscites conducted in Sabah and Sarawak, when their peoples had voted in favour of entering the Malaysian federation. Charges were made that these had been hurried and undemocratic, despite the supervision of a United Nations mission. When Soekarno's confrontation followed the setting up of Malaysia, Macapagal voiced no criticism of it, but refused to recognize the new State. Early next year he offered himself as an 'honest broker' to mediate between the two parties. After one abortive meeting in Tokyo, this unlikely brokerage was dropped. However, declared his foreign minister, Mauro Mendez, 'I still believe we can be a restraining influence on Indonesia. Soekarno holds President Macapagal in high regard. We hope to be able to win over Indonesia to the side of the free world.'

Sabah had the air of a master's opening in the chess game of south-east Asia. Yet Filipinos gave the Philippine Government's claim only lukewarm support, except certain influential Muslims in the south. Even if the Philippines had won its claim, it seems unrealistic to suppose it could either have occupied or defended so remote a territory. Soekarno's

2. *Manila Accord*, issued by the Republic of the Philippines, 5 August 1963, Manila.

forces were already on its frontier, which in turn was defended by British and Australian troops which would hardly have fought for Philippine interests.

It may be thought that subsequent events have made both this claim and Maphilindo dead issues. When President Macapagal lost office in November 1965 his successor, Ferdinand Marcos, proceeded to 'normalize' relations with Malaysia, while the Tunku denounced the Manila Accord for its racial bias. The disappearance of the P.K.I. as a force in Indonesian policies, following its unsuccessful coup, likewise ended any immediate threat of infiltration into the Mindanao-Sulu area. *Konfrontasi* has been abandoned. Yet there is still a possibility that Sabah, like Singapore, may one day leave the Malaysian federation, for which support is by no means unanimous. It is as well therefore to recall the discord created by Indonesia in recent years.

Soekarno set up a 'government-in-exile' for what he called Kalimantan Utara (North Borneo), with Sheikh A. M. Azahari as its so-called prime minister. Azahari, who had organized an unsuccessful revolt in Brunei in December 1962, announced early in 1965 that the new State of his dreams would absorb Brunei, Sarawak and Sabah. This would have given Indonesia possession of the entire island of Borneo. Filipinos, well aware of Soekarno's celebrated map of a Pan-Indonesia empire, would hardly welcome the extension of a socialist regime to the boundaries of their own unprotected southern islands, especially in the context of an overriding Islamic faith. Besides, the ancient links between north Borneo and the sultanate of Sulu would not easily disappear, even if these had now degenerated into smuggling. President Macapagal no doubt felt it necessary to placate the Muslims by some show of action, since his administration had done nothing to alleviate their poverty and sense of alienation. Also involved, according to the former secretary of foreign affairs, the late Salvador P. Lopez, were matters considered vital to Philippines defence. 'Sabah,' he told a large audience at the University of the Philippines, 'belongs to our national patrimony. It is essential to our national security.'[3]

It could indeed become a new 'cockpit for contending powers', as the Philippines Ambassador to Djakarta, Narciso G. Reyes, wrote a year later, unless political boundaries were once and for all defined. During the height of the 1964 dispute with Malaysia over Sabah, many bitter things were said by leaders in the region. Princess Tarhata Kiram, the late sultan's daughter, announced from Jolo that 'a war council was being convoked to assert sovereign prerogatives in Borneo through valour as in ancient times'. Though no more was heard of this, Governor Benjamin Abubakar excited the Tau-sugs by saying that 'if Malaysia would prevent us from travelling to and from Borneo, the results would be fatal'. He was having difficulty, he said, in attempting to stop his people from

3. 'The Crisis over Malaysia and the Future of Maphilindo', Address and Convocation of the Philippines, 4 October 1963, Manila.

taking matters into their own hands, and added that the Sabah population was mainly Muslim, with few Christians. Sabah's acting chief
minister, Harrie Bin-Mohammed Salleh, declared 'blood will flow in
north Borneo if the Philippines wins its claim', while another of the Sulu
sultan's heirs replied that more blood would flow if the claim failed.
The Sabah minister thereupon replied that the Philippines would have
to suppress his people by military invasion, which would require from
200,000 to 300,000 troops.

This was followed by a statement from Antara, the official Indonesian
news agency, that British officials in Tawao, Kalimantan Utara, had been
intriguing to set the Philippines against Indonesia. 'Filipinos and Indonesians living in Tawao,' the report went on, 'were recruited by the
British, armed and helped into business as smugglers. The Filipinos were
then sent into Indonesian waters, and the Indonesians to Philippine
areas. There they worked on the Malaysians to ignore the Philippine
claim to Sabah.'

The situation was acquiring the classical overtones of international
intrigue.

But who, after all, really owns Sabah? What basis is there for the
Filipino claim? Did Britain have the right to hand over a former protectorate to the Federation?

The facts have become so clouded with rhetoric that, if the case ever
reached the International Court of Justice, the judges would have great
difficulty unravelling the issues. They would have to examine obscure
documents hidden away in the archives of five nations: Britain, the United
States, Spain, the Philippines and Malaysia. They would also need Arabic
scholars as well as Spanish and Anglo-Saxon historians to resolve the
precedents involved. The antecedents for the dispute go back to the start
of the eighteenth century. It is a colourful story, but one that also reflects
the dubious origins of colonial power and its often slender legalities.

Until 1704 the whole of Borneo, with its neighbouring islands, was
ruled by the all-powerful kingdom of Brunei. In that year Sultan Abdul
Bubin, fighting his rival Sultan Muhaidin for sole possession, appealed
to the Sultan of Sulu for aid. The arrival of his Tau-sug fleet proved
decisive and Muhaidin made the Sulu sultan a gift of land approximating
the present area of Sabah. For one a half centuries these two sultans
remained the supreme rulers of their neighbouring kingdoms. Then, in
1851, the Spanish achieved their first victories over the Muslim south,
forcing the Sultan of Sulu to accept the domination of the Spanish
empire. Even so it remained a tenuous hold until 1878.

Britain's interest in north Borneo began in 1759, when an official of
the British East Asia Company, based on Madras, chose the Sulu Archipelago as a promising area for trade. Two years later the sultan gave
permission for a factory to be built, and in 1763 ceded all his Borneo
possessions, as well as part of Palawan. Wearied by the hostility and
corruption of the Sulus, the company abandoned the concession in 1805.

Fifty years later came Captain James Brooke, formerly of the East India Company, to persuade the Sultan of Brunei to cede what was later to become the British protectorate of Sarawak. The celebrated White Raja of Sarawak founded a dynasty that prospered there until family rule was replaced by a colonial administration after World War Two.

The next foreign intruder was a roving adventurer who had served on the lower decks of the United States Navy. Claude Lee Moses arrived in Labuan in 1865, having borrowed money for his fare from Singapore, proclaimed himself American consul and, within a few days, had coaxed the Sultan of Brunei and his heir, Pengeran Tumonggong, into giving him a ten year lease of a large part of the kingdom. There was British alarm in Labuan, followed by urgent despatches to London. Meanwhile Moses had sailed for the China coast, where he sold his concession to two American merchants. In October of the same year these men, with two Chinese partners, formed the American Trading Company of Borneo. One of these was a Hong Kong trader named Joseph W. Torrey, who styled himself a Colonel. He led an expedition of twelve Americans and sixty Chinese to the mouth of the Kimanis River, built a stockade and ran up the Stars and Stripes. Assuming the sovereign powers previously given to Moses, he equated them with monarchy and gave himself the grandiloquent title of His Highness the Raja of Maraudu and Ambong, Sri Maharaja of North Borneo. The *Straits Times* in Singapore dubbed him the first American King.

Though the Sultan of Brunei had given him the right to make laws and his own money, his palace was a grass hut beside the sluggish, equatorial Kimanis River, his court a handful of penniless adventurers from America and Germany, his musicians the local headhunters performing on nose flutes, and innumerable mosquitoes from the malarial swamps. After a fruitless fund-raising trip to Hong Kong, he returned to find his manager dead in the jungle, the other Americans preparing to leave and no prospect of empire-building beyond bad debts to Chinese money-lenders. In 1866 he set fire to the grass hut labelled United States Consulate, claimed compensation from the Sultan and when this was refused, sent for a United States gunboat, which took one look at the situation and departed.

Meantime another adventurous character reached Sandakan. This time a Scotsman. William Clarke Cowie, the Borneo manager for a small Singapore company, had made money running guns and contraband through the Spanish blockade to Sulu, using small ships manned by adventurers of all nations. In Sandakan he established his own Labuan Trading Company, refused to pay King Torrey the export duties he demanded, and said that the Sultan of Brunei had no powers to give away territory belonging to the Sultan of Sulu. Like Torrey, he failed to exploit a wild region populated largely by Dyak headhunters and sea-dwelling Badjaos.

The next arrival was a man of larger business acumen. Born in Germany, Gustavus von Overbeck had spent several years in the United States, become a whaler in the North Pacific, then settled in Hong Kong where he acted as consul for the Austro-Hungarian empire, which created him a baron. Though Cowie did not know it, Baron von Overbeck had meantime acquired Torrey's concession for £15,000, then travelled to London to raise capital. There he formed a partnership with Alfred Dent, a small businessman who raised £10,000 to form the British North Borneo Company. Von Overbeck, too, found the concession invalid, but was alert enough to cross the sea to Jolo, where in January, 1878 the Sultan gave him exclusive rights to develop Sabah for five thousand Malayan dollars (£570) a year.

It was said at the time that the Sultan had been only too happy to dispose of his territory, even for so small a sum, because it was infertile, barely populated and preyed upon by pirates and headhunters. The Spanish denied his power to sell, or even lease at all. In July that year they had been able to confine the Sultan's fleet to Jolo and, for the first time, forced him to accept their 'sovereignty over all his domains, including those in Borneo'. The Sultan was given sole rights to the internal administration of his islands, except for the control of arms, but was debarred from entering into any treaties with other European powers. However, he had to confess his dealings with Baron von Overbeck. At once a warship went to Sandakan. Von Overbeck refused to capitulate, even though the commander threatened to bomb the town, and appealed to the British Government for protection. For some unspecified reason he withdrew from the syndicate the following year, leaving Dent and his associates to apply for a royal charter. This was duly granted in 1881, with the blessings of Queen Victoria and Gladstone. Spain protested, carrying on diplomatic correspondence for several years. But Spain was too involved with a resurgence of Muslim hostilities to exert much control over the Sulu archipelago, let alone the coast of Borneo. Then, in 1885, a peace treaty was signed between Spain, Britain and Germany, all agreeing to recognize Spanish rule over the Sulu islands. But Spain also agreed to relinquish all claims to 'that part of North-east Borneo formerly ruled by the Sultans of Sulu, and now in the possession of the British North Borneo Company'.

This is one treaty which the Macapagal claimants appear not to have examined.

If further endorsement of Spain's disinheritance were required, there was the attempt made by the exiled Jose Rizal in 1891 to establish a colony for landless Filipinos in the Sabah region. The British company offered him 100,000 acres of land and a fine harbour for 999 years, free of all charges. The Spanish Governor-General at first ignored Rizal's request, then instructed his consul in Hong Kong to refuse the proposals on the ground that 'it is not very patriotic to go off and cultivate a *foreign* soil'. [My italics.][4]

4. Gregorio F. Zaide. *Jose Rizal: Life, Works and Writings*, op. cit.

There is thus no basis for the Philippine claim to portions of North Borneo on the count that they were originally part of Spanish domains. Whether the old sultanate still possessed legal rights of its own is another matter.

The basis for the Philippine claim, initially a private one put forward by the heirs to the Sultan, was stated by Princess Tarhata Kiram in 1957. She wrote:

> In the original contract of lease of 1878 between our grandfather Sultan Jamalul A'lam and Baron von Overbeck and Alfred Dent of London, the latter were invested with the royal titles of Datu Bandahara (treasurer) and Raja of Sandakan (ruler of Sabah) and were commissioned as the Sultan's administrative delegates in North Borneo.
>
> When these businessmen later constituted themselves into the North Borneo Chartered Company, the Royal Charter granted by Queen Victoria in 1881 expressly mentioned this fact to define the status of the Company as the administrative delegate of the Sultan of Sulu. So, when this company transferred its 'sovereign rights and assets in North Borneo' to the British Crown in 1946, what was actually transferred was nothing more than the rights of tenants and delegates of the Sultan of Sulu in North Borneo. The heirs to the Sultan now, therefore, believe that they are the sovereigns de jure and the landlords of North Borneo.
>
> The matter of our being the landlords of North Borneo was already settled for the heirs of Sultan Jamalul Kiram in 1939 when the Sandakan High Court of North Borneo adjudicated to them the right to the annual rentals which they are now receiving regularly from the British Government. However these rights to the sovereignty over the territory being a political matter, they can be enforced only by political action through the Government of the Republic of the Philippines.[5]

The strange fact is that very few people, even those most closely involved in the present dispute, have ever seen the document that has caused so much international dissension. It is not even known how many copies existed. The Sultan had one in Arabic, the company another in English, while the British Government is presumed to hold a duplicate. Since its contents have remained unpublished since 1907, I feel its re-publication is worthwhile here. It is, additionally, one of the most picturesque business contracts ever drafted.

> To all nations on the face of the earth whom these matters may concern: We, Mahasari Padukka Mawlana as Sultan Mohammed Jamalul A'lam bin al-Marhum Mahasari Padukka as Sultan Mohammed Dulalun, Sultan of Sulu and its dependencies, send greetings:
>
> Whereas, we have seen fit to grant unto our trusty and well-beloved friends, Gustavus Baron von Overbeck and Alfred Dent, esquire, certain portions of the dominions owned by us, comprising all the lands on the north and east coasts of the Island of Borneo, from the Pandasan River . . .
>
> Now, therefore, know ye that we, Maharasi Padukka Mawlana as Sultan Mohammed Jamalul A'lam (as before), Sultan of Sulu and its dependencies, have nominated and appointed and do hereby nominate and appoint the

5. *Philippines Free Press*, 6 November 1957, Manila.

said Baron von Overbeck Supreme and independent ruler of the above-named territories with the title of Datu Bandahara and Raja of Sandakan, with absolute power over life and death of the inhabitants of the country, with all the absolute rights of property over the soil of the country vested in us and the right to dispose of the same as well as the rights over the products of the country, whether mineral, vegetable or animal, with the rights of making laws, coining money, creating an army and navy, levying customs dues on home and foreign trade, and shipping and other dues and taxes on the inhabitants as to him may seem good or expedient together with all other powers and rights usually exercised. . . .

And we call upon all foreign nations with whom we have formed friendly treaties or alliances, and we command all datus, nobles, governors, chiefs and peoples owing allegiance to us in the said territories to receive and acknowledge the said Datu Bandahara as the supreme ruler over the said States and to obey his councils and respect his authority therein as his own. And in the case of the office of supreme ruler and governor-in-chief of the company's territories in Borneo shall likewise, if appointed thereto by the company, succeed to the title of Datu, Bandahara and Raja of Sandakan, and all the powers enumerated above shall be vested in him.

Done at the palace of the Sultan, at Likup, in the Island of Sulu, on the nineteenth of Muharam, A.H. 1295, being the 22nd day of January, A.D. 1878.[6]

One would have imagined this to be a trump card in the hands of the British. The designation of Baron von Overbeck or any successor as 'supreme ruler', the stress on 'absolute powers', the absence of any qualifying time limit on the original 'grant' imply a gift in perpetuity. Yet that one term 'grant' has been brought into question. It is claimed that the Arabic word in the Sultan's original document was *padyak*, which is open to different interpretations. Professor Harold Conblin, a Saudi-Arabian scholar of Yale University, has translated it as 'lease', but British historians, Maxwell and Green, claimed that it meant 'cede'.

To complicate matters further the Sultan's copy in Arabic has been lost. During a visit to Singapore in 1945, his son, Sultan Jamalul Kiram, told an American newspaper correspondent it had been stolen.

The whole affair has been filled with deviousness and mystery from its beginnings. As are so many crucial issues throughout the Philippines.

To prepare their case in 1947, the Sultan's heirs were obliged to engage lawyers and other researchers to look through Spanish archives in Madrid. In the Ministry of Foreign Affairs they discovered a number of documents. Among them was a letter from the Sultan, stating that he had not ceded Sarawak, as the Singapore press was then claiming. A despatch from the Governor-General also said that he had written to the Baron cancelling his lease. Von Overbeck's reply was that 'I fail to see how the said agreement executed about six months ago, and concluded for all times and perpetuity . . . could possibly be affected or cancelled by any subsequent treaty'. This ignored the fact that the Sultan had no power to make such treaties. Also found was a letter from the Commander-General of the Spanish squadron stating that nothing was known of

6. Najeeb M. Saleeby, *A History of Sulu*, Manila, 1908.

147

von Overbeck's claim to represent a powerful British company. 'Your Excellency is fully aware,' he wrote, 'that there are frequently fictitious expeditions of adventurers who obtain their capital by the pretence of colonization, working of mines etc., which parties sometimes collect funds of quite some importance and spend a small part of them in alleged preparations and travel, in order thereafter to prepare for another swindle if they can'. He then referred to the self-styled Colonel Joseph W. Torrey.

How ably he summed up the climate of the times.

Another Spanish version of the transaction suggested blackmail. The Sultan, it was said, had been a doddering old man. The Baron had persuaded his victim that the Sultan of Borneo was preparing to seize Sabah, while the Spanish Navy intended to raze Sulu if he put up any resistance. He had better make the best of it and rely on British support. He was offered a rental of $3,000, demanded $8,000, then settled for $5,000. It sounds like an authentic Tau-sug deal. The Sultan was reported to have said that the Baron's acquired title of Datu Bandahara did not originate from him.

'It was he who wanted to use that title . . . and as far as the contract he brought it to me already made up. We agreed to this for two reasons: on account of what he told us . . . that the Captain-General would destroy everything, and because the people of Borneo would seize Sandakan, and we would not be able to fight them because of the arrival of the Captain-General. . . . Without the threats of the English I would never have signed the contract of lease with Overbeck.'

These threats are elaborated in another letter from the Governor of Jolo to the Governor-General, which he forwarded to the Minister of State on 10 October 1878.

It gave the Sultan's account of his initial visit by von Overbeck, then styling himself the Governor Pro Tempore of Labuan, the British consul at Brunei and several others, including two unidentified Malayans. This party reached Maibung on a chartered British merchant vessel, *America*, escorted by H.M.S. *Fly*. After formal expressions of friendship, everyone returned to the ship except for the two Malayans, who remained in the Sultan's house under the pretext that no horses were available. During the official visit they had remained aloof, but now asked him directly if he had accepted the proposal. The Sultan professed surprise. He was told that the purpose of the visit had not been a mere courtesy call. The Baron was immensely rich, they told him. The proposition he intended to make would be a good one, for the Sultan of Borneo had already ceded his part of the island to von Overbeck. They told him also that the Governor-General of the Philippines was on his way with 5,000 men to raze Jolo to the ground. The Sultan was astonished at this news, especially concerning the Baron's ambition to acquire his Borneo lands, but promised to think about it. Then, a few days later, the party returned. Von Overbeck at once presented his contract, already drawn up, with only the amount of annual rental left blank. That was when they haggled over the sum.

Subsequently, reported the Governor of Jolo, the Sultan assured him that he had told the British they were wrong in believing he was free to dispose of his land, or that Spain had no jurisdiction over Sulu or Borneo.

One can imagine it. The double talk on the Sultan's part, the efforts to exonerate himself, the full deviousness. Perhaps the Baron had been too sharp for him. Perhaps he had been only too glad to accept, but it was now worth more than his independence to admit it to the Spanish. Finally — and how conveniently — the document is lost!

As for the only record of it in the Madrid archives, it carries the date 4 January 1878. Yet the version presented to the British was dated 22 January.

There was, as it happened, a Spanish translation in the archives. But its wording frequently differed from the English contract. Instead of the clause beginning, 'We . . . hereby grant and cede of our own sovereign free will to Gustavus Baron von Overbeck', the Spanish version reads, 'We have decided to conclude a contract of lease of Sandakan as proposed to us by Baron Overbeck'. The British, but not the Spanish, refers to the grant as being 'forever and in perpetuity'. The contract in English stipulates that 'this grant shall never be transferred to any other nation or company of foreign nationality without the sanction of Her Britannic Majesty's Government', whereas the Spanish reads, 'They cannot assign lease rights to foreigners nor to any other company without the agreement of the King of Spain'.

Comparison of the above phrases in both documents with the version published in 1908 by Najeeb M. Saleeby — who in turn drew on the version contained in an official American report from the Department of Mindanao six years earlier — reveals further variations again.[7]

Which contract is the right one? Which was the original signed by the Sultan, Overbeck and Dent? Who made the changes? The British company, the Sultan or the Spanish? The present heirs to the Sultan claim that the English version is a forgery, or 'doctored for colonial purposes'. It seems equally possible that the Sultan did the doctoring, or even the Spanish, for fear of censure from Madrid.

An additional contention by the Sultan's heirs that the British would not have paid rent if the territory had been ceded is not wholly valid. There are precedents. For instance, the Malayan State of Kedah was ceded during the nineteenth century, but the agreement stipulated the payment of annual rent which was still being paid up to the time the Malaysian Federation came into being.

The Philippines department of foreign affairs has not yet disclosed its hand.

It has, however, drawn consolation from two American opinions. The

7. George W. Davis, *Department of Mindanao Annual Report*, 1 August 1902, Manila.

first of these was made in 1915 by Governor Frank Carpenter, head of the Mindanao-Sulu division of the United States Government in the Philippines. He endorsed the fact that the territorial jurisdiction of the Philippines ended at the islands off the north coast of Borneo — as does the Philippines Constitution today — and added a rider to this effect.

> It is necessary, however, that there be clearly of official record the fact that the termination of the temporal sovereignty of the Sultanate of Sulu within the American territory is understood to be wholly without prejudice or effect as to the temporal sovereignty and ecclesiastical authority of the Sultanate beyond the territorial jurisdiction of the U.S. Government, especially with reference to that portion of the Island of Borneo which as a dependency of the Sultanate of Sulu is considered to be held under lease by the chartered company known as the British North Borneo Company.

The second opinion was voiced by a former Governor-General, the late Francis Burton Harrison, who was appointed special advisor to the Philippines on foreign affairs in 1947. He declared himself to have been 'scandalized' by the British action in transferring the North Borneo States to colonial government the year before, and made the first semi-official statement on the Sabah affair.

'In reviewing the subject of the claims of the Sultanate of Sulu to the ancient patrimony of North Borneo,' he said, 'we must come to the conclusion that the action of the British Government in announcing the annexation of the 16th of July, just twelve days after the inauguration of the Philippine Government, a step taken by the British Government unilaterally and without special notice to the Sultanate of Sulu, nor consideration of their legal rights, was an act of political aggression which should be promptly repudiated by the Government.'

Despite pressure from the Muslim interests concerned, the government took no stand on Sabah before Macapagal became president in 1962. He raised the question during his State of the Nation address to Congress in January the following year. Which is not to say that he had not hither to shown personal interest. This began when, as a legal officer in the foreign affairs department, he negotiated the reacquistion of the Turtle Islands from Britain. These islands, in the Tawi-Tawi group, had also been a concession of the British North Borneo Company, which had paid rental annually since the nineteenth century. However, they were within Philippine territorial waters, and considered essential for naval defence. It was not a question of recovering private property for an obsolete sultanate that no longer had independent rights.

The crux of the present dispute was the conflict between the functions of a constitutional republic and the relics of feudalism. The people of Sabah, despite cultural and racial ties, owe no allegiance to Sulu; the last sultan has long been dead; his heirs inhabit a free, capitalist society. The claimants recognized this by forming a business enterprise registered as the Kiram Corporation. In 1963 this was already offering Sabah timber rights, without legal title, to speculators. Its president and treasurer was a Manila lawyer, Nicosia Osmena, son of the late President Sergio Osmena. This lawyer, when interviewed by a visiting British journalist from Singapore in 1963, gave an astonishingly frank outline of his corporation's aims. Alex Josey, representing the *Straits Times*, had flown to Manila to see A. M. Azahari, leader of the Brunei revolt, who was then said to be going the rounds of night clubs. It was Nicosia Osmena who introduced him to Soekarno's future 'Prime Minister of Kalimantan Utara', informing him that he and his friends had helped to finance the revolt against the Sultan of Brunei.

Referring to the Sabah claim, Mr Osmena said, 'You can tell the Tunku we can easily arrange for a cash settlement. All we need is some money and a few concessions. We need some pieces of land from Borneo, a lumber concession, and the right to set up a Philippines development corporation to open up Borneo. We can settle this stupid revolt and the claim to North Borneo between us. But there is no time to talk. Our Vice-President (Emmanuel Pelaez) is going to London to talk about the Philippines Government claim. But don't worry, I can fix that, too.'

Osmena added that the Philippines Government was 'out on a limb' regarding the claim, but that all the corporation wanted was property rights, or compensation of £10,000,000. He said that the President had told him that, rather than risk the Indonesians taking over Sabah, he would prefer the British to remain. 'Frankly, I'm worried about the Indonesians myself. I'm worried about communism. We don't want the Indonesians becoming too involved. . . . Keep this secret or someone might get hurt. There are gunmen in Manila. For twenty pesos you can get your head blown off.'[8]

Osmena later denied having made this statement, while the foreign ministry stated that the Government was seeking no cash settlement. During Macapagal's eighteen months' re-election campaign, which began in 1964, he made little further reference to Sabah. Commenting that a successful presidential election costs at least a million dollars, Josey reported that his 'election backers are among the speculators heavily involved in the the Sabah claims', and that Macapagal, believing in the validity of the claims, 'is fully committed politically to guard their investments'. The new president, Ferdinand Marcos, was not so committed. It was officially stated in 1966 that the Sabah claim had not been renounced, though unofficially that it would not be pressed at the present time. A face-saving formula, no doubt. But a later change of regime could well revive the issue.

Besides, the ending of confrontation has not settled Sabah's problems. Local Communist agents trained by the P.K.I., strengthened by others sent in from China, are active underground. Malaysia may have difficulty in retaining a region with a large Chinese population. The threat of a future cockpit between nations remains.

8. *Straits Times*, 18 January 1963, Singapore.

CHAPTER 18

The Coconut King

> *What the Philippines needs most today,*
> *one hundred years after Rizal's birth,*
> *is an ever-increasing number of those*
> *clear-seeing and clear-thinking Filipinos*
> *who will dedicate themselves and all their*
> *waking hours to the development of the*
> *national patrimony.*
>
> TOMAS C. BENITEZ

'WHEN YOU GO to Basilan Island ask Juan Alano does he still plant a tree before breakfast each morning.'

So said a Manila friend before we sailed for Mindanao. One tree? It was an understatement. Don Juan Salonga Alano has earned the soubriquet of Coconut King of Basilan in far more energetic fashion. Within fifty years he has planted a quarter-million coconut trees, transforming disordered jungle and stripped timber concessions into fertile, productive parklands. All except 15,000 of these palms grow on his 4,000 hectare estate at Tairan, some twenty miles inland from Isabela. The remainder, mainly young trees, are on ten small, offshore islands he acquired more recently from their Muslim owners. If any one man could be said to have brought peaceful settlement to the formerly wild island of Basilan it has been this extraordinarily gifted, resolute man from the north. It required courage as well as persistence and vision, for he had not at first been welcomed. He and his wife endured hardships few people would have been willing to undergo: they lived for years at a bare subsistence level, and the prospect of lonely death by violence was a haunting reality. When Alano and his young bride first settled on Basilan in 1915, there was only one other non-Muslim living there, a former doctor from Luzon who began successfully growing rubber there against government advice. Today there is little land available for agriculture, so potent has been Alano's example.

His career is more than a story of personal success, even if his gross income from copra reached P3,000,000 a year during the 1960s. It has a moral for the Philippines at large. In a country obsessed with politics and self-advantage, with petty legal jousting, corruption and wholesale *lagay*, Alano has created a rich agricultural empire on this remote frontier, contributed vastly to the nation's productivity and given security and good wages to 750 local families who once lived in semi-nomadic penury.

As he pointed out to me one day, the former wasteland of Basilan was now contributing P1,500,000 in taxes alone to the government in Manila.

Alano was a poor man when he first went south. He was the son of a Malolos farmer who went bankrupt, largely through his own generosity. Alano senior had been a good agriculturalist, the land was fertile, but politics and fiestas drained his money away. It was his habit during Holy Week and December fiestas in Malolos to kill beef for the hundreds who invaded his farm, a practice that helps to impoverish millions of Filipinos still, prompting many socially-minded people to urge barrio and town councils to abandon these ancient festivals which, they claim, no longer suit the austere conditions of modern times. To my mind, it would be a pity to kill off one of the last colourful and ebullient expressions of the Filipino spirit, despite the tawdry and commercial nature that has overwhelmed so many of today's fiestas. It was an attitude that evoked little sympathy from Juan Alano. His father's bankruptcy had obliged him to look to his own education, to support himself as best he could. He left the province for Manila, studied at the Ateneo, took a job as stenographer in the law courts, read and studied in his spare hours, even plaguing judges and fiscals with questions to improve his knowledge of law.

He passed his law examinations without even attending university. Next he became a provincial journalist, believing this the best way of gaining a varied experience of life, then in 1911 attached himself to the staff of Manuel Quezon, who took him to Washington where he was the Philippine representative in Congress. On his return Alano became an assistant prosecutor in circuit courts around Mindanao, where few Manileños wanted to live in those aggressive times. 'I helped to hang a lot of wild and bad men in those parts,' he told me.

This legal work on the frontier brought an unexpected reward. Sent to Dapitan, Zamboanga del Norte, to prosecute a murderer, he became friendly with a Spanish planter who had remained after the Revolution, married a Filipina and experimented in growing coconuts. Antonio Maxias had learnt all he knew from Jose Rizal, during the patriot's four years in exile there. Rizal, who had once studied at Heidelberg University, where the theories of Malthus were then being debated, had been much impressed by Germany's scientific approach to agriculture and its colonizing successes in Africa and the Pacific. (Heidelberg, incidentally, now has a street named after Rizal.) He had also given Maxias the first textbook ever written on coconut-growing. This was translated from the German by the then governor of Lanao province, Colonel Wittenhauser, an American of German descent. Rizal had argued that the population explosion predicted by Malthus would create an unquenchable demand for foodstuffs. The Philippines, he said, had the climate and soil fertility to grow anything. But what could contribute more to mankind than the coconut palm? Its nuts provided food and drink and edible oils, its fronds produced thatch for housing, its trunks were ideal for structural building, even its fibres had commercial value. Finally the dried meat of coconuts was in demand for soapmaking, explosives and oil.

Alano was at once convinced, and set about looking for land. He found what he wanted on the small island of Malamawi, which protects Isabela harbour. He took his bride there in 1915, hired what reluctant labour he could and began clearing his first hillside for coconuts. Meantime he had to leave Doña Ramona there while he earned enough money by law to tide them over the crucial years until their trees began to bear.

'People said I was out of my mind,' he told me. 'Why put all my eggs in one basket? What are you going to do with so many coconuts, they asked? When the whole world is covered with coconut trees, what will you do then? I said I knew there would always be a place for them, however much copra was produced. I have been right. In fact, I'm just about to buy another island.'

He also said that everyone had warned him it was impossible to make a living from such a wilderness. Others had tried. One and all had retreated, if they were lucky enough to remain alive. 'If you don't starve to death,' one survivor told him, 'the Moros will cut off your head.'

Alano is among those who detest the term Moro. He went there with considerable respect for the Muslims, and by so doing gradually won their trust. It was not easy. He made it clear from the start that, though he came from the north, he was no Christian. Yet his early attempts to farm on Malamawi were resisted.

'The Spanish left this country to us,' he was told. 'Then the Americans did not interfere. The land was given to us by Allah. It belongs to us. Now you want to cut down the trees plough up the soil and plant things. How are we going to graze our cattle?'

They threatened violence. Somehow it did not come. The Alanos kept themselves armed nonetheless, though Juan confessed to me that he had another secret weapon, too. This was a phonograph. During his rare leisure hours records of Muslim music could often be heard drifting through the windows of his rough shack. The sullen peasantry were impressed despite themselves. He began to act for them in legal matters, always free of charge, and Muslims are great litigationists. At one time he became legal advisor to the Sultan of Sulu, drew up his last will and testament, and was offered — rare honour for an infidel — the freedom of his harem.

Doña Ramona, who was seventy-eight when she entertained us on Basilan — five years her husband's senior — was still a match for his astonishing energy and drive. In the weeks we spent in their two Basilan homes, or travelling about their present plantation at Tairan by jeep, I never saw her still. She was always doing something: supervising her household staff, making pottery or the fine tapestry she wove, visiting her wide range of friends and family. She had the vigour, looks, dynamic personality of a woman half her age. I shall always remember this handsome, white-haired, strongly-built near-octogenarian jumping from her

her chair on the verandah to dramatize the point of some story. Yet, at first meeting, one could assume her aristocratic, old-world bearing to have been the product of a life of ease.

'When you talk about what father has done here,' their elder son, Julio, said one day on the plantation he now manages, 'don't forget that mother was a good half of it.'

No one could question it. Born in Iloilo, she had been a schoolteacher when she met Don Juan, accustomed to a settled domestic life. They married in Zamboanga in 1913, when he had only ten centavos in the world. He had to borrow one peso to give the priest. When their first child was born, Chinese storekeepers refused him credit even for a can of condensed milk. Today it is the Chinese who seek his help when they want to enter the copra business. Left alone for long periods on Mala-mawi while he continued his legal practice, she had to run the plantation alone, grow the food they needed, run a school for her children, and supervise the labourers, who were mostly long-term prisoners loaned by the San Ramon colony, near Zamboanga.

'The only workers I could trust were murderers,' she told me over her embroidery one afternoon. 'I was all alone most of the time. I had to help clear the jungle and do most of the planting myself. We had a barbed wire fence around the compound, but I refused to have any guards inside it. They could have been as dangerous as the rest. I imposed a curfew at eight o'clock each night, beating a big brass Muslim gong. Anyone walking about after that time had to carry a torch of flaming coconut fronds so I could see who it was.'

She took to riding about the plantation astride a carabao, wearing a split skirt, with a Colt revolver strapped to her waist. Once she struck trouble with a Muslim employee, sworn to kill his father-in-law over some unexplained grudge. Probably some minor slight to his pride. As he sharpened his curved *barong* beneath her stilted homestead, he told her, 'I'm going to seek out that man tonight. I will have to kill him. Lend me your dugout canoe.'

She refused, saying, 'If you're going to kill him, you can't take my canoe. Take someone else's.'

Some days later, the man returned.

'Well, did you kill him?' she asked.

'No,' the Muslim said, though his eyebrows had been shaved. 'He was lucky. He had gone away. I didn't take your canoe either.'

When the coconut palms began bearing, Don Juan was able to give up law. They made such a success of the island plantation that in 1929 he decided to sell, taking up an even more fertile area at Tairan. By this time he had also been elected to Congress, which meant frequent journeys to distant Manila. One of those rare Filipino politicians with a reputation for being incorruptible, he is still honoured for his efforts in winning government finance and social services for both Basilan and Zamboanga. This was at a time when Manileños were notoriously indifferent to the

Muslim south. It put a great deal of added strain on his agricultural work.

Since there was no settlement at Tairan, they travelled to and from Isabela, lived in a thatched *nipa* shack and cleared the jungle with whatever labour they could hire. Nor was there even a road in those days. Sometimes together, sometimes alone, they would journey round the coast to Pangasahan in some fisherman's *vinta*, then go by foot through jungle to the embryo plantation. Many times, Doña Ramona told me, she used to walk half the night through the lonely, eerie jungle. They had to live off the country in those times, which was not difficult for a resourceful man with a gun: there was venison, wild pig, wild duck and other game, and plentiful fish and jungle fruits.

During the first year of permanent occupation, a bandit gang broke into the compound, murdering the overseer with his own gun. Another time Don Juan was attacked by a *juramentado* at his own homestead gate. The man was in a state of hysteria, threatening to kill everyone he met, because the father of the girl he wanted had given her to another man. Alano stood up to him. There was nothing else to do, he said wryly He asked the berserk Muslim if he was prepared to meet his God, seeing that he had yet done nothing with his life, not even produced a child to take his name. Would he offend Allah by bringing shame on his own father, his future wife? 'What wife?' the *amok* demanded. 'I tell you, they have taken her from me.' To have halted the man's murderous assaults long enough to argue was the first victory. The second was Alano's assurance that he could find him another, better bride. But he still thinks it was his onslaught on the man's pride that turned the emotional tide. Eventually the Muslim flung his blood-stained *barong* at Don Juan's feet.

It was only one of many crises in the early days, when only immense tact, patience and resourcefulness enabled him to tame those truculent people.

'I have a better weapon than the *barong*,' he told me. 'My tongue, and my two feet. When you can't argue any longer, run.'

Nonetheless, the Alanos always kept armed guards on the strongly-timbered gate outside their homestead. During a recent campaign by the Philippine Constabulary against large-scale banditry, a full company was stationed on Tairan. Alano was not happy about it. It would only encourage attacks, he said, and felt easier when the troops departed. On one occasion he met the bandit leader face to face, while driving through one of the more lonely paddocks. 'Don't come plundering on my lands,' he told the mounted bandit. 'I don't want you causing trouble among my people. If you do, I'll have the Constabulary brought back. But if it's only food you want — well, take it. There's plenty to spare. Just don't start shooting us up.'

Food was the least of his considerations. Basilan is an island of incredible fertility. It reeks of it. Everywhere you go you smell the rich, ripe earth, the perfume of the jungle, the scents of flowering shrubs and trees.

You put a stick in the ground, and it grows. You drop seeds, and the eternal rains smother the soils with new growth. Alano encourages his workers and tenants to scatter seed everywhere. He tosses seed out of his jeep. He dams small creeks and channels, diverts springs, puts down small wind-driven pumps. The whole estate is continually burgeoning.

I have spent many hours driving about his plantation without covering the same track twice, amazed at what he had conjured with such apparent ease from the humid soils, at the fantastic lushness and variety of his produce. In his large, timbered homestead with its wide verandah, he has set up a blackboard that lists the products of this immense venture he calls modestly his 'farm'. These are the items he chalked up:

> Copra, cattle, sheep, abaca, coffee (three varieties), tea, cacao, sugar, peanuts, vanilla, citronella, rice, sorghum, corn (four kinds), fresh and saltwater fish ponds, poultry, pigs, six kinds of citrus fruits, including Valencia oranges, pomelos, grapefruit, pineapples, lanzones, Spanish plums, three kinds of guava, pili nuts, duriens, bananas, papayas, avocados, mangoes. Spices including black and white pepper, cinnamon, lemon grass. Root crops including cassava, camote, ginger, gabi, ubi, timon.

There are people who claim that Basilan is among the richest islands in the Pacific, comparable only to the more prolific regions of Java and Sumatra. This was recognized by the few English and French intruders who reached it during the nineteenth century, but the inhabitants proved intolerably fierce. The keen eye of this Luzon farmer's son was the first in modern times to see its potentialities.

CHAPTER 19

Rice and Politics

*The new national leaders are
alienated from the intellectual
and emotional world of the mass
of their countrymen. Indeed,
even local leaders are incapable
of perceiving peasants realistically
(to say nothing of sympathetically),
because their orientation is towards
the new world of the city.*

PROFESSOR PAUL UREN

THE REMARKABLE achievements on Basilan Island, due largely to the pioneering of Juan Alano, reveal just how other fertile regions could be most vigorously developed. However, agriculture, even more than the rest of the economy, has suffered from two disadvantages, both of them political. With each change of administration, the directors of departments change, according to their party allegiances. Also few politicians have either knowledge of or sympathy with rural life. Congressmen are almost exclusively middle-class dwellers of cities and towns, having small regard for peasants or farmers once they have secured their votes. 'Most of our legislators are lawyers who can't tell an abaca plant from a banana,' said one farm school teacher. Yet the basis of the Philippine economy is a rural one. Eight per cent of its people work on the land. Their staple food is rice. Rice remains one of the perennial arguments of politics, an argument no one has yet been able to resolve.

'The rice situation in the Philippines is a case of sheer irony,' wrote Teodoro M. Ela, senior planning assistant to the National Economic Council in 1964. 'The country has enough land, the right climate, and the requisite manpower to produce rice. But each year we are plagued with the same dilemma: rice shortage. . . . In Asia the Philippines is a tail-ender in the productivity of rice. We produce an average of only 28 cavans of palay per hectare in 1962 against the yield of 106·8 cavans in Japan, Asia's number one rice bowl.'[1]

During the same year a well-known Senator, visiting South Vietnam, was highly impressed with what had been done in its famous Mekong Delta. He discussed the achievement with Vietnamese experts, spoke of urging his own government to send a study team across the China Sea, asked where agriculturalists had learnt their successful techniques.

'In your country,' was the reply.

1. Teodoro M. Ela, 'Why the Philippines is Asian Tail-ender', *Manila Chronicle*, 13 November 1964, Manila.

Here was the ultimate irony. The Philippines has the most advanced research centre for rice cultivation in the world. Sixty miles south-east of Manila, set in the fertile and beautiful landscapes of Laguna province, is an eighty hectare experimental farm run by the International Rice Research Institute. Los Baños, which is also a centre for agricultural work carried out by the University of the Philippines, has the best equipped, most handsomely laid out research unit of its kind I have seen. The Institute has gathered together some of the world's best rice scientists. There are twenty-four of them from six separate countries, with another thirty-six highly-trained Filipino research assistants. The director is a noted scientist from the United States, Dr Robert F. Chandler. Money for research is no object, for the Institute has been richly endowed by the Ford and Rockefeller Foundations. There are never less than sixty foreign scientists taking two-year study courses at Los Baños, and they come from almost every country in south-east Asia, which has derived tremendous benefits from the advanced study of rice-growing techniques. Since its foundation in 1962, the experimental centre has tested some 800 species, or 6,800 varieties of rice, and given advanced courses in agronomy, plant breeding, genetics and cyto-genetics, soil science, plant pathology, entomology, plant physiology, biochemistry, agricultural engineering and economics. The results in terms of increased production, better strains and stable crops throughout south-east Asia have been notable.

That is, in almost every country but the Philippines.

At home, despite the best intentions, something always seems to go wrong. Nor has there been any lack of government agencies to carry out President Macapagal's 1962 pledge to make the nation self-supporting in rice. Within two years the Office of the President, Congress and several government departments had set up nearly twenty separate agencies to stimulate production, many of them in conflict with one another. The only thing that did not multiply was the production of rice. In fact, rice shortages increased year by year. Yet the reasons for them were widely recognized. Teodoro Ela has listed the main ones in this order:

Lack of effective communication between rice scientist and farmer; absence of a co-ordinating plan between agencies; lack of incentive to farmers; poor credit facilities; the restrictive effects of share-cropping; low prices for raw *palay*; lack of irrigation projects; poor marketing; the ignoring of newly proven seeds of high yield; the non-application of fertilizers; antiquated farm practices; and the destructive forces of typhoons and floods.

'The underlying cause and final solution to the rice problem is evidently one of a political nature,' he concluded. 'Provided that the farmer is guaranteed higher net returns, he will apply fertilizer, use certified seeds, control pests and diseases with insecticides and pesticides and employ the approved methods of cultivation. However, all these measures will naturally increase production cost. The only assurance that the farmer will profit is by creating for him a realistic market.'

One would imagine that, since 32,000,000 Filipinos have a diet consisting very largely of rice, there would be little difficulty in finding markets. Yet the production of nationally-grown rice has actually been falling every year. The Philippines annual yield is the lowest in Asia. Each year enormous quantities have to be imported, imposing a heavy cost on the national economy. In fact, during recent years, rice brought into a rice-growing country has been the largest, most costly import.

The importing of foreign rice has been almost constant since 1901, apart from the Japanese occupation years, though it is only since the war that tonnages have soared in such astronomic fashion. In 1961, while campaigning against President Garcia, Diosdado Macapagal won wide support by his condemnation of a Nacionalista regime that imported 186,000 tons of rice, while giving no aid to Filipino farmers. He called it a conspiracy to buy votes by making foreign rice plentiful at cheap prices, while the administration paid dearly in subsidies. Hungry voters were angry voters, he declared. In 1965 President Macapagal's opponent levelled exactly the same charges against his Liberal Party regime. Only the import total had by then reached 600,000 tons. Instead of its promised self-sufficiency, the Macapagal administration had paid out P244,000,000 of public monies to foreign powers.

Most of these, as one critic observed, were in countries whose experts had been trained at Los Baños.

A curious feature of the situation is that rice cannot legally be imported at all, except under certain conditions, laid down by congressional law. There must not only be a shortage, but a proven one, certified by the National Economic Council. In August 1964 public protests greeted the N.E.C. forecast of a 100,000 tons shortage of rice for the following year. The influential Association of Rice and Corn Producers attacked the President for squandering public funds 'for electioneering purposes only'. It also pointed out that the current harvest was still taking place, so that no final estimate could be given, while planting for 1965 had not even started. By the time the presidential campaign was in full swing a year later, the import figure had been increased nearly sixfold. Costly imported rice was released, by government decree, at prices with which locally-grown rice could not compete.

The same situation had been created two years earlier, when the Liberals feared they would lose public support in provincial and municipal elections. Unfortunately, the N.E.C. had already announced a rice surplus for the year. The president thereupon said that, in view of the deteriorating situation in south-east Asia, it was essential to stockpile rice for the armed forces. More than 250,000 tons was at once imported. Though one Nacionalista senator declared that it would take the Philippine Army twenty years to eat its way through such a mountain of rice, all of it had magically disappeared by the following year. The import of a further 300,000 tons was called for. The estimated cost was P360,000,000. Amid a generally hostile reception given to the move by the Manila press,

The *Philippines Herald* coolly observed, 'even more important than importing the rice is distributing it, a process that must be attended by every possible safeguard to prevent the possibility of the cereal slipping into the hands of hoarders or winding up in bulk in the black-market'. Early in 1965 the Senate began an inquiry into the fate of the Army's rice, for there had been no observable increase in the bulk or girth of the soldiery involved in what must have been gargantuan feasts.

It was discovered that, within eight months, P91,000,000 worth of rice had been 'lost' in warehouses or trucking movements around the archipelago. Nor had the Philippine National Bank, which paid the total purchase price to overseas suppliers, received a peso in return. The vice-president of the Rice and Corn Producers Association, Mario Moreno, thereupon announced that P553,000,000 had been spent on imported rice within three years. Had this money been spent locally, he said, it could have irrigated 184,000 hectares of ricelands, producing more than 4,000,000 cavans — or 200,000 tons. In effect, government finance wisely spent could have achieved virtual self-sufficiency.

'Review the history of our political parties,' he stated, 'and you will invariably find the promise of cheap rice the principal plank of their platforms. If the prevailing price is low, the party in power boasts of it. If it is high, immediate and massive importations are made to bring it down and prevent the opposition from using it as an issue. Perhaps the politicians' worst fear is that they will wake up one day to find the Philippines so obviously self-sufficient in rice that the use of the industry as a political football would be untenable.

'The real reason for our continuous importation is not to cover shortages. Neither is the hypocritical assertion that rice must be as cheap as possible to be within the reach of the poor, for the really poor people are the rice farmers living in the rural areas. These are people whose only hope for survival is a profitable price for their produce. . . . As a direct result of the greatly reduced income of our 3,000,000 rice farmers, even our city industries are stagnating, for lack of a rural market for manufactured goods.'[2]

This diagnosis was clearly visible in 1965, when all governmental activities to prime the economy were dissipated amid the huge expenditure on election campaigns. It was impossible to estimate the outlay, for much of what administration candidates spent was hidden in normal government expenses. President Macapagal, for instance, spent from four to six days weekly touring remote provinces and barrios over an eighteen month period, travelling by chartered aircraft, air force helicopters, naval gunboats and administration vehicles on the pretext of normal visits, while millions in discretionary funds were allocated to projects favouring party policies and employing thousands of potential, if unqualified voters, or in assisting the private capital gains of industrialists providing cam-

2. Mario Moreno, 'Politics and Rice', *Philippines Free Press*, 24 October 1964, Manila.

paign funds. Elections in the Philippines are big business, even if investment in political parties is not listed on the Manila Stock Exchange.

'The government is bankrupt,' reported the *Manila Chronicle* columnist I. P. Soliongco five days before the elections in November 1965. 'According to the conservative estimates of fiscal officials who are more or less friendly to President Macapagal, a total of P515,000,000 has disappeared.'

The unfortunate effect of so much politicking is that even funds already earmarked for developmental plans often fail to materialize.

A searching report on these failures was published by the *Philippines Free Press* — the nation's public conscience — early in 1965. 'Perhaps the greatest irony of our time is that our country can afford millions of pesos for political campaigns,' it began, 'but spends virtually nothing in food production. In 1958,' the report went on, 'the government of the day began a P20,000,000 a year programme to increase rice and corn production. Farm agencies seldom received 75 or even 50 per cent of that amount. A National Irrigation Administration, designed to build small-scale dams, channels and storage waters for rice-growers, has remained a "ghost agency" because none of its P30,000,000 funds have ever been released. The land reform programme of the Macapagal era began with a budget of P15,000,000, but received only a small percentage of this money. Other urgent projects failed through nepotism, while trained officials were demoted or allocated to other departments, or were not even paid their wages. One farm agency employee,' the report concluded, 'claimed that his chief always had funds for trips to the provinces in the company of a large entourage of "information" men and "technical advisers" to promote the fortunes of his political party — but no funds for vital projects or for the travelling expenses of other personnel carrying out their assigned task.'[3]

To suggest that politicians alone are to blame for agricultural shortcomings (politics, next to cock-fighting, is the Filipino's favourite sport) would be to give an unreal picture of affairs. One has to appreciate the unique outlook of the peasant. The Philippines is not yet a scientific, industrial society, and the Filipino therefore lacks the sophisticated approach of the academic westerner. In many aspects this can be its strength as well. Juan de la Cruz may, by the standards of other nations, have a poor earning capacity. Yet he is able to exist, to endure, where others would starve. His basic needs are small. He grows much of the food his family needs, however low the price he can gain for it on the open market. He is in the same position as the Indonesian, whose economic collapse is always predicted by western observers. The Indonesian 'miracle' has its parallel in the Philippines, where inflationary trends have been comparatively mild.

The *tao*, however, is also too often ill-equipped to deal with his own multitude of problems. It is his nature to be a conservative. Ideally, the

3. 'Why The Food Shortage?' *Philippines Free Press*, 20 March 1964, Manila.

land reform programme of the 1960s appeared to offer obvious advantages, freeing him from an ancient serfdom. But it meant also a step into the unknown: towards a self-dependence hitherto undreamt of in his closed, traditional society. He tills the soil as his ancestors tilled it; he is accustomed to the lumbering carabao and iron or wooden plough, not tractors, and tractors, anyway, require larger areas than his tiny fields of camotes, corn or rice. He lives in fear of the eternal landlord, the powerful barrio leaders, the usurer, the next typhoon. Frequently he does not change his habits because he does not want to change. Change itself is something to be feared. The trained expert from the city, the agronomist, the government instructor tells him that his ideas are outmoded, wrong. But they have worked: they have brought up crops, and he has survived. Will he survive with the new-fangled notions they suggest? He is often a superstitious man, too. He plants according to the old rituals, he prays to the Virgin or older gods for a bountiful harvest. He tends to think less in terms of irrigation and fertilizers than in the esoteric lore of his forefathers.

If the politician takes advantage of these backward-looking trends, he cannot be altogether blamed. There is no time for crusading or scientific lectures, certainly not if the result is to lose votes. The problem is to break this recurrent cycle, the slow progression of rural ideas that seem never to emerge from the past. Yet gains are being made in the slow time-scale of rural advance, however sluggishly. More energetic prosecution of the land reform movement, the conversion of tenant farming to leasehold, could transform the countryside in future years. This does not seem likely under the Nacionalista administration that took office in 1966, for this party is dominated by large landowners.

During 1965 the government-sponsored National Rice and Corn Production Contest Committee announced significant advances in several provinces. More than 5,000 farmers had taken part in its annual rice production contest, one quarter of whom won awards for exceptionally large crops. The highest yield was 268 cavans per hectare, which made the national average of 28 cavans appear absurdly small. The Secretary of Agriculture, Jose Y. Feliciano, said that 'the feat of producing a hundred to more than two hundred cavans of *palay* from a one-hectare farm is no longer impossible. This proves that Filipino farmers truly are capable of raising the average of our national rice production.' His optimism was somewhat checked by the Director of Plant Industry, Eugenio E. Cruz, who cautioned him that the high-yield producers were still far too few to affect the country's total production.

Personally I refuse to believe that a people which, three thousand years ago, built those magnificent rice terraces in Mountain Province, a feat of fantastic engineering skill, cannot meet the easier challenges of today, whether they be posed by typhoons or tycoons in politics. I am assured that this is fallacious reasoning. Even such an authority as Robert E. Huke insists that modern rice farming can be expanded only on fairly level lands. The terraced *padis* of Benguet and Banaue were built on difficult slopes of at least forty-five degrees. These days, he writes, the practice would not be economic.[4]

I wonder.

A recent publication of the Chinese People's Republic described similar developments in five separate provinces, as well as Inner Mongolia. Some of these were extensions to the original rice terraces created by the Han Dynasty (206 B.C.-A.D. 220) in Szechuan Province. The author described, with impressive illustrations, how the Chinese government had greatly expanded these ancient terraces, having proved how effective they were in retaining soils and water, improving soil fertility and increasing grain output in mountain and hill regions. Experimental stations had also been set up in those provinces. In the Yellow River production increases of 50 to 100 per cent were claimed. Detailed photographs also revealed how hillsides above the terraces had been planted with trees to stop erosion.

This is not to recommend that the Philippines adopt collectivist techniques. It is unwise nonetheless to express contempt of the communist regime in China while its own economy stagnates or crumbles through corruption. In many islands, too, I saw distressing signs of neglect and official vandalism that no Chinese commune would tolerate.

Travelling through the Visayan islands, along the immense coastline of Mindanao, I was shocked by the devastation I saw upon once fertile landscapes. These are some of the world's most beautiful islands; or were so. Instead of fine timbers and lush grasses, hillside after hillside was scarred, eroded, plundered of its natural vegetation. The island of Cebu, whose beauty so impressed the early Spaniards, is today almost treeless, its central spine of mountains bare, sun-scorched, arid. The splendid mountains fringing the shores of Zamboanga del Norte, Cotabato, and Davao provinces frequently appear as if shelled by some remorseless enemy. Despite the fact that lumber is the third most profitable export, the great commercial forests of Mindanao are rapidly losing their fine timbers, because loggers gouge out the best trees as they please, destroying smaller ones and lesser growth as their tractors bulldoze their way through. No attempt is made by the forestry department to enforce replanting; rangers are scarce, venial, reluctant to enforce what laws there are upon truculent loggers. Above all, there are the destructive assaults of *kaingineros*, the semi-nomadic peasants who clear and burn a small area for planting corn or camotes, remain there one season, then pass on to burn and clear another.

An alarming report by Dr Lee M. Talbot under a World Wildlife Fund grant in 1965 stressed the dangers now facing the productivity of these islands. Forested areas, he wrote, have declined from 60 per cent of the total land area in 1911 to 30 per cent today. In the same period commercial forests have shrivelled from 50 to 20 per cent. Eighty per cent of this reduction has occurred in the two decades following World

4. Robert E. Huke, *Shadows On The Land*, op. cit.

164

Yakkans, Basilan

Muslim village, Sulu Archipelago

Fishing vinta, Sulu Sea

War Two; in effect, since the United States administration relinquished control. The destruction of forest cover was reducing the flow of rivers and streams during dry seasons, causing violent floods during the Wet, eroding topsoils at a rapid rate and silting up storage reservoirs. The rapid depletion of good timbers could well create a situation where the Philippines, once rich in forest reserves, would have to buy from other countries instead of profiting by its lucrative exports. Forest concessions were granted largely through political influence. Nor was the responsibility of most loggers in rehabilitating or protecting the areas they leased taken seriously. There was no attempt at selective logging, no replacing of fallen trees as in other countries. 'Foresters who try to enforce the law are often threatened with or subjected to reprisals,' the report said.[5]

Other surveys of the period gave an equally distressing account of fisheries being destroyed wholesale by dynamite and other illegal methods, of disastrous overcropping and the careless destruction of costly dam sites in Ilocos, the Mountain Province, Iloilo and Cebu, because no one bothered to police loggers smuggling large quantities of timber to overseas destinations. It should be noted that the foreign owners of timber concessions, notably Americans, strongly observe their obligations.

In 1965 this pillaging of forests was raised to a public scandal by the Angat Dam Affair. Drawn into it were several prominent congressmen, the President and two full companies of the Philippines Army. The Angat River Hydroelectric Scheme, due to be completed that year, was one of the most important projects devised to aid the national economy. At a cost of P217,000,000 it was to provide electric power, water supplies and flood control to Greater Manila, as well as much needed irrigation to the provinces of Bulacan, Rizal and Pampanga. A Philippine company had been engaged to clear 2,300 hectares in the mountains of Bulacan for the dam, yet at the expiry of its contract little more than a quarter of the area had been prepared. On the other hand, commercially rich timber had been felled for miles around, logging roads illegally cut through forbidden areas and thousands of superfeet of timber trucked away, despite Philippine Constabulary security posts set up to police operations. As the *Philippines Free Press*, which first exposed the scandal, commented, 'Illegal loggers are denuding the protected area, and, when it is completely bare of trees, the rains will wash away the soil in the absence of retaining trees; silt will rapidly accumulate and the dam be useless.' Even a reluctant embargo by the President two months later failed to stop the depredations. Eventually the army was forced to send reinforcements to stop logging operations in the hills and the heavy traffic of timber trucks coming and going. At one stage the commanding officer of a detachment of army engineers was warned that, if he interfered, machine guns would fire on his troops. Order was eventually enforced, but only when widespread publicity obliged the President to interrupt his campaign tour to issue fresh directives on the advice of forestry officials. A few months later,

5. Filemon C. Rodriguez, *Manila Times*, 28 December 1964, Manila.

following the change of government, illegal logging began again and is still unchecked. During 1966 Manila was forced to endure severe water rationing, while tens of thousands of citizens carried water by hand to their homes. It was also revealed that millions of pesos allocated to water supplies had vanished.

As Dr Talbot expressed it privately on one occasion, 'It looks as if the Philippines is hell bent on destroying what is left of her once abundant natural resources'.

One of the most touching — and poetic — 'Letters to the Editor' I have ever read expressed for me the full despair of the present climate of destructiveness. It was written by a city man, one Arsenio Espiritu, of Makati, Manila, and published in the *Chronicle* on New Year's Day, 1965. I cannot resist publishing this letter in full. It was headed 'Why Starve in Eden?'

> Sir:— Juan de la Cruz lives in a God-given Eden of 7,000 islands, watered by rivers and surrounded by seas teeming with fish of every variety. In this paradise are delicious fruits of every kind—mangoes, bananas, lanzsones, chicos, atis, papaya, melons, coconuts, star apples, etc. — so that rain or shine, Juan may have something delicious for every day of the year. Besides, the Lord gave him rice, corn, mongo, beans, peanuts, camote, cassava, ubi, yams, and sugar cane. In this Eden, where life is so easy and nature so bountiful, starvation would be a real tragedy. Those of us who have gone around the world and witnessed the often tragic struggles for bare existence declare that without doubt this land is still a natural paradise where food is so plentiful. And this in spite of typhoons, floods, pests, and the heart-breaking efforts of evil politicians to ruin us all.
>
> What if there are droughts? Juan must build irrigation systems to water the dry fields. Do typhoons and floods occur? Juan must build dykes to prevent rivers from flooding rice lands, and canals to facilitate the exit of flood waters. For what is the use of planting rice and watering it, if yearly floods will destroy all?
>
> Must we, Filipinos, starve? Why can't we live without eating rice? God gave us so many substitutes for rice so that we need not starve to death even if rice crops fail. Don't we have enough fish and fruits throughout the year? Bananas, papayas, and coconuts are always in season. We have plenty of sugar. We can always grow enough corn, camote, casava, mongo, and beans. These grow any month and anywhere with little care, especially during the dry season, when rice fields lie idle. If only every town worked hard, we would have, even without rice, an abundance of food. Until we attain self-sufficiency in rice — only God knows when — we must produce enough rice substitutes. Must we import rice? Only the barest minimum, which must not rot in bodegas, nor vanish mysteriously in the hands of thieves and politicians.
>
> Let us spend our millions, not in buying alien rice, but in producing our own rice and its substitutes. Let our scientists and nutrition experts concoct a meal composed of rice substitutes. With the New Year let this nation make an all-out effort to produce enough food for all, and with God's blessing we shall find abundant happiness in honest fruitful work in this our God-given Eden.

Who could quarrel with the humanity of such an appeal? And yet there is quarrelling. It concerns who shall own and control the land, the congressional seats of power, the popular vote. Until these matters have been resolved no further advance into the twentieth century is possible.

CHAPTER 20

Spirit of Bayanihan

*May our hands have the strength of the
roots of her kamagong
And the purposefulness of those of her
farmers in the ricefields.
May our hearts beat as the waves in
Nasugbu and have the courage
Of the Filipino heroes whose blood
colours every scarlet sunset in her
skies.
May our souls have the whiteness of the
foam of her seas
And the dedication of patriots as
Mabini to a nation that is free.*

REV. PATRICIO H. LIM

THE DISASTROUS eruption of Taal volcano in September 1965 forced a new appraisal of the submerged three-fourths of the nation's people. Here, within fifty miles of the capital, was an expression of the deprivations, poverty and latent fears under which so large a proportion of Filipinos exist; the unacknowledged, the patient, the mutely suffering. The explosive terror that overwhelmed some fifty thousand souls living upon and around that placid, picturesque lake, normally a postcard scene for tourists, created an interlude of common sympathy amid the bitter feud ing of a political campaign. Momentarily, at least, everyone became aware of the instabilities, the concealed threats to human life that brood upon what is, after all, a volcanic land.

To suggest that Philippine life takes place upon the brink of a volcano is almost a cliche. Yet Taal symbolizes more than a natural disaster. The eruptive forces are constants in these islands. The miracle is that, normally, they are so readily suppressed. The flashpoint of that eruption produced spontaneous reactions of a varied kind: panic, generosity, violence, greed, mutual aid and a selfless dedication to the sufferings of others.

The first report came from an airline pilot, flying in clear weather at 16,000 feet. It was 2.25 a.m. First came a gigantic explosion. A pillar of fire and smoke, like an atomic blast, towered ahead of him. Upon the small island of Pulo, heart of that once tranquil blue lake, at least five thousand inhabitants were shocked from sleep, breaking blindly out of their *barong-barongs*, driven by panic for some illusory safety. Mothers snatched up babies; men broke through flimsy walls and doors; children

167

rushed for the shoreline, sleep still in their eyes. The old, infirm, crippled, semi-blind blundered and wailed. Those who had boats dragged them to the already boiling water. Others crowded any craft they saw, till they sank beneath the weight of humanity desperate for escape. Some flourished guns, bolos, knives, forcing earlier occupants out of *bancas* and canoes. No one knows how many never left those shores; how many died beneath hot ashes and the breath of fire. Before long homes vanished beneath hot, suppurating mud. Frail shacks built laboriously, and with meagre earnings, were atomized like debris in a typhoon. Even those fortunate enough to reach Lake Taal's outer shores found more ashes falling, and ran for shelter beneath lightning bolts, thunder and sudden torrential rain, while a dawn yellow with fire filtered through black and rolling clouds.

Then came the rescue teams, relief bodies, mobile canteens, emergency clothing depots, all hurriedly improvised from distant Manila. Parties of Constabulary arrived, local police units, army jeeps and trucks, the Red Cross, church and women's organizations, gifts, food rations, bandages, drugs. And, inevitably, certain politicians anxious to expose their good-will for purposes of re-election. There were also those who came to be termed 'flying evacuees', slick characters from the city who drove from one relief centre to another, accepting handouts from the charitable un-wary. But what impressed most deeply was the impulsive generosity of the community at large: the food, funds, amenities so rapidly organized by government bodies, industry, social groups and private citizens. In all, there must have been 70,000 people within that disaster area, and fears grew rapidly that further eruptions might endanger the whole Batangas region. During the first few days three thousand were reported dead or missing.

It was as if Filipinos had for once found a common identity. Lake Taal was only the eye of the storm that might some time break over them all. One lived; one waited; one endured.

How else could people have accustomed themselves to living on that island of Pulo at all? This was not the first catastrophe. Since 1709 eighteen eruptions had been recorded, though only four within the past century and a half. During the eighteenth century Taal belched lava and fire at least once every decade. There was a perpetual cloud above it, electrified, and men raised a giant wooden cross on one barren slope to placate its fury. Having claimed a further 2,000 victims in 1911, the volcano went quiet. Many believed it to be extinct. The authorities periodically urged fisherfolk, rice-planters, the tenders of fruit trees and vegetables to leave this dangerous zone. Always they remained. The soils were too fertile, the waters too richly stocked. Besides, it might never happen again.

The fatal view. Fatalistic. This, above all, is Asia.

And the Philippines.

So is the spirit of mutual aid. There is a special Filipino word for it.

Derived from the Tagalog. Not much is heard these days of *bayanihan*. It is a fine word. It represents the best in traditional barrio life. To translate it is not easy. Literally, it means to work together: co-operation. It has spiritual connotations that are not so readily transcribed. One thinks too often of this as a fragmented society. In its urban, petty bourgeois, mercantile regions anyway; in the ruthlessness of politics; even in the desperation of the common *tao* to survive; landlord against tenant, usurer versus debtor, man in conflict with man. There is also *bayanihan*.

Significantly it comes from the bottom levels of society. One peasant family will help another, without expectation of reward; except for some later return of aid, unsolicited. In the *padis* neighbours frequently plant and reap and winnow together, lend one another ploughs, or seed, or carabao. When government promises fail, as they do so often, villagers will band together to meet their own needs: to build dykes on a fishpond, a jetty for fishermen, irrigation systems, roads, bridges. The essential goodness of the Filipino is too often discoverable only in remote corners of the countryside, in the more primitive barrios. It is a perpetuation of the ancient *barangays*, the clan groupings which sought out and fashioned a common life together.

There was a perceptive touch then in giving this name to one of the nation's two leading dance groups. The Bayanihan Dance Company has done more to create a warm image of the Philippines abroad than all its government agencies or globe-encircling politicos. Since its formation in 1954 to present almost forgotten folk dances at an Asian festival in Pakistan, a succession of brilliantly-trained student groups have toured the United States, Europe, Latin America and Australia, enthusing large audiences with the richness and diversity of Filipino folk arts. Characteristically, the warmest tributes have come from abroad, though I attended one moving performance in Manila's huge Araneta Coliseum, where the company earned an excited reception after its triumphant return from New York and Mexico City. The cynics claimed that it is mere romanticism to revive ancient folk arts in the twentieth century, that these only generate a sense of nostalgic unreality. This is to miss the significance of the Bayanihan troupe. It is essentially an expression of national pride, of a strong and individual culture too long neglected. It is also good theatre. Here you rediscover the varied and colourful elements that have made the modern Filipino, the richly-costumed dancing by one of the Muslim courts, the Pagdiwata ritual that follows rice harvesting in Palawan, the savage exultation of Ifugao and Kalinga dances, the Spanish influences of the traditional Paseo de Ilo Ilo and Jota Caviteño, and the freshness and exuberance of barrio fiestas.

'I have sometimes been asked why we can't produce something like the spectacular, harsh, fighting dances of the Russians,' the Bayanihan choreographer, Lucrecia Reyes Urtula, once said. 'All I can answer is that our people aren't like that. They have a different attitude to life. They are gentle. They have grace and a sense of fun. They can reflect the languor-

169

ous mood of the Carinsa and the Fandango, the mystic quality of the Mountain Dances and the fierce pride of Muslim dancing. This is the Philippines.'

Significant, too, are the influences which brought this venture into being, as well as creating a permanent research group to recover the authentic music, poetry, literature and dance from a discarded past. The Bayanihan Folk Arts Centre was created by the Philippine Women's University, whose principals are among the most socially-aware people in the country. They are the inheritors of the *ilustrado* system. The dancers and musicians themselves are largely students, the sons and daughters of prominent families, devoting themselves to performances of quality and high professionalism, with no commercial overtones. They are not even paid. The group consciousness engendered by these dedicated young people is in the proper spirit of Bayanihan.

You have to savour the normal patterns of Filipino life, in Manila especially, to appreciate how rare this attitude has become. One Bayanihan performance prompted the *Manila Times* columnist, Alfredo R. Roces, to reflect on certain other national characteristics: 'Many Filipinos copy contemporary American singers who emphasize more their gyration and less their singing,' he commented. 'At basketball games cheer leaders have become more and more exhibitionistic. Big shots love to strut around in the *rigodon* in the big social events of the town. The Santa Cruz de Mayo had become, not a religious event, but a spectacle with movie stars and fabulous gowns. Our houses, our cars, our love for banlon and "blue seal", what are they but reflections of this exhibitionistic trait? Our big weakness has been our vanity and one expression of this is exhibitionism. In the dance it is loveable, but in real life it is our undoing.'

Conspicuous consumption is the term in vogue today. The usual inference is that it stemmed from America. Bayanihan researches tend to disprove this. 'Don't forget,' said one pre-war politician, 'that the usurious money-lender makes his living from marriage feasts, births and fiestas.' The hungry society that greeted post-war independence had a hunger for more than food, clothing and basic shelter. It was for nylons and lipsticks, Scotch whisky, two-tone convertibles, mistresses, the neon glitter of hotel lobbies, the flash nightclub and discreet, off-colour bar. In a society where only one per cent is rich, such goals are not easily attained, or not by gentle means. Yet esteem goes, as it has done since pre-hispanic times, to the affluent, the free spender, the man of patronage and *chiarismo*. One has only to read the extravagant society columns in Manila, the credits to certain expensive couturiers, or watch the chauffeur-driven limousines drawn up outside the Forbes Park mansions or the hotel reception, the luxurious political conventions, the lush furnishings of restaurants, night clubs, gambling halls to delineate the ambitions of the élite and would-be so today.

'In an attempt to bridge the big gap between the rich and the poor,' the

Jesuit sociologist Father Jaime Bulatao told a seminar of women journalists in 1964, 'I would urge society women to talk and listen to others outside their own groups. Let them become part of the people sharing the feeling of a daughter who weeps when there is no rice; of a fisherman who has to sell his boat to buy medicine for the tubercular wife. Let the society woman sit beside such people and the diamond necklace around her neck will begin to choke, the half-million-peso tiara become an unbearable weight upon her head. How much do I wish that the women in society pages could direct their energies, their brains and their beauty to a cause greater than their own selves, to their own country which now so sorely needs them.'[1]

These attitudes, of course, are by no means uniquely Filipino. However, you do question in a context of mass poverty, the wisdom of publishing photographs of champagne receptions at Malacanang, the prices paid for evening gowns at a wedding party or the fact that ladies at resplendent luncheons carry home oversize steaks to feed pet dogs. It says much for the tranquil nature of the Filipino that so little unrest exists, unless you look more deeply into the ever-rising graph of violent crime. The dogmatic Marxian would be baffled by a social order of this kind. There are no comparable societies in the West, except possibly Spain. The roots of this acceptance of privilege can be found in much earlier times. A revealing social study on peasant attitudes, carried out by the University of the Philippines in 1955, suggested that common attitudes have changed little in centuries. Its leader, John E. de Young, concluded that, at barrio level, the social structure has always been authoritarian, creating a constant 'father image' and still finds a ready acceptance. The image of the leader is almost always associated with power, wealth and prestige; it is paternalistic; it stands for protection against the unknown enemy or hostile force of nature beyond. The *tao* looks always to his elders for guidance and leadership, he fears change or youthful inexperience. He accepts.[2]

Status symbols, it seems, are not wholly an American invention.

Superimposed on the Malay heritage is the equally authoritarian outlook of Spanish Catholicism. This was transplanted during the most illiberal period in Spain's history, undermining the more open structure of native life: the easier relationship between classes, the clan structure, the principles of *bayanihan*. No humanistic values were imported to replace them. The seventeenth and eighteenth centuries were periods when the Spanish hierarchy attempted to stifle the spread of scientific thought. Copernicus, Leonardo, Galileo were anathema; the Renaissance did not penetrate the boundaries of Spain, while Sinibaldo de Mas, an early nineteenth century diplomat, recommended the closure of men's colleges in Manila for fear they might breed liberals and rebels. It was

1. *Manila Times,* 23 September 1964, Manila.

2. 'A Pilot Study on Communication Problems in the Barrio', Social Science Research Centre, University of the Philippines, Manila, 1955.

not, in fact, until the twentieth century that the Philippines faithful were allowed to know of Galileo's theory that the earth moved round the sun, and not vice versa. Not that Filipino fisherfolk, or any others charting their existence by the stars, were ever so deceived. The effect of this cosmology on education, as Rizal frequently observed, was a crucial one.

'The clerical intellectual tradition in the Philippines looked down on the Filipinos — the *Indios* — as either less than human, or as perpetual children who were not endowed with enough reason to be responsible for their acts.' So wrote Professor Leopoldo Y. Yorkes, of the Graduate School of Arts and Sciences, University of the Philippines. 'During most of the Spanish regime (the tradition) could hardly deserve to be called intellectual, because the friar-missionaries that came here were as a rule not endowed with a high quality of intelligence and were not well educated, in contrast to their confreres in Europe.'[3] Questioning the claim that the main object of the friars had been to stamp out superstition among the pagan natives, Professor Yorkes referred to a nineteenth century monograph written by T. H. Pardo de Tavera, one of the leaders of the Propaganda movement. De Tavera wrote:

> The patron saints recommended by the missionaries took the place of the ancient *anitos*, representatives of their ancestors who intervened in their former idolatry in all the incidents of life. . . . When the missionaries preached their religion, they condemned the ancient pagan superstitions, but they taught another new superstition more powerful than the primitive one . . . because of the prestige of the new patrons, who are all members of the celestial court organized like a celestial aristocracy . . .[4]

Hence Juan de la Cruz tends still to pray for rain rather than conserve water, makes his harvest offering at wayside shrines, carries the image of the Virgin through the streets at fiesta time, dances the *Pit Senyor* before the Santo Niño in Cebu City and perpetuates his miraculous legends of Our Lady of Pilar outside the ancient fortress in Zamboanga. Rural folk in Badian, Cebu Island, struggle to catch the calachuchi petals showered by infant 'angels' upon holy images on Easter Sunday, believing these will bring them good luck, while farmers bury them in the fields knowing they will increase crops. During Holy Week the *penitentes* of Marinduque roam the streets in the guise of Roman soldiers, while the famous *flagellantes* of Vinzon whip one another publicly with iron chains, thereby attaining 'desperate wishes' and cleansing the soul. In other rural areas Palm Sunday inspires peasant folk to decorate their doors and windows with palm-leaf crosses to exorcise evil spirits. In Tanauan, Leyte, Our Lady of the Assumption is known to have saved the town from the typhoon of October 1889 by walking on the crests of a wild sea, while

3. Leopoldo Y. Yorkes, 'Two Intellectual Traditions', *Asian Studies V*, 1964, University of the Philippines, Manila.

4. T. H. Pardo de Tavera, *The Character of Rizal and the Legacy of Obscurantism*. Manila, 1960.

church bells carried parishioners to prayer. Eight years later, during a cholera epidemic, her image vanished nightly from the local church, appearing at the bedsides of those who were not sick to comfort them, persuading them thereafter to carry her through the streets every day for seven days. She was seen again during the disastrous floods of November 1928 when she was said to have dug with her bare hands a canal that miraculously carried the raging waters out to sea. Her last appearance was in 1939, during a fire that destroyed a large portion of the town. The Virgin, it is claimed, was seen measuring certain street blocks with a length of abaca string, and by this action confined the flames only to that section of Tanauan.

While I was in Mindanao during 1964, a college student in Bukidnon was inexplicably struck blind. For no known reason she fell unconscious in her dormitory at Mountain View College, Malaybalay. Prayers were said for her without avail. She was then flown to Manila where, according to one newspaper report, an eye-specialist examined her and could find no physical defect, while X-rays of her skull produced negative results. 'Then,' reported the *Manila Bulletin*, 'on the night of September 28, at 9.20, it happened. While a nurse was praying at her side, Elsa felt a big cold hand on her chin and went through her face to her forehead. "It frightened me very much," she said. Slowly she opened her eyes and saw the hand that touched it until she saw it no more. She said she even felt part of the sleeve which touched her face. . . . Now she could see. . . . Excitement rose to a high pitch among the nurses. . . . She believes that miracles are not only for Biblical times.' The report noted that Elsa had decided not to go back to Bukidnon, transferring to a Manila college instead.

Psychological studies are still rare in the Philippines. However, sociologists have been carrying out much significant research. They have come to recognize a curious duality in the common Filipino outlook that makes adjustment to the demands of modern living excessively difficult. Most modern societies have their deep-rooted frustrations; it is all part of the increasing pace, complexity and competitiveness of life. The Philippines has been subjected to far more exacting pressures. The drive towards industrialism and urban living, the uprooting of the once stable peasant order, the crowding of millions into cities where worse poverty awaits them, the appalling rise in crime, the paucity of educational facilities and standards, the heritage of superstition that leaves people ill-equipped to cope with increasing materialism, the economic hardships, corruption and ungovernable expansion of population, the failure to repair wartime devastation in the moral as well as physical sector; all this has fashioned a rigid, iron-cased jacket that gouges, bruises and jars the flesh at every turn.

What has happened to the joyous hopes that greeted liberation, and republican independence? The people were at once plunged into an authoritarian regime as ruthless as the Japanese had been. The guerrillas who had emerged as heroes found themselves discarded, unrewarded, often treated as criminals, while the collaborators took control. What had they fought for, after all? Disillusion, cynicism, a grab-what-you-can philosophy replaced the relatively easy-going attitudes of pre-war days. This has been accompanied by a break-up of a once firmly-ordered family organization, widespread juvenile delinquency, parental irresponsibility and a corrosive feeling that the whole world was out of control. A paternalistic past had left modern citizens wholly unable to deal with such an anarchistic age.

From this, I feel, has arisen the present preoccupation with creating a favourable 'Filipino image'. What the foreigner thinks has become all-important. It appears to involve questions of national pride, as well as a sense of inferiority that is often as painful as it is undeserved. Perhaps a sense of inadequacy expresses it better. This finds expression in the common 'I am ashamed'. The Tagalog word *hiya*, though usually translated as shame, really comes closer to embarrassment. Its equivalent among the Polynesians is *haama*, and has the same connotations of shyness that finds expression first in excessive modesty and then, only too often, in compensating arrogance or pride. Is this due, I wonder, to heredity or the pressures of environment? It was most clearly summed up for me by a highly-educated Filipino friend of mine.

'You couldn't understand how we feel,' he told me. 'For nearly four centuries we were under the heel of the Spaniard. He made no secret of his superiority. Then came the Americans. They, too, made it clear how much better their civilization was. When the Japanese came, they made us bow to their soldiers in the streets. We have never had the chance to be ourselves.'

Hence the gentleness of the Filipino that has so enchanted foreigners can give way, quite unexpectedly, to an aggressive outlook, even to violence. Offence is often taken without apparent reason. In the midst of some smiling conversation, the mask abruptly falls, and you do not know why. You are reminded that Filipinos are a proud people. Yet, only too often, this pride becomes indistinguishable from vanity. These symptoms have been analysed by an American sociologist, Professor George M. Guthrie, formerly attached to the Philippine Normal College, the teacher training centre in Manila. Filipinos, he wrote, were an ambivalent people: their private outlook frequently contradicted social practice; they lacked pride in the civic sphere, yet had a highly-developed personal pride. 'People are quite outgoing to strangers,' he added, 'but very competitive among themselves. It may be more than competitiveness, because so many carry guns and have bodyguards. . . . The Philippines has been called a shame society rather than a guilt society, because of the importance of each individual to the opinions of others.'[5]

He listed a number of social trends inherited over many generations.

5. George M. Guthrie, *The Filipino Child and Philippine Society*, Philippine Normal College Press, Manila, 1961.

These were:

Amor proprio, a high degree of sensitivity and pride which, if wounded even unintentionally, could lead to revenge. *Bahala na*, equivalent to the Russian *nitchevo*, representing passive acceptance, fatalism. *Ningas cogon*, quickly waning enthusiasms. *Mañana*, procrastination. *Pasikat*, showing off. *Extravagance*, closely related to *pasikat*, and evidenced in many fields from fiestas to high society. *Striving for status. Imitation*, especially in the adoption of supposedly superior foreign styles, notably American. *Inferiority*, as expressed in a preference for imported goods, ideas and judgments. *Utang na loob*, literally a debt to insiders, and involving exclusive loyalty to a family or special group at the expense of society at large. This provides the basis, in the political field, for nepotism, graft and an apparent indifference to the national welfare.

It is no accident that Malay languages have two forms of the first person plural. The inclusive We, *tayo*, means you and I; the exclusive We, *kami*, means he and I. In social practice, too, there is a significant difference. 'The Filipino's *kami* is still very limited,' writes Father Bulatao. 'His *kami* does not include the nation. It is circumscribed within a limited in-group composed of friends and relatives. The government employee does not realize that his new duty as public servant binds him to serve the nation, that the nation cannot be hurt without hurting him, too.' The result is all too frequently *lagay*, the expected bribe as a stimulus to action. However, as the priest concedes, the *lagay*-conscious man often uses the questionable money he gains to support his parents, find jobs for his nephews and put his near relatives through school and college. What strikes the foreigner as public immorality is not necessarily immoral to the Filipino.[6]

The perceptive Father Bulatao's remedies are better education, more emphasis on individual as opposed to group values, and a gentler hand in ruling family life.

'One may suggest the unifying concept of an ego highly in need of security and protection,' he wrote. 'Possibly as a result of the tender and highly protected upbringing received by the child, the ego seeks to maintain a similar environment when it grows up. . . . It protects itself against the harsh world outside the family by great carefulness not to take unnecessary risks (traditionalism), to be careful of what other people say (*hiya*), not to antagonize others or create potential enemies, to seek the approval and protection of important people (authoritarianism). It prefers to suffer a loss in patience, since suffering is preferable to insecurity. Only when the self is attacked, as when the authority figure withdraws its approval and the ego is hurt (*amor proprio*) does there come the possibility of explosive retaliation.'

This was my first key to the puzzling outbursts of violence that happen so frequently throughout the archipelago. The amok is a well-known Malay phenomenon. The victim of it does not give expression to normal

6. Father Jaime Bulatao, S.J., *Philippine Studies*, X, 1962, Manila.

anger. It is an uncontrollable reaction. Like the *juramentado*, to which he is clearly related, the amok will often attack without provocation, indiscriminately. It appears almost as a form of temporary insanity. When this passes, the man will usually be unaware of what he has done and show no remorse. I remember one case in Manila of a young clerk going berserk in a city office, killing one of his fellow workers with a dagger and wounding two others. The subsequent explanation was given as wife trouble at home. What startles the observer is the senseless savagery with which such assaults are committed. A random list of amok cases reported during two months of my stay in the Philippines reveals a barbarity unknown this side of the Congo.

On Christmas Eve, of all days, a man stoned his brother to death in Negros Oriental for selling a pair of trousers; a Samar policeman was shot trying to prevent someone exploding dangerous fire-crackers; a fireman, also in Samar, beat his argumentative colleague to death with a stone. On Christmas morning one straphanger in a crowded Manila bus accidentally bumped another, whose friend immediately stabbed him. Less exuberant times of the year brought their own violence. In Zamboanga del Sur a housewife was slashed to pieces by a young man she had 'spread gossip about'. A Laguna farmer was hacked to death for refusing to pay a boatman the price of a fish. In Rizal a servant girl hacked off her mistress's arm with a bolo because of unspecified 'scoldings'. The Santiago mayor, his brother and a bank officer quarrelled over the mahjong table and all finished in hospital with multiple knife and gun wounds. In Davao an *aficionado* stabbed another for 'untying the gaff of his fighting cock', whereupon the stabber was beaten to death with a length of lumber. In Leyte, for disturbing their assailants with songs, two brothers were sliced to small pieces with bolos. A Dipolog ranch hand, caught in the act of stealing a carabao, later ambushed his accuser, shot him three times, hammered his face with a heavy stone and threw him into a crocodile-infested river.

One of the most appalling cases concerned two identical twins from Samar who ran amok on the Bicol Express in 1965. I had been on the point of taking this train to Legaspi, because I wanted to visit the Mayon volcano. I was persuaded not to do so. To call this 400-mile journey an express route is overstating things, for it averages less than twenty miles an hour all the way from Manila to Legaspi. This does not include derailments, inexplicable halts miles from anywhere, breakdowns caused by corroded sixty-year-old tracks, unstable bridges and the fact that much of the rolling stock are mere survivals of Japanese bombing. Hot, airless, overcrowded coaches wear tempers pretty thin, especially when crowds surge aboard at every station, many without even buying tickets. It is commonly said that the only people who profit from this almost bankrupt government railway are the conductors and inspectors who make private deals with travellers. On this particular journey the Toleng brothers found themselves jammed among the sweating, third-class passengers.

176

Samar people are superstitious and moody at the best of times. Jose and Antonio Toleng were especially so, with bony faces and dark, sunken eyes, sitting there silent and withdrawn. No one knows what started it. Some said they had been twitted for their peculiar likeness to one another; others that a woman slapped their faces for refusing to give her a seat, or that a man had demanded money.

Whatever it was, they went suddenly amok. Jose pulled out a six-inch knife; his brother sharp scissors. Panic surged through the coach, which was crowded with women and babies, though some never woke again. The conductor was swept off his feet, panicked and forgot to pull the alarm cord. One bystander let go with his pistol. When the train pulled into Calamba twelve were dead, eight wounded, while six more corpses were scattered along the track. The Toleng brothers, when police came, showed neither emotion nor remorse. It was as if they had no awareness of what they had done.

Obviously there must have been abnormal psychological tensions to produce an explosive violence of that kind. Not even the hazards and discomforts of the Bicol Express alone could have done so. In hundreds of cases the situation becomes more deadly because of the prevalent habit of carrying guns, daggers, knives and bolos. Essentially, the bolo is not a weapon of offence, because it is the peasant-farmer's tool of trade. But two feet of bare steel can be put to other uses than cutting rice plants or coconuts. In other lands the most savage quarrel usually ends in a fist fight or a broken skull. Here, too often, the result is death. Initially the assault may often be explained in terms of offended pride. Unfortunately, this pride — and its allied exhibitionism — encourages the carrying of lethal arms.

How can this be reconciled with the gentle characters you meet in the barrios, the smiling peasant who offers you the modest hospitality of his *nipa* hut. He will offer you food and drink which he can ill-afford. He enjoys himself in relaxed fashion at fiestas, cock fights, dancing and picture shows. The labourer in the city, too, is friendly enough, if shy, on first acquaintance. Then, without warning, the volcano blows its lid.

The nearest I have come to an explanation is Professor Guthrie's monograph on the Filipino child. 'He is circumscribed in his opportunities to show anger,' he writes. 'He may have a tantrum, but must expect humiliation, for he cannot strike back without fear of reprisals. He is often the subject of teasing, for which there is no easy retaliation. It would appear that he learns to deny the anger which children in a different society express. Children are raised to be humble, respectful and obedient. Lower class Filipinos are very authoritarian with their children. There is little room for rebellion. It is tempting to try to relate this suppression of anger to the amok phenomenon in adulthood.'

If this is really so, you can only imagine what passions continually simmer below the impassive or smiling exterior. It is at least one explanation for the prevailing climate of fear.

There is also strong medical evidence to suggest a very high rate of schizophrenia and paranoia, though even normal health services are so rudimentary in most provinces that this can be little more than conjecture. In 1965 the chairman of the Philippine Mental Health Association, Dr Alvaro L. Martinez, told a conference in Manila that he believed psychiatric treatment to be an absolute essential for combating modern crime, especially among youthful delinquents. He discussed the characteristics of a number of well-known Manila gangsters and criminals in pathological terms. He estimated that between 20,000 and 30,000 crimes committed the previous year called for specialized treatment. He attributed much of the social disorder to the effects of Japanese torture during the Occupation, the wartime privations of the young, their lack of schooling and incitement to robbery and force as a means of livelihood, followed by the excesses and corruption of the post-war period. All this, he said, had produced a sick society, a desperate confusion of frustrated and troubled egos, and the self-destroying struggle to climb the rice ladder. When one visitor to the Association's psychiatric clinic — the only one of its kind in the entire country — complimented a specialist on the 'sweet nature' of the patients, the psychiatrist replied:

'They are very shy people. Their shyness can easily be turned to savagery.'

A notable factor of all this social instability is that it appears largely restricted to the behaviour of the male. Women seldom seem to be involved in acts of violence, nor in mental aberration. The women are the strong sex in this land, the stabilizing influence. It has always been so. There is evidence that, in some regions at least, the pre-hispanic Malays had a matriarchal society. In the Visayan Islands, for instance, pagan worship was largely in the hands of sibyls and priestesses. There were certainly more of them than male priests. Pigs sacrificed to the gods had to be consecrated by women, who called upon their own sex to carry out the ritual eating of the meat. Women also carried out ceremonies for the dead, and conserved the idols. There are records of rajas, attending ceremonies, who were expected to walk behind their wives. The main resistance to Christianity is said to have come from the priestesses, not the gaudily-plumaged male warriors. Ironically, when the male leaders of the 1898 Revolution wanted to destroy the power of Catholicism, so embittered were they against the friars, it was their womenfolk who remained within the Church, providing the main support for a native priesthood. Yet it was this same Church which had attempted to remove the power of women over public life, reducing them to inferior status, the mere bearers of babies.

In Malay times woman had been the important figure. And, of course, lacking in the coyness and pseudo-virginity a celibate priesthood demanded under Spain, though by no means always enforced upon the peasantry's luckless daughters. Nick Joaquin, a man of considerable religious insights, has written of the Conquistadores waging their early struggles in terms of sexual symbolism.

'The emulation between moon and sun explodes in every encounter of Christianity with paganism. The drama of Philippine conversion was really mostly a struggle between old native female cults and the new masculine religion. . . . The painful sexual contraptions the males had to wear from childhood, because the women required them, indicates not only an extreme sensuality (indeed noted by the early voyagers) but also a rather sadistic domination of the male. The Filipino's *machismo*, on the other hand, may spring from a nervous memory of the old order, when his phallus was fettered; and he asserts himself both to deny the past and to prevent its recurrence.'

There is no question that, in modern times, this *machismo* is being vigorously asserted.

Yet it would be wrong to assume that the women of today are in any aggressive sense matriarchal. I know no other country where women grace public and social life in quite such a natural way, even in the United States or England, where women have long taken for granted their place in parliament or the universities. Filipino women — at a sophisticated or middle-class level — are among the most beautiful and elegant in the world. At peasant levels, of course, life is too hard to acquire much elegance. Yet there, too, women have always had an important role. They not only plant rice beside their men, winnow the seed, drive the carabao, trade in the markets and wayside stores. They are also masters of their families, concerning themselves with financial affairs, negotiations with landowners, selling the crop and lending money. The women of ancient Malay times had equal political rights. Property was divided equally between sons and daughters and, when a husband died, the wife not his eldest son succeeded as head of the family. Any man who insulted a woman in public was harshly punished by the law. If she was of high rank, he was sent into slavery. The Tagalog name for a wife is *maybanay*, whose literal meaning is 'one who owns my house'.

In the creation myths of the ancient Malays the first woman was not a spare rib drawn from the Filipino Adam. Both man and woman were said to have emerged together from two different stems of a bamboo tree. They were, in fact, created equal — and it has been hard to persuade women of anything else since. There are also women historians who like to remind people of the famous Princess Urduja, who once ruled over the people of Pangasinan. Legend has it that she led an army of Amazons against a neighbouring tribe, with a body of women councillors for her own retinue.

Not that the modern Filipina is by any means an amazon. The most feminine of creatures, she delights in the elegant *terno* and Maria Clara, with their butterfly sleeves and fine embroidery. However, none can doubt her active role in public affairs. In Manila I knew a number of women who ran large business enterprises, others who were executives in banks, insurance companies and private firms. They have, of course, one advantage over the women of most other countries. Servants are plentiful, and still remarkably cheap to employ. Nor is it only the wealthy families who employ them. In most middle-class homes you will find two or even three servants, though my own experience was that the normal housewife — if she stayed at home — could do the work more easily and efficiently than the primitive women from the provinces she engaged. Without them, however, it would be impossible for mothers of eight and nine children to take so energetic a part in social life and commerce. As Professor Guthrie expressed it: 'In the Philippines the woman's place is in the home — and in the office, too.'

Yet, even here, the quickening pace of life is having its effect on the domestic stability of earlier times. In this predominantly Roman Catholic country there is no divorce, though the number of separations and 'common law' wives has become very considerable. It is to these broken homes that much of the juvenile delinquency has been attributed. As one prominent Malineña expressed it to me: 'It is the women who have let home life down today. The wealthy ones. They think too much of their social affairs, their business careers, making money. They are neglecting their families.' And another, a young university graduate: 'We used to be a people with high standards of morality. Now we have double standards. Our lack of ethics has become so widespread that I don't see how we can ever recover those we once had. I believe that one of the worst aspects today is the perpetual reliance on servants. They are left to look after the children from the time they start walking. It is the un-educated maids who bring up children now. You can imagine what they teach them — all the old superstitions, the worst values, the shoddiest of ideas that cultured families in the old days would never have allowed their sons and daughters to acquire.

Chief among these shoddy ideas, infinitely pervasive, are the values spread by television and local Tagalog-language films. Psychologists throughout the world are divided on the impact that filmed and televised violence has upon the impressionable young. But there is no doubt that, in so anarchical a society as the Philippines, the effects are unsettling and destructive. Mass culture is one of appallingly low standards: literature, the visual arts, music — even indigenous music of a folk or national kind — are restricted to a small cultivated minority. The government takes no interest whatever in the arts. Commercial television — there are no pro-grammes of a more enlightened kind — has nothing to offer beyond the more sensational of mass-produced American fare. There is a large and thriving local film industry, but its productions merely imitate the most banal, low-grade Hollywood crime films and westerns. I know of few things more absurd than imitating America's 'Wild West' in Philippine settings, complete with gun-slinging Filipino heroes in American cowboy dress. These find an enthusiastic market among what is called 'the *bakya* mob' (the clog-wearing set) .

The hero of the masses is no longer Jose Rizal, despite the number of city and provincial statues, the lip-service paid to him by politicians and the study of his writings in school. The modern heroes are the rugged, sharp-shooting Jose Estrada, with inexhaustible revolvers and ten-gallon hat, and Romeo Vasquez riding the crook-infested *pampas* to rescue kidnapped, brown-skinned heroines. On the TV and cinema screen no solution to man's problems is ever depicted that cannot be made with bullets. The Filipino is given no answer to the stresses of modern life but guns, just as he was under the Occupation, in the post-war epoch of grafting and blackmarkets. And tens of thousands among these audiences are daily familiar with the feel of their own concealed guns.

What better symbol of a diseased climate of culture than the real-life love triangle that ended with death by gunshots in a Manila cinema during 1964. A Tagalog 'western' was actually being shown at the time.

The volcano still rumbles.

CHAPTER 21

Climate of Fear

*Economic malnutrition, not juvenile
delinquency, is our biggest problem. Once
the basic needs — food, clothing and
shelter — are beyond reach, you have
insecurity, and that leads to an overt act
against society. Poverty is a vacuum; and,
in this instance, the stopgap is crime.*

ALVARO L. MARTINEZ

I HAVE lived in some fairly hazardous places in my time: Panama City,
back country Mexico, the restricted frontier of New Guinea. But I have
yet to experience tensions comparable with those of Manila, or, to a lesser
degree, the provinces. You soon learn to watch every figure approaching
along the street, the loiterer, the man who asks you for a light, the taxi
driver ('Never travel by taxi without taking down its number'), the
figures strolling behind you, or standing outside your door by night.
Perhaps, if you were warned less often, if Filipinos themselves were less
uneasy, these fears would seem irrational, not worth a moment's thought.
At times it seems almost like childhood fears of the dark.

It is almost impossible to believe that, somewhere in the Philippines,
twenty murders take place each day. Yet these are official figures from
the National Bureau of Investigation. In 1963 the homicide figure rose to
a total of 7,403. A year later it had reached the 8,000 mark. The N.B.I.
has followed American precedents by publishing what it terms a 'crime
clock'. It is a grim way of reading modern times. Among its major listings
in 1965 were these: murders and homicide, one every hour; rape or sexual
assault, one every two hours; robbery with violence, every two hours;
theft, every half-hour; *estafa* and falsification, one every two hours.
'Such crimes as murder rose by 28·3 per cent in Manila,' the report
stated, 34·9 per cent in the Ilocos region, 37·9 per cent in Cagayan,
Isabela and Nueva Vizcaya, and 32·3 per cent in the Bicol region. There
was also a 50 per cent increase in juvenile arrests on charges of murder,
homicide, parricide and infanticide. In Manila many of the hoodlums
are youngsters, including scions of prominent officials or businessmen.'[1]

No wonder the Philippines ambassador to South Vietnam remarked
undiplomatically as he was leaving Manila's airport in 1965, 'I'll be glad
to get back to Saigon. It's safer. In Saigon at least you don't see so many
tough-looking characters hanging around the lobbies of hotels.'

1. *Philippines Free Press*, 19 September 1964, Manila.

A Manila columnist replied: 'Didn't the ambassador know? Those toughies in the hotel lobby weren't gangsters. They were police. Nowadays it's not easy to tell the difference.'

The Manila press has a cynicism matched only by its candid reflection of administrative and private scandals that most newspapers overseas so often, and not always for the best motives, prefer to evade. If Filipinos complain, as they do frequently, of having an unfavourable 'image' abroad, it is the candour of their own newspapers they should deplore, for they are fearless in reporting uncomfortable truths. The Philippines press must surely be the freest in the world. Its uninhibited reporting, though sometimes short on facts, is one of the guarantees of democratic thinking. Several efforts to impose some form of censorship, mainly by sensitive or angry congressmen, have so far failed. There are three reasons for the remarkable freedom the press enjoys. It was a principal inherited from the United States; it is written into the constitution, and it allows the influential newspaper owners to conduct political campaigns in which they are so interminably involved in a manner free enough to discredit their rivals. I would hate to think of the Philippines under a controlled press. It could only exacerbate the climate of fear.

Yet how real are these fears so constantly haunting the general citizen, rich or poor, politician or elector, gangster or policeman on patrol? How dangerous is it to leave the bedroom window open on humid nights, live in a house without a fifteen-foot protective wall, not to have uniformed guards outside banks, offices, apartment blocks, or to drink in a Pasay City bar without a gun? In the foyers of most government and commercial buildings, nightclubs or even restaurants you are greeted with a prominent sign that reads:

> Pursuant of Ordinance No. 3820, possessors of firearms and other dangerous weapons not authorized as security guards and other special services are requested to deposit their weapons here.

Of course, nobody complies.

At times I felt that Manileños were hypnotizing themselves with their fears, deepening them each time they bolted the front door or iron-grilled gate, sent their daughters off to school in the chauffeur-driven car, put the oiled revolver under their pillows at night. Perhaps it was a heritage of Spanish times, a form of paranoia. Look around the streets and towns Spain built, not only in Manila, and the dominant architectural forms are the walled courtyard, iron window grilles, immense doorlocks — the expressed fears in stone and metal of a hostile outer world. The Spaniard seldom went out to meet that world, took no social action to placate it. Instead, he locked himself away inside his domestic fortress, and was finally overwhelmed.

Today, on the other hand, it could be dangerous to hold these fears illusory. The daily crime reports occupying columns in the newspapers carry their own alarm. It has been reflected in the reluctance of overseas tourist agencies to recommend travel, despite a government-sponsored conference in 1965 to discuss ways of protecting tourists from assault, thievery and confidence tricks. The existing practice is to restrict recommended tours to a handful of reasonably safe resorts. Day tours to the beauties of Lake Taal, for instance, are still listed, though motorists are advised to return well before dark. I have friends who will not drive to Batangas and other nearby provinces along a certain stretch of highway, even if police road-blocks check passing cars and Cavite bandits keep mostly to the hills. Most Filipinos travelling north to the mountain resort of Baguio, preferably in daylight, keep a gun in the glove box or under the seat. Highway Three is one of the world's most scenic, but it runs through provinces where the Huks are once more terrorizing farmers and holding motorists to ransom.

Public alarm over the continued rise in crime was touched off late in 1964 by what came to be known as the Grand Opera House Affair. It was a theatrical event. Gunmen burst into the crowded foyer of this vaudeville theatre late one afternoon, fired pistolized carbines at random and drove off as a traffic policeman answered their shots, more to the peril of pedestrians than the fleeing protection gang. For weeks police were curiously unable to trace the bandits, though their whereabouts were reported almost daily in the press. Finally, the ringleader — who had been hiding first in a film star's house, then on a politician's country estate — promised to give himself up, if the chief of police would come for him in person. Subsequent interviews on television increased the gunman's glamour.

Investigations revealed that another gang member, long ago charged with murder, had never had a warrant served on him. This led to the discovery that more than 9,000 warrants had gone unserved since 1960. Many, which had been served, failed to bring anyone into court. In July 1964 alone, 240 listed cases had to be abandoned because no one turned up. Another 355 men accused of homicide, robbery, rape appeared to have vanished from the earth. Frequently key witnesses failed to arrive. The reasons given were intimidation, money changing hands, political interference and the fact that bail was usually arranged, at high rates of interest, by at least one hundred different surety companies with long records of unrecovered debts. None of these had been prosecuted, but remained in business and were not asked to recompense the courts.

A few weeks later criminal investigators found that at least 3,000 convicts had escaped from the maximum-security Muntinlupa gaol. No attempt had been made to search for them, while police departments had neither dossiers nor photographs. A minor traffic accident in the city brought further revelations. A plainclothes policeman happened to be visiting the office of a lawyer, then handling the insurance claim, and recognized the two men involved as convicts under life sentence. It seemed they had taken french leave from Fort Bonifacio army camp, where they had been given light duties cutting grass. A further inquiry revealed that 1,721 criminals had been secretly released 'on parole' long before their terms were due to expire.

One congressman, a Nacionalista, attempted to explain this by claiming that, since the appointment of a new director of prisons by the Liberal administration in 1962, '665 hardened criminals, life termers and death convicts, among whom are homicidal maniacs, pathological killers, kidnappers, rapists, Huks, swindlers and sex perverts, were let loose with scant security from Muntinlupa prison for as long as three days at a time, ostensibly to seek monetary contributions, forage for supplies and confer with political leaders'.

A campaign initiated by the *Manila Times* forced the administration to call a police conference, after which the commanding officer of the Philippine Constabulary ordered a nation-wide drive against bandits. Evidence showed that more than a hundred armed gangs were preying on highways through the country. No arrests had been reported a year later.

In November 1964 Manila police discovered that a gang of one hundred escaped criminals was terrorizing city and suburbs. By day they worked at gasoline stations, hamburger stalls, sidewalk *sari-sari* stores, or as shoeshine boys and car-watchers. All, according to the records, were still in jail. Police estimated that the gang had killed at least twenty people, apart from carrying out an average of ten hold-ups, assaults and bag-snatchings nightly. In Quezon City similar terrorism was being practised by the *Bahala Na* gang. It was said to operate without police inter ference, because 'sons of local government officials are involved'. A retired army colonel, who had been assaulted with an iron bar and robbed, told the press that the Quezon City police force took no action 'because it is under the thumb of politicians protecting the gang'. When one over-zealous policeman tried to make an arrest he was stabbed to death and a city councillor was charged with his three sons. The case was subsequently, in the common phrase, 'lost'.

Commentators who suggested that the crime wave might be ended by bringing criminals to trial, producing key witnesses and keeping the guilty in gaol were considered somewhat naive. Justice just did not operate in this fashion.

Nor it seemed did the curfew system introduced some years earlier. Every night at nine — ten o'clock in Quezon City — the wail of air-raid sirens warns juveniles to leave the streets. The wartime sirens still wail. The juveniles remain on the streets, and no action is taken by the police. Yet it is among youth that crime has taken most serious root. Seventy per cent of Manila's knifings, according to a 1964 survey, were committed by juveniles.[2]

Poverty is the mother of crime, said Addison. Had he lived today he might have revised his judgement, especially in the world's affluent societies. In the Philippines, too, crimes with violence are frequently

2. *The Plain Truth About Child Rearing*, Ambassador College Press, Manila, 1964.

unrelated to want. In Capiz a municipal judge shoots his wealthy friend, before the police chief's eyes, at a party; in Ilocos Sur a vice-governor's son kills the labourer who insults him; on the campus of one Manila university a student shoots another for slapping his face; in nightclubs along Roxas Avenue rich young bloods stab, pistol-whip and wound their rivals over hostesses or gambling debts. In such cases the law can often be persuaded to take a lenient view, as with the son of a former Congress speaker who 'vanished' on bail after allegedly shooting and assaulting gambling den operators in 1964, then had a later charge of murdering the doorman of a nightclub revoked, because the chief witness changed his evidence. Finally he 'escaped' to Hong Kong the following year as police crowded the airport to arrest him for allegedly killing his wife. The violence of that murder shocked Manila, for she had been a noted beauty whose wedding was once the social event of the year. She was shot nine times at close range, then thrown to the floor of her apartment beside the body of a friend. From Hong Kong 'Banjo' Laurel, grandson of the puppet president of Japanese occupation years, had his attorney-uncle announce that he would not return to stand trial, because 'we do not trust the Manila Police'. Besides, he suggested, it was probably a political plot to discredit his father and an uncle then standing for Congress in the 1965 elections. Young Laurel was persuaded to return the following year, but a series of complicated legal manoeuvres has so far prevented a trial.

The murder rate alone appears to argue a case for laws to restrict the possession of firearms, which almost anyone can obtain today. The Philippine Constabulary reported in 1965 that 365,000 licensed revolvers, rifles and other types were in private hands. As for unlicensed firearms, these were estimated by other sources to be at least 750,000. This fantastic armoury hidden in private homes was more than twenty times the number possessed by the entire Philippines Armed Forces.

This passion for guns goes back to World War Two, when the many, sometimes mutually-warring guerrilla bands roamed the countryside. Mass poverty following liberation persuaded many of these bands to continue living by the gun. The possession of a lethal weapon also has prestige value. Young men toy with them in jeepneys and hotel lobbies; daring high school boys display them under their desks. Some newspapers even whet the popular appetite with lavish advertisements which stress the glamour and status to be gained by their possession. 'This little weapon carries a real punch,' announces an illustrated advertisement in the otherwise socially-conscious *Philippines Free Press*. 'It's called the ... Baby Automatic, but don't let the name "baby" mislead you. It's the toughest little "baby" you ever saw. Wood penetration around four inches.'

No mention of skull penetration? The same journal even publicized specially reduced prices of revolvers for Yuletide gifts. Happy Christmas indeed!

The last festive season I spent there saw the largest upsurge in crime since the war. It was allied to mass dismissals in government and private industry, designed to save money during an unusually slack season. It was a criminal notion, considering the average Filipino's sentimental and extravagant approach to their month-long Christmas celebrations. The homicide rate jumped; so did robberies with violence. In one raid alone a Cebu City pawnshop lost P1,000,000 worth of cash and jewels. In the Manila suburb of Marakina five men with machine guns broke into a lumber firm, hog-tied employees, raped a housemaid and escaped with jewellery and P5,000. In San Pedro, Laguna, three armed men in a jeep snatched a coconut planter's daughter as she walked to church. She was held to ransom, but never seen again. Another, a fifteen-year-old school-girl was kidnapped in Quezon City the same week, and held for three months in a wartime air-raid shelter by six men, who were discovered only by chance when P.C. troopers raided a counterfeiter's lonely hut in Central Luzon.

Shortly before Christmas that year the *Manila Times*, running a lone crusade for crime prevention, published the findings of its own city-wide poll. Thirteen out of every 100 Manila families, the *Times* said, had been victimized by armed robbers, prowlers, extortionists and snatchers of handbags, watches, jewels. In its vast suburban areas 12 out of each 100 reported robbery under arms or burglary. Fifty per cent of the victims had never troubled to inform the police, regarding it as a waste of time.

No wonder the nation's capital so often looks like an armed camp. Or that public cynicism has been swollen by so many reported cases of miscarried justice and police inaction.

Almost daily news stories show the police to be anything but inactive. Despite popular cynicism, they have frequently shown courage, initiative, sometimes heroism in the course of their work, especially the Philippine Constabulary, which is a semi-army organization. They have arrested armed gangsters single-handed, fought tough campaigns against Muslim bandits in the Sulu Archipelago and Mindanao, run smugglers to ground in remote, unfriendly barrios and carried out smart detection work on large-scale frauds, embezzlement and political subversion. Such achievements are less often publicized than the other side of police activities, which make headlines of this kind: NAB FORMER COP CHIEF FOR HOLDUP. COP TAGGED ON JEEPNEY 'TONG'. COPS LEAD ROBBERS. These are random instances of police officers who robbed country bus services, led a protection racket over Manila jeepney drivers, gambling dens and brothels, or organized a gang of armed shopbreakers. There was also the case of a P.C. raid on a Pasay City narcotics and prostitution den, whose madam identified a local policeman as the brains trust of a gang extorting money from wealthy Chinese patrons. He had persuaded her to plant morphine packets on her gentlemen friends, who were thereupon arrested and allowed to buy their release.

My introduction to modern police ethics came soon after the Grand

Opera House Affair. This time it was pure comic opera: the Mystery of the Gold Bars. Six members of the Pasay City police force, including a major, were charged with relieving a Lebanese traveller of forty-five gold bars he had somehow smuggled through the airport, carrying them in the pockets of a concealed vest. Why Farouk Chaffei, making an overnight stop on his way to Australia, should have preferred these heavy objects to travellers' cheques remained a mystery. As one woman journalist wrote, he was after all 'a transient and hence fair game in this city of thieves and whores'. A police motor patrol stopped the airline bus as it was taking him into town, then drove him to a local motel noted for its drinking parties and prostitution. Next day he complained to police headquarters that he had been robbed, and the gold bars were returned. At least, fourteen of them were. Defence lawyers for the policemen fought a delaying action for four months, after which time Chaffei applied for Christmas leave, flew home to Lebanon and never returned. Eighteen months later several of the policemen were found guilty, but immediately lodged appeals that may never reach the higher court.

Pasay City became a test case for law and order. This neon-lit, honky-tonk suburb with its bars, nightclubs and brassy hostesses, its motels devoted to prostitution and police parties, has long been notorious as a germ-carrier of crime. Its autonomous police force — there are 1,200 separate forces in the Philippines — had been so often under fire that the Philippines Constabulary was ordered to take over. What they found was comic opera. Of Pasay's 290 officers and men, 175 were officers, including 32 majors, while only 63 rank-and-file men patrolled a district of 200,000 people. Sixteen others were facing criminal or disciplinary charges, the remainder were said to be 'in smoke'. Few of them, even commissioned officers, were paid more than a normal labourer's wage.

Sometimes it is difficult to distinguish cops from crooks. Not even the uniform is proof enough. Crooks have a habit of buying them from manufacturers supplying police. Frequently the men you meet in the dark streets or entering your house may not be police at all.

'The deteriorating peace and order situation,' reported the *Manila Herald* in 1965, 'has killed the livelihood of the travelling salesman and other occupations that require knocking on doors. Almost nobody opens doors these days and with very good reason. Even a police or army uniform no longer opens doors.'

In 1965 the N.B.I. reported that policemen throughout the Philippines had averaged one crime a day for the previous twelve months. Amongst those charged with murder, rape, robbery with violence and extortion were seven provincial police chiefs, two majors and six captains and lieutenants. One of the comparatively minor crimes included a raid by two Manila patrolmen on a funeral parlour where they systematically robbed the mourners of all the money they had put together to bury a dead relative around whom they were then gathered.

The question of police morale was a major item on the agenda of a conference late in 1964, when 200 Luzon police chiefs discussed the accelerating rate of crime. Addressing them, N.B.I. director Jose Lukban asserted that it was impossible to make improvements while politicians exerted so much control. He outlined the 1965 Police Act which President Macapagal had sent to Congress. One of its main clauses, he said, was to penalize any outsider attempting to influence police, meaning, of course, congressmen themselves. The bill became 'lost' almost immediately, prompting press commentators to ask whether congressmen preferred to have criminals and 'goons' employed in the local forces they patronized rather than in gaol.

An ironic footnote to the conference, made abortive by rival jealousies, was a debate on what had happened to a national association set up by all 1,200 chiefs in 1955. To protect their interests each had paid P30 a year until the association became inactive five or six years later. The P100,000 fighting fund had likewise 'disappeared'.

Who is to police the police?

Investigations, reports and complaints from all over the country in the past few years have produced an alarming picture of police demoralization. One report from the 'smuggler's paradise' of Laguna, asserted that high-ranking P.C. officers were rendering ineffective the administration's 1965 drive against smuggling by almost daily changes in provincial commands. In Cavite and the two Ilocos provinces, Constabulary officers arresting bandits and their political protectors 'would immediately be transferred to some remote area, there to expiate their nameless crimes of meddling in the affairs of politicians and gangsters.'[3] In Quezon City the P.C. commander, ordered to investigate the local police force, told the press that it had broken down completely, because its officers were loyal only to politicians and had gone unprosecuted after many shootings, assaults and robberies. In Manila, a mayoral investigation during October 1965 led to the discharge of more than one hundred policemen, many of whom had criminal records. The report also mentioned that one in every five members kept more than one wife. These were Christian policemen, not Muslims. Some policemen, the report added, had as many as five wives or *queridas*, and appeared to regard 'changing women as no different from changing their clothes'. This, the report concluded, was a prime cause for extortion and other criminal activities. The Cebu City police chief likewise found that 500 security guards had criminal records, and that his own men had insufficient firearms because so many were issued to 'so-called confidential agents, informers, investigators and un-skilled labourers on the city payroll'. Perhaps it was as well, for a hundred of those Cebu policemen later failed to pass psychiatric tests.

Seldom, however, do police indulge in such dramatic displays as did a Manila detachment in October 1964. Ships' crews in South Harbour were awakened during the early hours by the sound of shooting. Swift action by army authorities stopped what threatened to become a battle.

3. *Manila Chronicle*, 3 November 1964, Manila.

An official inquiry found that two armed units, one military and the other police, had both been sent to guard valuable cargo against looting by a known waterfront gang. Instead the soldiers and police fought for its possession, while the cargo itself was last seen travelling in a police jeep uptown. One Manila policeman had been heard to threaten that 'blood would flow', unless the soldiers gave up the spoils. Later, I asked a city councillor friend of mine how the issue had ended. 'Quite simply,' he said in an offhand way. 'They split it fifty-fifty.'

Clearly there are complex factors influencing the decline in police morale. Chief among them are poor pay, the *padrino* system that runs so deeply through Filipino life, and the inducements offered by well-placed criminal elements, smugglers and ambitious politicians. 'The country's not going to the dogs,' said one Manila wit. 'It's going to the police.'

Since independence the Republic's major failure has been to organize effective police control of a sometimes restive population, which in turn has yet to recover from the anarchy and violence of war. Added to that has been the post-war aggravation of widespread graft, blackmarketeering, poverty and unemployment. No overall police organization exists. Each city and town has its own force, an autonomous one, subject to the control of the local mayor and council. As mayors and Congress representatives change, so do police chiefs and many of their personnel, for municipal posts are seen as rewards for services rendered at election times. It is the American system, grafted on to an already corrupt heritage from Spain. This is how one police chief in the provinces explained it to me: 'When a politician stands for office, he needs all the support he can get. Someone who wants a job comes to him and says, look I can promise you so many votes. Afterwards, he's got to give you something. Being police chief, after all, is one of the best jobs. You've got to find jobs for hundreds of others. Then one day he comes down from Manila and breaks a traffic regulation. Usually, it's something much worse. I'd be a fool to run him in, wouldn't I? In many places politicians employ gunmen, who get votes for him by straight intimidation. They've got to be protected too. Protected against the law. And yet do-gooders talk of passing laws to stop men carrying guns. Who's going to stop them? It's no good asking us.'

In recent years a number of local police forces were found to be so inefficient or guilty of misconduct that they were taken over by the Philippine Constabulary. This disciplined, quasi-military body, with a tradition of courageous service going back to 1901, once had a reputation for incorruptibility. Evidence shows this to be less so today. Late in 1965 one of its own retired officers, Lt. Col. P. C. Milan, published his proposals for restoring its somewhat tarnished reputation. 'The Constabulary,' he wrote, 'has failed to discharge its duties and responsibilities efficiently since the end of World War Two, because of reasons beyond its control. The adverse effects of war and fast-changing conditions in the

Philippines have contributed. . . . The despicable practice of officers and men seeking the intercession of powerful politicians and influential persons or pressure groups to get choice assignments or gain undue benefits should be stopped. Top commanders must resist political pressure exerted on behalf of an officer or enlisted man. Commanders should have the courage to resign if undue interference is brought to bear upon their functions.'[4]

One Constabulary officer, at least, took this advice seriously. In July 1965 Captain Jacinto Guinto, a decorated veteran of the Korean War, asked for a court-martial rather than accept a reprimand from his superiors. Disciplinary action had been taken against him after he had charged his company commander with attempted bribery. He said he had been offered money to ignore the landing of contraband cigarettes in Pampanga, Constabulary dealings with known smugglers and the free passage of logs smuggled from the Angat Dam area. The charge against him was of 'conduct unbecoming to an officer and a gentleman'. The result of the court-martial was not revealed. During the same period a congressman, who had served with the N.B.I., claimed that the Constabulary was frequently unable to deal with gangsters and hoodlums protected by politicians, and that any attempt to do so led to their immediate transfer to innocuous posts elsewhere.

Another enlightened Congress member, Joaquin Roces, said during a newspaper interview that 'the system of bodyguards and the presence of hoodlums in ward politics have contributed to the rise of gangsterism. To divorce politics from gangsterism and personal bodyguards, the political parties must clean their rosters of hoodlums, city fixers and promoters of illegal cockfights. Organized crime can only exist with the protection afforded them by government officials. In many cases there are unsavoury characters in the payroll of Manila politicians.'[5]

Two days after Christmas his views gained unintentional support from a high-ranking police officer. Col. Felix Maniego, P.C. zone commander in the restless provinces of Central Luzon, told staff officers he expected the rate of killings and civil violence to increase during 1965.

'It is election year,' he said briefly.

Even more candid was the police chief in Cagayan de Oro who delivered a Christmas Day message in 1964. Condemning his political masters, he classified the inefficient members of his force under three headings. *The Untouchables:* political proteges who could afford to choose their own assignments or reject them, who had no training or qualifications whatever. *The Drunkards:* again political appointments who refused to be disciplined by their superiors. *The Illiterates:* appointees who barely knew how to read or write.

The concealed pressures exerted upon police organizations have their counterpart in the courts of law. In certain provinces the influence

4. *Philippines Free Press*, 1 May 1965, Manila.
5. *Sunday Times*, 10 October 1964, Manila.

exerted on judges and fiscals is obvious and unashamed. No one is any longer surprised at delays in hearing even the most flagrant of criminal cases, the temporizing of court officials, the vanished witnesses, the easy provision of bail for those charged with violent or even capital crimes, the freedom accorded to numerous criminals if they have the money or connections to continue without interference their normal lives. The situation was recently discussed in public by Justice Roman Ozaeta at a convention of district judges in Manila.

'Political pull has become a necessary consideration,' he said. 'Influence peddling has supervened in the selection and promotion of judges. Self-respecting, capable, honest lawyers and judges who do not care to kowtow to politicians and to barter away their dignity and independence are liable to be by-passed in selection or promotion. On the other hand, mediocrities and misfits who pull strings and play politics can be appointed. In such an atmosphere the confidence of the public in the judiciary — the bulwark of our liberty — is being subverted.'

So much for general terms. The august rituals of law courts usually make it difficult to discover the hidden influences at work. A lawyer friend of mine expressed it in these terms. 'Things have to be done with a certain finesse,' he said. 'If a big case comes before a certain judge, we first look up the congressional records. We find out who sponsored his appointment. Then, when the case opens, we bring the congressman along. We introduce him to the court. If he happens to be a lawyer, which so many congressmen are, we tell the judge he'll be assisting us during the course of the trial. If he is not qualified, we just mention he is to be called as a witness for our case later. Very often it has the desired effect. The judge is usually most friendly to him. Of course, it means the defendant has to pay a rather large fee. To the congressman, of course.'

Meantime public disillusion grows. Law-abiding citizens, by the hundred thousand, feel themselves powerless to cope with the drift in social order. The United States commission of inquiry which visited the Philippines in 1921, finding many thousands of cases hopelessly awaiting trial, would have been horrified to learn of the chaotic situation reached in the law courts by the end of 1965. It was then estimated that 80,000 cases were listed for the courts of first instance alone. Thousands more had still to be dealt with by the Supreme Court and Courts of Appeal. One legal authority stated that if all judges were to work double time, accepting no new cases, it would take them twenty years to catch up.

However, 1965 happened to be an election year, and crimes with violence sharply increased. In the twelve months preceding polling day on 9 November 1965, a number of town mayors and other officials were assassinated in central and northern Luzon. Their assailants were either Huk terrorists or hired gangsters from Manila. Nine of them were never identified, let alone arrested. Most of the violence occurring in the seven Ilocano-speaking provinces of the north were attributed to the extreme bitterness that has existed between rival political factions since the post-war years when General MacArthur forced an unpopular leadership upon the restless peasants. In one Nueva Vizcaya town during September 1965 two long convoys of jeeps, led by rival congressmen, fired upon each other in the main street, killing seven and wounding four. In Capiz an escaped convict, a notorious bandit, made a door-to-door campaign threatening to kill anyone who voted for the former Speaker of the House. In Ilocos Sur five senior P.C. officers were arrested because they refused to be transferred from regions in which they were accused of giving protection to certain candidates. Violence and threatened violence flared in almost every province, though the worst sectors were, as always, in the Ilocano-speaking provinces of northern Luzon. Reported the *Philippines Free Press* one week before polling started, 'A poverty-ridden region racked by political feuds, Ilocandia is virtually a gigantic powder keg, its fuse waiting to be lit by hot-headed politicos. Last month alone, 16 persons were killed, 11 wounded and countless others either shot at, mauled, threatened or intimidated. Of eight provinces in Ilocandia, seven — Ilocos Norte, Abra, La Union, Cagayan, Mountain Province, Neuva Vizcaya and Isabela — are considered critical. . . . Though some of the reported goons have been rounded up, the heavily-armed security guards and pistol-packing cronies of politicians have yet to be disarmed. . . . Only about six months ago, re-electionist Rep. Delfin Albano of the lone district of Isabela, the tobacco-famous province, his brother and 13 others were accused of murder. Some twenty towns of Ilocos Sur are in danger of a political shooting war . . .

'From January to July this year over 300 persons were killed in Ilo-candia — roughly two killings a day. Ilocandia has about 820,000 voters and roughly 40,000 assorted firearms, excluding home-made *paltiks*. In the second district of Ilocos Sur alone about 1,000 "secret agents" owing allegiance only to political *padrinos* carry firearms. There can never be political peace so long as some Ilocano politicians act like dictators in a banana republic . . . who uphold the power of bullets insted of ballots.'[6]

The successful candidate for president, Ferdinand Marcos, who was himself an Ilocano, was given an overwhelming vote in these northern provinces.

A week before the poll, the Chief Justice, Cesar Bengzon, made an appeal for more democratic attitudes before the exclusive Philippine Columbian Club, which in pre-war years had been a forum for *ilustrados*, professional men and the political élite. 'A massive wave of extremism has of late enveloped our society,' said the Chief Justice. 'It seems as if contempt for law and order has become the fashion of the day.' He invited congressional candidates to remember that the Philippines was the only country in Asia where democratic elections had been held regularly for more than half a century. A nation that takes pride in being 'the showcase of democracy in Asia' should remember that the only alterna- tives to orderly election processes were tyranny or rebellion of the masses.

6. *Philippines Free Press*, 6 November 1955, Manila.

'It would be interesting to inquire whether the heat and frenzy gene-rated by the race for the elective posts betray the open secret or confirm the spreading suspicions that such posts offer opportunities not so much for service as for sudden wealth. With such prizes at stake, it is no wonder that to some candidates, ambition comes first, and hence any plot, any scheme is permissible, including falsehood, vote-buying, force and co-ercion.'[7]

When Marcos was declared president, the chairman of the Commission of Elections, Juan V. Borra, announced that only fifty people had been killed in election disputes since the first of August. This compared with eighty-five during the same period in 1961. These somewhat arbitrary figures excluded the hundreds who had been killed before the beginning of August. However, it allowed him to claim that 'We Filipinos are growing in maturity in our attitude towards elections'.

7. Ibid.

CHAPTER 22

Wealth of a Nation

*To be a Filipino nowadays is to be
alone. Each fights his lonely battle for
survival. No one joins another to fight
the total war for the survival of the
nation. . . . When will he learn that
nationalism is the sense of belonging to
each other; that, when one of us dies,
everyone else dies a little and the bells
toll for the rest of us . . .*

HILARION M. HENARES

VISITING economists have frequently been baffled by the nature of the
Philippine economy, which often appears to follow peculiar laws alien
to the West, or even to quasi-colonial nations. There is no lack of information on most sectors: reports and surveys issue from many sources, yet
they seldom agree. During the heated pre-election year of 1965, for instance, the supporters of President Macapagal claimed a growth of the
national income of more than 6 per cent. His opponents proved equally
convincingly that it was little more than four. Nor did this take into
account the annual population increase of 3 per cent. Looked at in that
light, the economy was stagnating.

It is equally difficult to find accurate figures for primary or industrial
production, for employment, the exact quantities of goods imported or
raw materials sent overseas. Exports and imports are usually expressed
in percentages, or approximations. The Central Bank, for instance, pub-
lishes the quantities of logs shipped to Japan, yet in 1964, when its
officers wanted authority to remeasure them on arrival, exporters protested violently. Between 1959 and 1963 large numbers of log shipments
so mysteriously expanded when crossing the China Sea that their value
increased by P378,000,000, which the smugglers salted away in overseas
banks free of tax. This is locally known as 'technical smuggling'. While I
was in the Philippines a number of warehouses and ships carrying copra
to Europe were destroyed by fire, enabling the consignors to collect heavy
insurance though cash payments had already been received from buyers.
In 1965 one shipper was found to have relieved banks and insurance
companies of P16,000,000 by the simple process of borrowing the original
warehouse delivery receipt 'to have photostatic copies made', using these
as further collateral. The copra did not even exist. While in the port of
Davao, I also witnessed the clandestine transhipment of Celebes copra
from Indonesian to Filipino freighters, which enabled the consignor to

gain higher prices overseas for an inferior, illegally imported product. In the port of Manila there is seldom much relation between customs returns and actual imports, for textiles, machinery and other valuable cargoes have a habit of being cleared by officials under classifications that require smaller dues, if they are not smuggled through duty-free.

Estimates of the gross national product are difficult to assess for other reasons. This is inevitable when so much of life is lived at subsistence level. There are almost as many intangibles as those attaching to the Indonesian economy, which westerners have frequently predicted to be on the point of collapse, without appreciating the peculiar virtues and resilience of peasant production.

The peasant lives very largely on what he grows or catches, he is often engaged in small-scale barter trade, and what he sells may often be a mere surplus over his immediate needs or the percentage he has tradition- ally to pay his landlord. Rice production figures, for example, do not include what the tenant farmer consumes or exchanges for rent. What goods he buys are additional to his basic food requirements, and, fortu- nately for him, these are not large. The real victim of inflation, high living costs, high indirect taxation — income taxes themselves are not high — is the comparatively small middle class. The one per cent of wealthy citizens are beyond worries of an economic kind. Their estates, their capital, their investments at home and abroad, the overseas interests they represent set them among the richest, most influential people on the globe. These are the people who determine political as well as economic life, and the two are inextricably woven, thus accounting for the sterile, change-resisting character of Congress, whichever of the two parties happens to be in power.

'To most outsiders looking in,' writes the Australian economist Ian Shannon, 'the fundamental problem of the Philippines is not only to ensure that the national income is spread around somewhat more. The corollary is that the income itself should increase quickly enough to run ahead of population expansion. Although lip service is given to this laudable aim by the politically powerful Filipinos, the major emphasis nonetheless (with some notable exceptions) boils down to a discussion about the distribution of the existing national income. In fact, instead of looking upon economic development as a concept concerned with expanding income as quickly and soundly as possible, too much emphasis would seem to be given to disputing about which sectors should be encouraged and who should be *allowed* to participate.'[1]

The emphasis on 'allowed' is an apt one, for ultimate control still rests with the United States, despite the gift of political independence in 1946. The fact has led to much embittered dispute in recent years, though such arguments pass over the heads of the people, who are little concerned as to who employs them so long as they are employed. To remove Ameri-

1. Ian Shannon, *The Philippines: Australia's Neighbours*, Committee for Economic Development of Australia, Melbourne, 1965.

Bayanihan dancers

Juan Alano, Coconut King

Confiscated firearms

Gangster arrest, Manila

can domination at present, assuming that it could be done, would be catastrophic. The desirability of economic independence is another matter. The Philippines lacks the large capital required, the technical experience and, too often, the managerial integrity. There is no doubt, however, that the brakes have been kept full on since the American regime ended. This was outlined in candid fashion by Professor Taylor in his study of Philippine-United States relationships.

'It has to be admitted,' he wrote, 'that the United States set up for its citizens monopolistic advantages not only with respect to other countries, but also with respect to the Filipinos themselves. . . . It is also clear that the United States used pressure to secure advantageous terms for its nationals, for in practice the reciprocity has not meant a great deal to the Filipinos.

'Through their own Chamber of Commerce in the Philippines and through the embassy, the Americans can bring pressure to bear on a weak government and, in some instances, this pressure may well make it more difficult for that government to carry out reforms. More serious, there is sure to develop an alliance between foreign interests and certain domestic interests — commercial, producing, or financial — and enmity with others, thus splitting the Filipino middle class.'[2]

Conceding the American businessman's argument that this so-called reciprocity was destined to create heavy investment for the Philippines, Taylor pointed out that, in recent years, this had been much smaller than similar investment in Japan, Mexico or Peru. Since 1956, when United States investment in the Philippines reached $275,000,000, no more than $25,000,000 in capital has come annually. Each year since 1946, he wrote, revenues transmitted to the United States exceeded new investment. The principal safeguard has been the Laurel-Langley Agreement (1954). This stemmed from the Bell Report of 1950,* extending the system of trade and investment preferences to 1974, an issue that is now fiercely debated. The Nacionalistas, who represent the section wanting to industrialize as well as being landowners, have consistently agitated against any further extension of the present relationship, in order to minimize competition from American imports and subsidiaries, while primary exporters would be happy to see them continue.

These exports are practically the only dollar earners today. Two-thirds of the entire export trade is provided by three products: sugar, copra and timber, and all of these, despite occasional booms, are notably unstable on the international market. The nationally-minded are highly critical of this perennial shipping away of raw materials, asserting that this reduces Filipinos to mere 'hewers of wood and drawers of water', while United States' enterprises gain all the benefits. Understandably, they would like to see processing plants built in the Philippines: sugar refineries, timber factories and coconut oil distilleries. Meantime the massive importing of

2. George E. Taylor, *The Philippines and the United States*, New York, 1964.
* See Chapter Nine.

197

consumer goods is largely in the hands of American enterprises or their Philippine subsidiaries. This has severely limited Filipino ambitions to develop industrially. What secondary industry does exist is on the light side: textiles, tobacco, clothing, food and light metals. Three-quarters of the industrial work force is in Luzon, most of it in and around Manila. For the rest the only sizeable employers of labour are the sugar mills of Negros, American gold, copper and chrome mines, fruit-canning plants in Cotabato and timber mills in Agusan, Cotabato and Basilan.

No one has yet attempted to exploit fully the mineral resources of these islands, which have never been properly surveyed, though work has lately begun on large-scale copper deposits in Cebu Island. Two regions in Mindanao are known to have enormous reserves of iron ore, which should one day make the long-delayed building of a steel plant in Iligan a reality. Yet, as far back as 1954, the country's mineral reserves were estimated to include, as well as 1,200,000,000 tons of iron ore, 15,000,000 tons of gold and silver, 20,000,000 tons of copper, 10,000,000 tons of chromite, 200,000 tons of manganese, 12,000,000 tons of coal and 66,000,000 tons of other metallic and non-metallic ores. These reserves, based on surveys covering only 16 per cent of the total land area, were then estimated to be worth some P160,000,000,000. At present forty-four mining companies, principally American-owned, are producing about P450,000,000 annually, most of it naturally being remitted out of the country. The forgotten Macapagal programme specified that P399,000,000 should be spent on the development of mining between 1963 and 1967, 4 per cent of this being produced by the government. However, tight credit policies made the promised private capital unavailable. The government did nothing on its side either.

The main prospects for future development at present rest with the primary industries so long neglected. The aborted five-year 'socio-economic plan', introduced by the Macapagal regime in 1962, achieved nothing beyond turning a small percentage of tenant farmers into lease-holders. Its concurrent aim of diverting capital to the industrial sector, mainly by taking idle lands, was rejected by the landowning majority in Congress. In fact, it was widely claimed that congressmen themselves had quickly acquired what lands were available, keeping them idle for specu-lative purposes. On the other hand, most free capital has gone to profit-able real estate ventures in Manila rather than to promoting new industries the nation desperately needs.

By far the largest industry is government. Employing more than a million people, this has become a massive bureaucracy of truly Parkin-sonian proportions. Much of it acts in a kind of vacuum, with no apparent purpose beyond perpetuating its own monumental inactivity.

Each time I visited a senior public official, I was mystified to find three or four others seated beside his desk, like the acolytes of a high priest. Perhaps I had interrupted some important conference. Later I discovered that these people had no function whatever, did no work beyond drawing pay. They were somebody's nephews or uncles, and helped to give the senior man prestige. Yet life can also be perilous at the top of the bureaucrat's rice ladder. The Customs Department, for instance, has had twenty different commissioners in six years, most of them being transferred because they attempted to reorganize procedures, which meant interfering with vested interests in smuggling, co-operating with smugglers, misdeclaring dutiable goods or extracting *lagay* in profitable areas of the waterfront. A little backstairs pressure, especially through Congressmen, can always restore the *status quo*.

Yet the top Customs post is not only a sensitive, but an all-important one to the national exchequer. Ships from all the major nations crowd South Harbour, whose chaotic wharves are the heart of the country's commerce. At least 45 per cent of the government's revenue derives from customs duties. Yet the collection of them seems almost beyond the realms of the possible. No wonder each succeeding administration forever verges on bankruptcy.

I had only just arrived in Manila during 1964 when the press grew excited over the disappearance of twenty-nine heavy trucks destined for army use. Neither police nor customs men saw them leave the wharves. 'Gargantua swallowed them,' said one report. Another, 'Were they seized by men from Mars?' There were rumours of politicians involved, of the trucks being 'cannibalized' for the spare-parts market or used by illegal loggers in the mountains. And there the incident ended. Reports are frequent of valuable, misdeclared cargoes passing untaxed through the heavily-guarded port gates with uniformed escorts. The ruinous effects of pier smuggling — not even including contraband cigarettes, transistors, perfumes and narcotics brought in through the 'back door' of Mindanao-Sulu, nor the undeclared shipments of copra, logs and other products overseas — has been estimated to total 50 per cent of expected customs revenues. The *Philippines Free Press* summed it up in this fashion:

> The country is being deprived yearly of some P800 million in additional customs revenues, an amount that could have been used to build roads, bridges, schools, hospitals and other essential public services or invested to provide employment for tens of thousands of jobless Filipinos.
> Behind the P800 million yearly loss are official laxity and dishonesty, and graft and corruption at the waterfront. Misdeclaration, undervaluation, double manifest and wrong paragraphing are costing the government more than P2 million a day in uncollected customs revenues. One more evil is pilferage, now a syndicated operation which has become a P40 million a year racket.
> Central Bank Governor Andrew V. Castillo is deeply worried over the terrible effects of smuggling on the economy, not to mention the country's monetary stability. 'A substantial outflow of dollars from 1962 to 1964,' he said, 'went into the financing of smuggling operations and in undervaluation.' For about eight years now, according to a customs insider, a number of packaging and assembly plants here have been defrauding the government of hundreds of millions of pesos through misdeclaration. Finished goods have been declared as spare parts, thereby lowering the rate.

Undervaluation of imports has also become the rule at the piers. Textile yarns, fabrics, cereals, equipment, appliances, and electrical apparatuses have been brought in practically tax-free, thanks to graft and corruption at the piers. In the past, brand-new cars were taken out of the customs zone without a single centavo in taxes being paid on them. For a 'reasonable' fee, pier syndicates reportedly had worked for the immediate release of imported goods. Many smart operators have cheated the government of taxes with the use of old tax receipts. This, of course, would not be possible without ignorance or connivance on the part of customs employees.[3]

In two years between 1963 and 1964, commented Senator Alejandro Almendras, 22,118 imported items were 'lost' while still under bond. To protect themselves, marine insurance companies raised their rates by 200 per cent in that period, while shipping companies threatened to set a 25 per cent premium on Philippine cargoes or by-pass Manila altogether. Small wonder that the cost of living in an already poor community has risen so disastrously. The impact on economic development was summed up by the president of the Philippine Chamber of Industries in 1965 when he said that 'the ultimate effect of smuggling has been to strap the industrial, commercial and banking sectors in a financial strait-jacket within the confines of which they can hardly squirm. . . . The malaise is one that demands a correction of the market situation, a massive financial reorganization, a redemption of the fiscal position from the unsound basis on which it rests today.' The National Economic Council chairman, Eleuterio Adevoso, had already advised President Macapagal that the funds of which his administration had been robbed could have built 21,000 classrooms for 840,000 poorly educated children, 625 hospitals to accommodate 300,000 patients now unable to gain treatment, irrigation systems to produce 800,000 tons of rice, 3,080 kilometres of desperately needed roads, power plants to meet the entire industrial needs of Mindanao or 10,000 child care centres in the barrios.

President Marcos began his term in 1966 by threatening smugglers with the death penalty. Spectacular threats of this kind cannot hope to eradicate such practices, however unethical, because they have been fostered by grave weaknesses in the economy. The Macapagal decision to abolish monetary controls in 1962 did much to end currency smuggling, but it had the result also of halving the peso's value in the principal overseas market. Hitherto pegged at two pesos to the dollar, the rate jumped to 3·90. Importers of raw materials found their costs doubled. To protect already insecure industries, the administration imposed tariffs on a wide variety of foreign goods. To defeat these raised costs came smuggling.

Three years later New York's *Wall Street Journal* asserted that 'fully one-third of all imports enter the Philippines illegally. General dissatisfaction with the government has been heightened because of the involvement of many high-ranking officials with big-time smugglers, and this, in

3. Edward R. Kuinisala, *Philippines Free Press*, 10 April 1965, Manila.

turn, has emboldened communist subversive elements to greater radicalism. Foreign capital has become increasingly shy, and prospective investors have given up plans to open factories. The smuggling of jute bags has discouraged a local investor from setting up a plastic bag factory, electronic assemblers groan under the competition of contraband radios, and textile mills operate at only 58 per cent capacity, because half of the clothes and clothing materials are imported illegally. Impetus for industrialization has all but dissipated.'

It is not surprising that the *Manila Times* reported enviously that, during the month of June 1965 the tiny colony of Hong Kong had exported $U.S.134,635,879 worth of goods to the United States and imported $85,283,850 worth, at least six times the volume of Philippine trade. It pointed out also that Hong Kong, whose textile industry had started at the same time, exported $U.S.6,882,594 worth of finished garments to African countries during that month.

In the Philippines, only the exporters of raw materials showed much gain, for their profits doubled after decontrol. 'Sugar barons and the new aristocracy of loggers are not by temperament industrial investors,' commented the London *Financial Times* in 1965. 'There is a nagging feeling among government officials that these earnings from American, Japanese and other markets are being wasted in foreign exchange spending and unproductive activity.'

The *Manila Times* economist, Filemon C. Rodriguez, noted that huge amounts of money were being spent abroad on pleasure trips, the proliferation of travel agencies and the growth of expensive residential subdivisions in Manila. 'The smugglers and racketeers have prospered,' he wrote, 'and, with them, the politicians and the influence peddlers who abet and protect them. But the high incomes generated in this manner did not go to productive investment. The beneficiaries enjoyed high living, went on junkets abroad. Dollars flowed out of the country, tax collection broke down, goods came in untaxed and choked local industry. . . . In the "new era" of free enterprise that promised to usher in a new unprecedented period of growth under its co-called socio-economic programme, we have failed.'

Confronted with so much vanishing wealth, President Macapagal pledged himself in 1965 to provide more government funds by raising taxes, but was unable to summon the special session of Congress needed because the treasury lacked even the money to call it together. Yet the Bureau of Internal Revenue had already admitted that uncollected taxes amounted to between P200,000,000 and P300,000,000. It seemed that few people troubled to pay tax, nor was there any official attempt to make them do so. That tireless seeker after discomforting truths, the *Philippines Free Press* observed that, out of a population of 32,000,000, only 100,000 declared a taxable income at all. Yet there were known to be 200,000 car owners in the country, surely not all 'paupers', 117,000 professional people including doctors, lawyers, chemists, engineers, pharmacists and dentists — as well as 1,000,000 government servants. Only 13,000 of nearly a million Chinese, the richest group in the country, were paying income tax. The huge San Miguel brewery grossed P300,000,000 annually, yet only 12,376 merchants or stores admitted to selling beer. The government had given a P300,000,000 subsidy to the tobacco industry, yet recovered only P12,000 in taxes.[4]

This was a strange bureaucracy indeed that apparently kept no files or records. Yet anyone you speak to knows what happens. Like the customs assessor, the B.I.R. man will give you a sympathetic hearing. Rather than have you mail an official tax return, he will call at your home or office. If an assessment of, say, P5,000 seems too high to pay, he will generously reduce it by perhaps 50 per cent, providing that you split the difference with him. As for the *sari-sari* stores selling beer, the Chinese emporiums, the provincial retailers, the hundreds of thousands of market stalls, the local police make their regular calls and 'protect' them from paying tax. In addition, there are numerous 'anomalies' committed by other departments. No one seemed much surprised when, in November 1964, the Secretary of Public Works casually announced that P30,000,000 had vanished and that a syndicate involved had offered him a P75,000 bribe for another contract. This syndicate, he announced, had secured a monopoly of Public Works contracts by using fake signatures and requisition slips, gaining control over everything from nails to bulldozers. 'A member of the syndicate will get the signature of a certain district engineer,' he said. 'Then he brings the supposedly signed papers to the bureau, which in turn would stamp its approval on the requisition which would start from P10,000 to P5,000,000. As the papers go through the bureau, they are coddled and protected by employees, who get a cut out of the anomalous deal.' The loss was later estimated at P100,000,000. In almost any other country it would have become the subject for a commission of inquiry. As in so many other cases no more was heard of it.

I gained some insight into these practices when trying to leave the country. Entering it had certainly been much easier. It took two whole days to secure our exit visas. The first visit to the Immigration Department resulted in a demand for P350. No one could explain what this was for. I refused to pay, insisted on seeing the Commissioner in person, told him I would sooner go to gaol than pay such charges and explained that I had been invited to come as a 'guest of the country', whatever that meant. I produced my official invitation from the then Commissioner for Travel and Tourism, Col. Teofilo Zosa, whom I met only once in all my stay during a vague three-minute conversation. After a while you begin to understand the airy nature of 'Filipino promises'. When the Immigration chief confessed himself unable to reduce those inexplicable fees, I asked for the redoubtable colonel's assistance. Reluctantly, he provided me with an aide, supplied with government funds. We spent the next two days on a pilgrimage of *lagay*, passing under-the-counter money to at least

4. Napoleon G. Rama, *Philippines Free Press*, 15 May 1965, Manila.

a dozen officials. It was an exhausting two days, for we had just had renewed cholera injections as well. Yet we had to stand in crowded vestibules hour after hour, lined up with illegal Chinese and Indonesian immigrants about to be deported, and had our fingerprints taken exactly ten times. Meantime the offices were hung with Christmas decorations, religious texts and streamers announcing *Peace and Goodwill to All Men*, while the crisp new banknotes went surreptitiously under the desks of officials.

'When I was Commissioner for Customs,' that knight errant for clean administration, Cesar Climaco, told me the same week, 'I thought that was the only place in the government saddled with corruption. Now I know there is no government office free of it.'

Once Zamboanga's most efficient and sympathetic mayor, Climaco had achieved miracles in cleansing the Customs Bureau, only to find himself moved to another post. In 1964 he was appointed chairman of the Presidential Anti-Graft Committee, where he shocked many influential people by his assumption that his functions really meant what they said. His official notepaper carried the heading, 'Thou Shalt Not Steal'. He refused to accept his salary until his organization produced results. His early investigations were so thorough that several politicians, as well as others close to Malacanang, privately advised him to 'go easy'. In January 1965 he published his first report in which he said:

> To minimize graft and corruption in the public service, it is imperative that government crooks be convicted and jailed. A number of public servants today do not behave as servants. By and large, public servants act as if they were lords and masters of the people!
>
> It is the general tendency of many public servants to take advantage of their positions by misusing and abusing their powers and authority, and in the process they resort to wholesale stealing, bribery, extortion and oppression. And, as if adding insult to injury, hordes of public servants would still demand and get promotions in rank and/or pay. High and big officials oftentimes cannot be found in their respective offices during office hours, and if they are in, it is difficult for the public to see them. This not only gives way to feigned overtime work which the indolent, delinquent, thieving public servants immorally get paid for but also breeds graft and corruption.
>
> One primary reason responsible for the steady deterioration of morality in the public service is the failure of all administrations to substantially fulfill the loud and solemn promise repeated during every election — to jail big crooks in the government!
>
> Where are the masterminds in the big cases of graft and corruption of yesteryear? They are still very much around and not in jail where they belong. They are free to roam all over the country and the world over, occupying prestigious government positions, always in the centre of high society, residing in palatial mansions, and well-entrenched in the midst of multi-million-peso businesses; not one is in jail where all of them should be.

In the uproar that followed this report, Climaco publicly stated why PAGCOM had been unable to achieve any progress. Senators and Congressmen, he said, were quick to charge others with graft, but refused to allow him to inquire into their own affairs; prosecutions were made almost impossible by endless delays in court; his investigators were prevented from obtaining bank evidence on 'big time public crooks', its organization lacked police powers to search and seize incriminating documents; too many of his own staff were 'political recommendees'; while documentary evidence had been frequently pilfered within his own offices. Finally, frustrated by the administration that had appointed him, he resigned and in 1965 was narrowly defeated in the Senate elections, due to officially recognized frauds by both political machines in electoral returns. One of the first actions of President Marcos in 1966 was to abolish PAGCOM altogether, replacing it with a new body of more vaguely defined aims.

If I appear to have set a good deal of emphasis on the more questionable practices of government and commerce, this is simply because graft, smuggling, tax evasion, nepotism and other vices have become such consistently damaging factors in the economy. As Denis Warner expressed it of Indonesia, 'Among the rich corruption is a vice, among the poor it is a necessity'. There are other, more hopeful aspects. This is especially evident in the younger generation, which has frequently expressed its impatience with the corruption of its elders, born of the agonizing aftermath of war and the struggle for survival. The trend among young men today is away from politics, due to a certain disgust with electoral and congressional malpractices. The educated, the alert, the university-trained are these days going into the world of commerce and, if they are given the chance to revitalize the economy, the whole concept of public affairs could well change within a decade or so. They can perhaps gain comfort from Professor Taylor, who wrote that 'no nation has ever developed to maturity without violence, corruption, greed and injustice'.

Historically, this has been partially true of many countries, notably the United States, Australia, Mexico, in their earlier stages at least. The crucial difference was that their legal systems were more firmly grounded, and given more respect. The problem here is how to achieve any advance in creating secondary industry. 'Present economic trends,' said Felix K. Lirag, the head of one large textile manufacturing concern, in 1965, 'indicate that the economy is sliding back into the colonial type of exporting raw materials and importing finished products. If we don't snap out of the old mould and build industries that produce substitutes for imported finished goods, the country cannot move forward.'

Rodriguez, in the *Manila Times*, argued that the tight control of credit since the peso was freed in 1962 has strangled local growth while 'foreign companies operating here are free to bring their unlimited resources from their mother countries, and therefore have a competitive advantage'. He added that 'of course, decontrol and free enterprise have been urged upon us by our foreign mentors all along. When we succumbed and adopted it, the applause of those foreign mentors must have been music to the administration's ears. What our leaders did not know — or did they? — was that those who are vehement in urging us to abolish all controls and follow free enterprise are not following the same doctrine in their home country. They want it only for their own advantage. There, in a nutshell, is the one great "accomplishment" of the present [Macapagal] administration. In one swoop, it has liquidated much that has taken this country years and sweat and tears to achieve.'[5]

This accounted for the extreme bitterness that greeted a statement by the American Chamber of Commerce of the Philippines which, in 1964, expressed a hope that the Laurel-Langley Agreement would continue beyond its legal expiry date of 1974.[6] The Philippine Chamber of Commerce responded angrily.

'Parity,' said its spokesman in October 1964, 'has only succeeded in giving a certain sector of the foreign community the feeling that they own this country, and that any effort on the part of Filipinos to assert their mastery in their own economic house is . . . to quote the American Chamber in "very poor" grace. The poverty of the Filipino masses today is directly attributable to the effects of American economic policy . . . [which] for almost sixty years was designed to prevent the Philippines from industrializing.'[7]

Even more to the point was an unusually candid statement by a highly respected business leader and educationalist, Salvador Araneta, published by the *Manila Times* under the heading of 'U.S. Ideals and Reality'. He charged American enterprises with dumping competitive commodities; selling fertilizers, flour, electrical equipment at prices lower than in their own country; building competitive factories to produce paints, motor tyres, air conditioning, refrigeration units and cement; and, more specifically, that when a Philippine group planned to establish an aluminium smelting plant, the powerful Reynolds group immediately announced that it intended to do the same.[8] None of this could be reconciled with the genial expressions of brotherly accord made at the inauguration of the Republic nearly twenty years before.

The Liberal regime, historically linked with United States commercial interests during the MacArthur era, was unmoved by these pleas. Today, with a Nacionalista president, the issues, despite a generally friendly attitude towards Americans, will certainly become a major element in the struggle.

However, the task ahead — two decades after the first attempts to restore a war-shattered economy began — are enough to intimidate the most utopian administrators. Professor Taylor, a sympathetic observer, listed these immediate necessities: a better educational system to produce enlightened leaders; improved and more rapid communications; electric

5. Filemon C. Rodriguez, 'Decontrol as a Failure', *Manila Times*, 31 December 1964, Manila.

6. *American Chamber of Commerce Journal*, September 1964, Manila.

7. *Manila Chronicle*, 4 October 1964, Manila.

8. Salvador Araneta, 'U.S. Ideals and Reality', *Manila Times*, 7 October 1964, Manila.

power for the barrios; more tax-raising powers for local authorities; the abolition of present 'pork barrel' allowances whereby opportunistic congressmen unfairly gain the credit for supplying public funds.

It is the Filipino's classical ambition to become president. Candidates will engage in the most ruthless, spendthrift actions to achieve it. But who could want to be president at a time like this? How would he know where to begin?

Surely there can never have been a more agonizing appraisal of a nation's plight than the speech made by President Marcos at the Luneta on 30 December, 1965 on the day of his inauguration, held by tradition on the anniversary of Rizal's execution. Having appealed to the vast gathering, which included diplomats of many nations, to give him a 'mandate for greatness', to the public service to practice self-sacrifice and to the people at large to restore the rule of law, he said:

> We are in crisis . . . our government in the past few months has exhausted all available domestic and foreign sources of borrowing. Our public financial institutions have been drained to the last loanable peso. . . . There are no funds available for public works and little remains of the appropriations for our government for the present fiscal year. Industry is at a standstill. Many corporations have declared bankruptcy. Local manufacturing firms have been compelled to close or reduce their capacity. Unemployment has increased. Prices of essential commodities and services remain unstable. The availability of rice remains uncertain. . . . Syndicated crime has been spawned by smuggling. The democratic rule of law has lost all meaning and majesty; since all men know that public officials combine with unscrupulous businessmen to defraud the government and the public — with absolute impunity . . .[9]

It was a speech whose passion and sincerity had a profound effect on his audience, though subsequent assessments — notably by *Philippines Free Press* — compared his post-election promises with those of President Macapagal exactly four years earlier. The evils to be eradicated were phrased in almost identical terms. As Napoleon G. Rama expressed it: 'A cluster of power blocs, spurned or sidelined during Macapagal's regime, ascended the ladder of power with President Marcos. . . . Most presidents enter Malacanang with political debts to pay. For good or evil, Malacanang and the people will in the coming months and years feel the influence and impact of these powerful pressure groups. Already they have demonstrated their power over the new regime by securing for their men positions of authority.'

The first presidential year has always been a year of promises.

9. *Philippines Free Press*, 15 January 1966, Manila.

CHAPTER 23

Democracy in Asia

If we do not espouse 'Asia for the
Asians', if we do not speak out for
the freedom and independence of the
Asian nations, and if we do not come
out in defence of the rights to
equality, to self-determination, of the
Asian peoples, then the communists
will, for their own purposes; and the
results will be tragic both for Asia
and the rest of the free world . . .

CLARO M. RECTO

LOOKING back at the prolonged Gethsemane that has been Philippine history, I am often reminded of G. K. Chesterton's poem: 'We are the English people; we have not spoken yet.' The Filipino people have never had much chance to speak. It has always been done for them: by the policy-makers of other nations, by a few nimble climbers among their own countrymen. A Ramon Magsaysay is not given to every generation. Too frequently, like President Kennedy, he does not live long enough to complete a crusade only just beginning. The Philippines has at least been fortunate in the quality of its patriots and martyrs. It has had gifted and eloquent men like Rizal, Mabini, Manuel Quezon. These have also been subjected to a depth of suffering paralleled only by the Russians, Spanish or the Chinese. To say that Filipinos have consequently produced a fine literature may be largely to concede a genius for survival, for continuing their national aspirations despite defeats and hardship, and nurturing a rare sensitivity under conditions that were often brutalizing. High art tends to thrive on a tragic vision much admired by the detached spectator, but desperately uncomfortable to live with. 'The Philippine race, like all the Malays,' wrote Rizal, 'does not succumb before the foreigner, as do the Australians, the Polynesians and the Indians of the New World.'[1] *Adios*, his last poem, written with a firm hand shortly before they led him from Fort Santiago to the firing squad, is a profoundly moving one, though the agony of his emotion can only be felt completely in the almost untranslatable Spanish:

> I die just when I see the dawn break,
> Through the gloom of night to herald the day;
> And if its colour is lacking, my blood take,
> Poured out for your need at this ripe hour
> To dye with its crimson the awakening ray.

1. Jose Rizal, 'The Philippines A Century Hence', *La Solidaridad*, 30 September 1869, Madrid.

Nick Joaquin has written many brilliantly evocative short stories of the modern dilemma, as well as one novel, *The Woman Who Had Two Navels*, that offers a symbol for the Filipino's ambivalent allegiances in Asia. Where does he truly belong — to the Orient or the West? Is it that the great political adventure begun by del Pilar and Mabini has merely become, in one character's words, 'ninety per cent scandalmongering'? Is the future to be only the lost vision of frustrated patriots or the decadence of Manila society? — 'He had resumed his solitary explorations of the city but what he now saw increased his discomfort; the heat-dazzling panic-edgy streets darkened in his brain with doom, dirt, danger, disease, and violent death. Some venom was at work here, seeping through all the layers, cankering in all directions. . . .' There was irony in the fact that this searching, bemused novel should have won the first Stonehill Award in 1960. Only one further award was made, for early in 1962 Harry S. Stonehill was arrested and deported for what President Macapagal described as 'economic sabotage, tax evasion, political interference, mis-declaration of imports, schemes and machinations inimical to the state . . . and influence-peddling and corruption of public officials'.

The event was the grand climax of post-war politics. In fact, Stonehill — 'the G.I. whose brass turned to gold', as one American writer described him — had been himself at the hub of those politics. It was said that he shared one privilege with the Cardinal of Manila: no government could be formed without him, no minister remain in office, nor could high administration officials ignore his wishes. Though police took three truck-loads of documents, telephone tapping and jamming equipment, tape recorders and walkie-talkie sets from his luxurious offices, while his suppressed Blue Book was said to contain scores of prominent names, little has yet been published so significant as the memorandum Stonehill addressed to a prospective cabinet minister after the 1961 change of regime. 'You will shortly be appointed under-secretary of finance,' he wrote, 'and we want to congratulate you for having done such a wonderful job during the campaign and are sure we can together keep the country in the next four years. Nobody of importance helped Macapagal significantly, so we are, through you, most powerful in the nation.' The unexpected election of President Macapagal had been largely due to the late withdrawal of a third candidate, engineered — or so he claimed — by Robert P. Brooks, the kingmaker's business associate. Campaign funds also said to have been given to the incoming president — P120,000 according to a statement in the Senate by his former executive secretary — were later to become a major issue in the following presidential elections. Interviewed by a former employee in New York during 1966, the exiled financier 'laughed and told everybody present that he had spent very much more — about P3,000,000. He said he did it because he was "double-crossed" by a kin of the former president.' According to the same newspaper report, Stonehill said also that several pages missing from the Blue Book, which detailed his transactions with politicians and government officials, had also listed close associates of the president. The fact that this remarkable American, who began as a private in the United States Army, could have made a fortune estimated at P200,000,000 within ten years had disturbing repercussions on the state of contemporary politics. This was derived from real estate, tobacco manufacture — including imitation 'blue seals' manufactured within the country — and other industrial activities at a period when no others could import the machinery and raw materials needed for such large-scale enterprises. Years after his expulsion he still owed P32,000,000 in taxation, in addition to $U.S.34,000,000 to the United States Bureau of Internal Revenue.

It is probable that he would still have been in a seat of power, had not one of his managers, Mienhart Spielman, already threatened with murder, taken information to the N.B.I. This included his claim that Stonehill had made P69,000,000 from illegally manufactured cigarettes, whose packets even bore forged certificates of tax paid. His former patrons expelled Stonehill as soon as possible, before any public inquiry could reveal further embarrassing information. Spielman's body has long been at the bottom of the Sulu Sea.

Under such pressures — and who can say how many exist still? — it is difficult to make parliamentary democracy a workable affair. It is not enough to create democratic forms, even though guaranteed by an enlightened constitution, nor to await the distant hope of creating an informed and educated public. The Philippines, by comparison with other Asian countries, Japan excepted, does have a high literacy rate. That is, nearly 60 per cent of its people can read and write. What they read, apart from American or Tagalog 'comic books', is another matter. So are the marks written upon ballot papers, all too frequently dictated by the exchange of a few pesos. Philippine democracy is not unusual in offering its electors a choice of only two candidates, whose influences, aptitudes, often names even are unknown. Representation, as in most Western democracies, is limited to those pre-selected by party bosses for their own unstated purposes. It would be tragic if, at its present stage of immaturity, the mass of Filipinos should become disillusioned with a parliamentary process that has so far reproduced little more than the paternalism, benign or dictatorial, of earlier times. The pressing problem is just how to make these democratic institutions work.

A two-party system narrows the scope of national policies at any time: what is not white is black. But the two parties that have dominated the Philippines since independence are not, in the true sense, parties at all. They stand for no principles, have neither continuity nor grassroots organization. Neither has ever produced a coherent programme, no recommended reforms. Both stand for unrestricted private enterprise, without regard for minority interests or the least vestige of social welfare. Apart from personal ambitions, they are almost indistinguishable from one another, for they depend entirely upon personalities. Fundamentally, as critics have so often said, they are mere quarrelsome branches of the same

party, which was split by the Roxas breakaway group backed by General
MacArthur in 1946. Renato E. Aglapo sees them as governed by four
unchanging principles: the dominance of certain family interests; *utang
na loob* or nepotism; *hiya* (shame) ; and pragmatic realism, by which he
means personal alliances for survival. '*Hiya* and *utang na loob*,' he writes,
'both extremely personalistic values, usually go together, prescribing to
the political participant that he honour his debt of gratitude to another,
which came into being after some kind of favour was bestowed on him.
The favour could be anything — a job given to him, a recommendation
for some position, a personal service of some kind. . . .'[2]

Professor Taylor attributes this outlook largely to inherited Spanish
influences. 'To the Filipino,' he writes, 'that man was corrupt who failed
to pay his political debts with the spoils of office, or to promote the
interest of his kin group. The concept of honest and efficient government
as an end in itself . . . found little support in theory or in practice.'[3]

Hence it is not surprising that so little legislation emerges from the
annual hundred-day sessions of Congress, for which salaries and expenses
paid are the most extravagant in the world. Every year has seen a higher
secret vote. Since the president is elected by separate vote, it happens
frequently that he has to send his recommendations to an unsympathetic
Congress, though a skilful chief executive, endowed with greater powers
than even American presidents, can usually arrange matters to his liking,
especially by calculated inducements to change party allegiances. 'Turncoatism' is the Filipino phrase.

The classic statement of these 'principles' was made by the youthful
governor of Tarlac province, Benigno S. Aquinas, during 1964.

'I became governor of Tarlac in 1961,' he told a press conference.
'When President Macapagal took over I was a Nacionalista. Barely a few
weeks after the Liberal Party's victory my provisional health officer, who
was very co-operative, was "resigned". Then it became the turn of the
provincial [Constabulary] commander. Then the district engineer. Then
the divisional superintendent. Then the auditor. One year after the
Liberal Party victory, the Tarlac provincial government had been completely overhauled, except for the elective officials. As a Nacionalista Party
governor, I was a governor who did not govern. When my constituents
ask for better roads, schoolrooms, irrigation water, doctors or medicines,
can I face them and ask them to bear their sufferings longer because their
governor refuses to sell his political soul? I cried goodbye to a political
idealism I held sacred. While I still hold that turncoatism is morally
wrong, I am equally of the firm belief that given the same set of circum-
stances I will act the same. And to President Macapagal's credit, barely
a year after I joined the Liberal Party, much of the things I set out to do
are no longer plans but realities. Roads are now being built all over my

2. Renato E. Aglapo, *Philippines Free Press*, 13 March 1965, Manila.
3. *Philippines Free Press*, 7 November 1964, Manila.

province. A tractor and machine pool helps our farmers and residents in ways never before imagined. The University of the Philippines has set up a new unit in Tarlac. We have our new hospital. We have the begininngs of a real life in Tarlac. I paid the price — with my honour.'

You wonder how such regimes have fared since the Liberal president lost power in 1966. Tarlac, incidentally, is one of those sensitive regions where the Huks exert a subterranean influence on municipal affairs, as well as both political parties, so that attempts to govern must be trimmed to potent pressures below and above.

Similar tensions oblige congressmen to read their party seismographs with care. Their native talent for survival has lately made them 'instant millionaires'. The secret allowances they have voted themselves annually aroused such violent criticism that, shortly before the 1965 elections, the president was obliged to veto at least part of them. He did so reluctantly, for the honourable members rely upon these immense sums to buy their way back to power. It was later revealed that Macapagal surreptitiously restored the vetoed monies by transferring to Congress amounts that had been allocated for the aid of rice and corn farmers, land reform, regional development schemes, the Mindanao State University and government salaries. Congressmen have their own measure of national prosperity.

The precedent for these allowances goes back to the 1945 Congress, when the first action of its members was to legislate for 'compensation' to cover their collaborationist activities during the Occupation. Then, in 1958, without making it public, congressmen of both parties allocated themselves P8,900,000 annually for expense allowances. This was in excess of the P7,200 per member laid down by the Constitution. Year by year the amount rose: from P12,000,000 in 1960 to P56,000,000 in 1965. This allowed each member P250,000 a year above salaries, *per diems* and other expenses for a maximum of three months in the House. During their four year term, in fact, they became peso millionaires. Officially, these sums were supposed to cover expenses for travel, research, reference, office repairs, special materials and 'technical services'. Senator Antonino, opposing them in a week-long filibuster in the upper house, said that Congress should have been piled to its domed roof with reference books, the entire building rebuilt at least once a year, and every junior employee taken at least two free journeys around the world. As it happened, most congressmen do spend nine months of the year in paid overseas travel. Special sessions of Congress have had to be cancelled, because a quorum could not be found within the country at the time.

'While criminality stalks the land and grinding poverty grips the people,' reported the *Philippines Free Press* late in 1965, 'Congress has been on a protracted vacation. After three months of talk, interrupted only by travel, the congressional score is zero. No bill of any significance has been passed.' The writer listed a number that had been awaiting passage for several years. Among these were proposals to tax idle land to aid the lapsed socio-economic programme, to enforce the collection of income and other taxes, and the long-avoided police reform bill that would have helped to suppress the crime wave.

'Filipinos Unite!' read one placard during a mass protest of university students outside Congress. 'YOU HAVE NOTHING TO LOSE BUT YOUR CONGRESS-MEN.'

These undeclared expense accounts stirred strong reactions against the two monolithic parties. It brought wide support for an entirely new movement, which offers great promise for a fresh approach to Philippine democracy. The idealistic Philippine Party for Progress, despite its lack of campaign funds, gained further support from the obsessive feuding of the two major presidential candidates. Each accused the other of public graft, commercial dishonesty and even, in one case, murder. The aggressive 'blow for blow' arguments between Diosdado Macapagal and Ferdinand Marcos — dubbed by Manila wits as 'psychological warfare' — diverted several million votes to the new party. While the president-in-office asserted that everything was for the best in the best of all possible republics, his Nacionalista challenger could offer nothing more positive than a catalogue of administrative corruption, said to have cost the nation some P900,000,000. The misdemeanours he listed were little different from those voiced by Macapagal when he unseated his Nacionalista predecessor four years earlier: racketeering in rice importations, smuggling, tax evasion, scandals in business and banking, the disappearance of huge Japanese war reparation funds into the pockets of government officials. The public, grown blasé about such occurrences, found them as inevitable as typhoons.

Perhaps the last word on the subject was made by a convict in Negros Oriental, where none but prisoners had offered to give blood for an emergency operation. Asked why he had committed his crime, he answered, 'I'm just looting as everybody else is. Everyone in the government is looting. Many get P250,000 a year and nobody cares. During the last war looting was encouraged, provided the guerrillas got a share. Today we have to share the loot with government officials. The judge who sent me to gaol was joking. Looting isn't a crime.'[4]

During the elections it was said that, had only the intelligent voted, the youthful, 45-year-old Senator Raul Manglapus would have become president. With his vice-presidential candidate, Senator Manuel Manahan, he drew many thousands of young people and the intelligentsia to their public rallies, voicing a new faith in the integrity and aspirations of Filipinos, a weariness with what one of their campaigners, a retired Korean War general, described as 'the cynical attitude which regards elections like cockfights, horse-racing and gambling'. Reporting one huge midnight rally of university students on Manila's Plaza Miranda, significantly beneath the shadow of the Quiapo Church of the Black Nazarene, one observer wrote that Manglapus 'might have been addressing French intellectuals on the Left Bank'. Wherever they went, candidates

4. *Philippines Free Press*, 24 April 1965, Manila.

spoke beneath large portraits of Rizal, 'the man who embodies the virtues of all our heroes, the greatness of our people'. Both leaders are men of unusual intelligence in Filipino politics, which no longer attracts the best minds. Manglapus, an outstanding scholar of the Ateneo de Manila, has the backing of liberal Roman Catholics. Manahan, a wartime guerrilla leader, is a former Customs Commissioner, who did much to suppress graft and topped the previous Senate poll. Because of the Tammany Hall character of machine politics, they had little hope of winning congress or the presidency. But the movement promised to generate popular enthusiasm that would carry through to the ensuing elections four years away. It could well change the character of contemporary politics. The manifesto, published just before the movement's formation in May 1965 carried an inspirational force, a sense of responsibility and vision that has not been voiced since the Malolos Constitution of 1898. The document was given the bold heading: A CALL TO FILIPINISM, CHANGE AND GREATNESS; *An Alternative to National Despair*. It is a declaration that deserves publication in full, for it summarizes so much of Philippine history as well as its present dilemma.

OUR DESPERATE CONDITION

In the history of a nation, there are times that call for a change, change not only of men but in men, not only of leaders but of systems. Today is such a time for our nation.

The fabric of our society is fast crumbling. Law, order and justice — those great cornerstones of civilisation — are fast breaking down. We are so swamped with the tide of criminality that our citizens no longer feel safe in their homes and even the members of the Supreme Court have become the object of intimidation.

Despairing over the public acts of their public officials, our people are losing their faith in government. The cancer of corruption has spread so wide and deep in the body of this nation that its members have ceased to feel its pain, have accepted the malignancy as part of their normal state.

Today our people are coddled and deceived as they were in colonial days by a paternalistic government and by a paternalistic feudal land system. Being made to depend upon others, they have not learned to depend upon themselves.

Our country continues to be weak. We are outstripped by other nations of Asia which are bounding forward, propelled by well-defined and dynamic ideologies.

Our people have looked for that leadership which will unite them, set out for them the goals they are to strive for, the roles they are to play, inspire them to act, to work, to build, with their own sweat and their own hands. They have looked for that sense of direction which will move them to national discipline.

But they have not found it.

NO POLITICAL DIRECTION AND VISION

Political leadership in this county rests in two groups — the Nacionalistas and the Liberals.

The Nacionalistas once discharged a noble and indispensable role in rallying our people to the cause of immediate and absolute independence.

This cause was so popular and so brilliantly pursued by outstanding leaders that the Nacionalistas in the end found themselves without an opposition party.

To provide this democratic alternative was the valid and patriotic reason for the foundation of the Liberal Party. In its early days, this Party performed this function.

To insure that our people were given alternatives — and to insure that these alternatives were reduced to two — we established a system by which government-paid inspectors in effect became the exclusive prerogative of the two original groups.

Such a system has eliminated the necessity of parties to stand on political ideology and pursue consistent programs in response to the demands of our developing nationhood.

The first question that is asked of a party is not 'How many good ideas and how much moral integrity have you got?' but 'How many inspectors have you got?'

And so our parties have in fact been reduced to one — one party with two factions.

Many men of high motives in each faction are frustrated by this artificial condition. Neither faction now embodies a vision or a set of ideals principally because there is now no need for vision and ideals to get elected to power.

Thus we are presented with a spectacle that is to be seen nowhere else and is the laughing stock of the world. Members of each faction freely jump back and forth and change 'loyalties' as often as they would change their shirts in pursuit either of Presidential patronage or of nominations to high office.

Instead of wrestling with the mighty task of charting the course of this nation, they dissipate their energies in endless bickering and personal conflict, in those local affairs best left to the local government and local communities.

Instead of the truth, they weave flatteries. Instead of rallying the people to work and sacrifice, they would pretend to do everything for them.

TIME FOR CHANGE

The time has come to change this state of affairs. We can no longer tolerate this artificial party system. We can no longer continue to be a democracy in name but an oligarchy in fact.

The people must take back their government from the factions that have hitherto shared it between themselves. They must take control of their government at last.

We must destroy, once and for all, these ragged remnants of colonialism.

What is the remedy?

The remedy lies in the people themselves — so cruelly exploited by our insidious party system — uniting into a Force stronger than any and all factions combined.

A Force made irresistible by the three basic nationalist virtues of our people: Faith in the Filipino, Hope in the Filipino, Love for the Philippines.

FAITH IN THE FILIPINO

Here is the substance of our faith:

We believe in the Filipino as a citizen.

We believe that he has the innate capacity to be an enlightened, self-confident, self-reliant, progressive, productive, creative and self-governing citizen.

We believe not only in the Filipino as an individual, but in Filipinos as a nation.

We believe that this nation can stand on its own two feet, on a footing of equality with other nations, self-governing and self-reliant.

214

We believe in total participation of the people in the political and economic life of the nation.

We believe in a people's capitalism, in a private capital welfare state, for only ownership, specially that of productive property, can make a man truly free and secure.

We believe in spreading the ownership of productive property, thus promoting an equitable distribution of wealth and closing the widening cleavage between the levels of our society.

We believe in integrating political decentralization with economic regional planning under national policy direction.

We believe that any program for agricultural and industrial development should be based on private investment with planned participation of national and local government in support.

We believe that the investment necessary for the building of a responsible and stable society can be made only by a change in the values and attitudes of our people, in our outlook in life.

We believe in the kind of co-operative assistance and investment from abroad that will help to bring about this change without impairing our national patrimony and dignity.

We believe in a political movement that shall not be of the extreme right for we reject the *status quo*, not of the extreme left for we value democratic liberties, and not just of the dead center for we do not believe in moderation for moderation's sake.

Ours shall be a movement for change within the framework of freedom, and therefore left of center.

HOPE IN THE FILIPINO

Victory can begin only with hope, and in the hour of national despair such as we see today, hope alone can save us.

We rest our hope on the rugged strength of the Filipino, on his self-reliance.

Self-reliance calls for an educated people. It calls for the possession of the modern tools of science. The greatness of our country will depend on the sacrifices we are willing to make to strengthen our educational system on all levels. In this endeavour we must not rely on government alone, but encourage the maximum participation of all segments of society.

We place little value in tactical victories. We seek big changes in the very fabric of society. This must take time and infinite patience. But we are ready to dedicate the rest of our lives to this endeavor.

LOVE FOR THE PHILIPPINES

The inner life and strength of our faith and hope is love.

Love of country is creative. It builds; it does not destroy.

It is expressed through nationalism.

We reject as bogus nationalism any movement that would destroy the Filipino and remake him according to some alien model, whether it be Western or not.

We reject that brand of nationalism which seeks only personal gain for a few and sacrifices the interests of the many.

We love the Philippines as she is, as our patriots and heroes of the past — Lapu-Lapu, Silang, Rizal, Bonifacio, Mabini — made her and gave her to us to cherish.

We will see to it that she emerge from the slough of despond in which she languishes today as he truly is, as Rizal dreamed she would one day be:

'. . . lofty the upright brow:
unclouded, unfurrowed, unblemished and unashamed.'

215

FILIPINISM IS THE ANSWER

Freedom is the atmosphere, nationalism is the vehicle and here is the road: Faith in the Filipino, Hope in the Filipino, Love for the Philippines. In brief, Filipinism.

For this, we are ready to give in a total commitment all that we are and possess and if need be, our very lives.

With Filipinism as the instrument of change we shall forge a Force that will give back to our people their government, offer them direction and lead them to greatness.

This is what we must do.

In God's name, let us begin.

This forthright, idealistic appeal had a far-reaching influence on the 1965 elections. The party's campaign against Congress allowances forced the president to take public action, even if they were subsequently restored by the back door. Both parties were also obliged to inject promises of social reform into their campaigns. The Commission for Elections took more forthright action to police polling areas and reduce gangsterism. The large vote for Senator Manglapus helped to swing the election against Macapagal and, since the Philippines has no preferential system, put President Marcos into office. It was not so much a victory for the Nacionalistas as defeat for the Liberals. The Macapagal regime paid the price of its inability to control crime, corruption and smuggling. Marcos, the much decorated veteran of Bataan, resistance fighter and noted lawyer, won the presidency despite many vitriolic charges by the opposition against his public and personal life.

The result was further evidence that Philippine democracy is traditionally fashioned by a kind of anti-vote. No president has yet been re-elected for a second term (Roxas and Magsaysay both died in office). Misgovernment brings its own reward. The problem has always been to find a better alternative. Furthermore, the fantastic cost of elections is having a ruinous effect on the economy. The Philippine Constitution Association, basing its figure on elections in 1959 and 1961, estimated that it cost each man P50,000 to be elected to municipal or provincial office, P250,000 to Congress, P500,000 to the Senate or a provincial governorship. To become president costs anything up to P10,000,000. In 1965 the two leading candidates were believed to have spent between P20,000,000 and P40,000,000. Where did these vast amounts come from? It was a question asked in particular by Senator Manglapus. How was it, he wanted to know, that the past two presidents had appropriated P356,047,360 for urgent irrigation programmes, yet passed on a mere P6,448,000?

The Philippine Party for Progress has given electors their first chance to view government in constructive terms. Its policy statements advocated the decentralizing of political power, now dictated almost wholly from Malacanang: elimination of the 'pork-barrel' approach to public works; the merging of semi-bankrupt public utilities into large and efficient combines; creation of a national police authority; aiding commerce by a

216

more realistic rate of exchange; improving labour relations through liberalized laws and worker participation in investment; the ending of special relations with the United States, especially the Laurel-Langley Agreement.

Professor Taylor is one of the few American allies who endorse this explosive Filipino stand on parity rights. He believes that Washington treated the Philippines unjustly by forcing through the Bell Act after the war. 'The sooner special relations are done away with,' he writes, 'the better for both countries.'

Resentment against the strong grip the United States still holds over the economy burst into the open with mass demonstrations in Manila immediately after Christmas, 1964. The spark was struck by protests against the shooting of Filipino nationals at Clark Airfield and the Subic Bay naval base during previous months. In November a sixteen-year-old youth had been shot dead by an American sentry at the air base while foraging for scrap metal. Popular indignation soared when accusations were made that some thirty others had been killed in similar fashion in recent years. The fact that they had no business within restricted military areas was ignored, especially as unofficial permission was sometimes given for these salvage operations. United States authorities then pointed out that some action had to be taken, because pilferage had become a highly organized affair. During 1964 alone 564 large bombs were stolen, sold to local Chinese who extracted the powder, then resold to Filipinos for illegal dynamite fishing. Truckloads of frozen meat, clothing, aircraft landing lights and electronic equipment had been hi-jacked. It was no occasion to examine long-established misunderstandings between two races, the prejudices based on colour and status, nor the searing contrasts between squalid poverty and the affluence of highly-subsidized American nationals. Angeles City, at least in its Filipino sector, is among the most depressing areas of the country, a centre for vice and prostitution (hence the slogan, 'Angeles welcomes Yankees with open legs'), and almost any kind of criminal activities are to be expected. But what inflamed popular sentiment further was the hitherto unknown fact that the inhabitants of Crow Valley were so desperate for a livelihood that they competed to catch live bombs dropped on the air force practice range. 'Filipinos hang around the site like vultures,' said a Philippines Army officer. 'They race each other to snatch at the still smoking bombs. Many of them have lost fingers or hands or eyes, but are still there, hovering and quarrelling, like vultures, when the bombs are exploded.'

All this provided a new image of Philippine-United States relations.

The real dispute involved the question as to who should conduct legal inquiries into the shootings. Filipinos suspected that servicemen involved in previous incidents had been exonerated or posted elsewhere, and demanded that trials be conducted by their own courts. But the United States had sovereign jurisdiction over military bases, despite sporadic discussions over many years to change the situation. For the first time in

Philippine history anti-American feelings were popularly voiced. In January an official of the United States embassy blundered by making an 'off-the-record' statement to a press conference, involving the finding of an unexploded bomb in the American school playground at Clark. The ethics of Manila pressmen do not allow such confidences. The incident was at once given headlines. Americans were charged with false propaganda, provocation, attempts to 'frame' innocent Filipinos. When the bomb was later found to be the invention of a Filipino sentry, apparently anxious to impress his American superiors, hostile demonstrations only increased. The bomb report was an insult to Filipino honour; demands were raised for the Ambassador's recall; his image astride a huge bomb was publicly burned; thousands of demonstrators marched through Manila to the embassy on Roxas Boulevard, bearing cardboard coffins and placards denouncing 'American Imperialism', 'Go Home, White Monkeys', 'Down With American Murderers'.

This sudden explosion of anti-American feeling came as a profound shock. There had been nothing like it before. It has always been assumed that Filipinos had a deep regard for the nation which had helped them to develop, freely given them independence. It did not augur well for future relations, unless skilful diplomacy could heal the wounds. Initially, this skill was conspicuously lacking. Attempts were made to prove that the demonstrations were communist-inspired. Bogus leaflets bearing hammer-and-sickle emblems appeared mysteriously on Manila streets. Their origin was at once attributed to the C.I.A., especially when paper and type were identified with work done by a job-printer for the embassy. The political atmosphere worsened when demonstration organizers produced a twelve-point programme of demands that included the cancellation of the military bases treaty, parity rights, American requests for Filipino troops to fight in Vietnam and the presence of all foreign agencies, especially the C.I.A. and United States Information Service.

Fortunately the period coincided with a year-long presidential election campaign, which proverbially clouds all other issues. The excitement faded, and better relations were restored in August 1965 with the revision of the base treaty, giving Philippine courts jurisdiction over both Filipinos and Americans involved in civil crimes. It could so easily have been done years before. The question of parity, however, may be expected to remain a lively issue until 1974.

The events of that December-January period still need serious consideration by both governments. The rising nationalism throughout Asia has influenced the Philippines more profoundly than the leaders of either country have yet realized. Independence is, and will continue to be a touchy question in the Philippines. American officials, in my experience, have been insufficiently aware of present-day Filipino thinking. There is little contact, perhaps even little sympathy, with any but the social élite. Surely what happened in China has not already been forgotten? Support for the wealthy and corrupt, indifference to mass poverty brought the

Communists to power. It is perhaps no accident that many middle class people patronize a Mabini nightclub called the Ugly American. The middle class, after all, is the one solid anchor that can stabilize this restless, impoverished nation. This is a comparatively small class still, but growing in influence and sophistication. It can continue to grow only if United States interests create an economic climate where more industrialization becomes possible, which means essentially setting restraints, preferably voluntary ones, on continuing efforts to monopolize the Republic's commerce. As Dean Conrado Benitez once put it to me, 'The reason why we won't go the way of Vietnam, Cuba and other former Spanish possessions is the existence of an educated middle class. Those countries never had them. Education, secondary industries, a pride in our national culture — these are the essentials for stability.'

The United States has contributed far more than its critics concede, notably in its aid programmes through A.I.D. (Agency for International Development), the Big Brotherhood Movement and the Philippine Rural Reconstruction Movement, and numerous government-sponsored agencies and corporate bodies such as the Rockefeller and Ford Foundations. However, it was ill advised in attempting to involve the Philippines in the Vietnam war. The setting of Asians against Asians, could, in the delicate power balance of the present time, have perilous consequences. Maintaining friendly relations with Indonesia, a major power on its borders, are equally important to the Republic as purely American prestige on Asia's mainland. Besides a strong antipathy exists to war of any kind. The Philippine constitution is the only one in existence that specifically 'outlaws war as an instrument of policy'. This, in itself, has considerable propaganda value on the Asian scene. The nation suffered cruelly under the Japanese, and is devoid of aggressive militarism. Commenting on the number of Australian memorials 'glorifying' war, the *Manila Times* columnist Alfredo R. Roces, recently wrote: 'The Australians have a heroic concept of war since they have never had any enemies occupy their territories or any actual war in the homeland. . . . We Filipinos, like most Asians, have a less glorious picture of war. This monster straddled its haunches on our shores. The fear, the pain, the hunger and disease, the futility and the depths of barbarism and inhumanity have made us all a little weary of sword-brandishing. We do not ask for peace at any price, we are too aware of the fact that this means submitting to a horror equal to war if not worse, that of appeasement. But we are for more diplomatic and calmer methods to seek reason. We are just not too eager to don a plumed helmet and dash into the trenches.'[5]

Now that the Dulles theory of falling dominoes has been discredited, the virtues of neutrality in at least one south-east Asian region have much to recommend them. During 1965 President Macapagal promised the United States to send 2,000 troops, mostly engineers, to South Vietnam. The Liberal majority in Congress approved the project, but the Senate,

5. Alfred P. Roces, 'A Climate of Tension', *Manila Times*, 5 September 1964, Manila.

largely for political reasons, refused assent. Those of independent mind declared that the heavy expense involved, initially P35,000,000 a year, would be better spent in combating communism at home; through increased educational facilities, social services and the alleviation of poverty upon which the Huk movement at present breeds. When the United States offered in 1966 to finance the expeditionary force, Filipino opposition was strengthened by Senator Wayne Morse, who told Congress in Washington that American money for such purposes would reduce Asians to the despicable role of 'foreign mercenaries'.

The most eloquent voice opposing involvement in the Vietnam War during 1965 had been the then president of the Senate, Ferdinand Marcos, who called President Macapagal's proposals 'canine devotion to America . . . deception . . . typical demagoguery and mental dishonesty'. After his election as President of the Philippines, Marcos took up the same arguments he had condemned in his predecessor, while his opponents quoted extensively from his 1965 speeches. They accused him of having made a secret pact with Washington to have the failing economy underwritten if troops were sent overseas. The embittered debate occupied the entire 100-day session of the 1966 Congress, which overlooked his appeal on inauguration day to concentrate on urgent economic problems, and did not attempt to deal with the many urgent reform bills. Majority support for the expeditionary force was finally secured in both houses, but only after twelve months of impassioned public argument, mass rallies, demonstrations and the engendering of fresh cynicism that a new president, confronted with his publicly admitted problems, can ill afford. Meantime the climate of poverty and violence at home continued. It had also been Senate President Marcos, not his present critics, who drew attention to that clause in the Philippine constitution that forbade recourse to war.

In any event, as qualified observers have so often pointed out, the Philippine Army is not equipped for fighting. It has more officers than men, more generals, colonels and majors than privates. In fact, there are 3,500 senior officers, 37,000 sergeants and corporals and only 131 privates in an army of 45,000. It is largely a prestige corps in which promotion is based less on skill in the military arts than in cultivating political friends.

The most constructive course, to quote Professor Taylor again, is for 'the middle class to make an active ally of the army, supporting and extending its present activities in civil affairs, such as engineering projects, land clearing, communications and the enforcement of election laws'. There is probably no more forward-looking text for the times than this American historian's appeal to his own government to help the Philippines achieve a true position of independence:

> At a time when the United States is trying to bolster the political institutions and the economies of the independent countries of south-east Asia while protecting them from Communist aggression, it is politically essential that these objectives should be achieved in the Philippines, a country in which the United States has had unique opportunities to create so many of the things

that it wishes now to see elsewhere. For good or for ill, the U.S. record in the Philippines is part of our political stock-in-trade in Asia. Because we made an open commitment to prepare an Asian people in the ways of democracy and because the Filipinos themselves have proclaimed their adherence to democratic institutions the United States is involved in their success or failure. Not to succeed here would reflect adversely on us much more than would failure in other parts of Asia. It would be a serious matter if the Filipinos made a mockery of democratic institutions; it would be disastrous if they were lost to Communism.

At a period in history when we no longer have direct control over its destiny, the Philippine Republic is more important to us than ever before; our good intentions and our prideful boasts are equally at stake. Put in very general terms, the prestige of American democracy is involved in the Philippines in a way that it is not in other parts of south-east Asia.[6]

What the Republic requires is to be allowed to live in peace, to be given all aid possible for peaceful development for its economic and human resources — massive financial aid, technical aid, and aid to create more employment, more social services and welfare, more food production for its hungry millions. These things cannot be achieved without some fairer distribution of the nation's income, which is at present largely concentrated in the bank deposits of the one per cent who are wealthy. The Philippines is almost the last remaining country to retain a free enterprise system virtually without checks or controls, and certainly without any social legislation to aid the totally unprotected mass of the poor. In view of its runaway population growth, it is difficult to see how this can ever be achieved. Yet Japan has done so; India is making the attempt; even China has revised its earlier illusions of grandeur to adopt birth control. Equally essential is more recognition of the special problems and potential of the Philippines by the world outside. It is no longer a closed preserve for the United States, and neither Filipinos nor intelligent Americans would wish it so. In recent years there has been a slow advance in cultural and trade links with Australia, Germany, the United Kingdom and independent Asian States.

The fact that, somehow, the Philippines has retained its democratic status without falling to revolution from the left or right, is a sign that its people have the necessary stability to order their own affairs. There are major difficulties yet to overcome: notably in establishing the rule of law, curbing criminality, gaining some political philosophy beyond self-interest. At least there are signs of a maturing in election practices, a shade less violence, a freer vote, more candidates with a social consciousness, or conscience.

The danger zone remains, as it has always been, the restless rice bowl of Central Luzon; the Huk stronghold. Unless positive action on land reform is soon taken, the persistent anarchy could well lead to a more serious upheaval; even revolution. The terrorism that overshadowed the 1965 elections was no passing phase. In July 1966 President Marcos was obliged

6. George E. Taylor, *The Philippines and the United States*, op. cit.

to offer large rewards for the capture of thirteen underground Huk leaders. This followed the assassination of a provincial mayor and five aides driving to Manila for a conference on measures to combat subversion. The warning of South Vietnam is clear for all to read. A future set-back to the economy could create the kind of unrest that gave the Huks mass support after World War II, again prompting intervention by the West in defence of an unpopular landlord-dominated government. There is still time, through enlightened policies, to prevent a new disaster of this kind. Economic action now could avoid military action later, as the Nhu family as well as Magsaysay have taught.

The next stage must surely be to create an awareness that the Philippines is Asia, not merely an appendage of the West. In the existing context of Asia, the West has need of an authentic ally in the region. Essentially, the Filipino needs to recover his Asian character, so long corrupted and diffused. Despite the present confusion of national politics, the trend towards a common outlook with the newly emerging nations around the China Sea is discernible already. The Association of South-East Asia was the first tentative attempt; so was the illusion of Maphilindo. President Marcos has expressed his belief that, sooner or later, some economic union will develop between the Philippines and its immediate neighbours, perhaps a form of south-east Asian common market.

The Filipino, as a tactical ruse, put on the mask of the foreigner Adrian E. Cristobal once wrote. When the time came for taking off that mask, he found it had become part of his face. What mask is he wearing now? Both Westerner and Oriental are part of his heritage. It may now be the time to put on his authentic Asian face.

'The Philippines,' Cristobal concluded, 'must take to heart the lessons of Asian nationalism, both for its dignity and survival. It cannot afford to be a tail-ender to the Asian revolution; by keeping in step with it, the Philippines may yet be a better nation, commanding the respect of its neighbours and allies. And when the time comes for its representatives to address the assembly of nations, they can do so without appearing like trained lackeys to their enemies, untrustworthy wards to their allies, and spineless conformists to themselves.'[7]

The sharpest, most penetrating criticisms of the Philippines have always been made by Filipinos themselves. These are healthy signs. Self-criticism is essential to self-knowledge. Many of the world's nations are much less aware of their true nature and potential.

7. Adrian E. Cristobal, *Manila Times Annual*, 1958.

Bibliography

Hernando J. Abaya, *Betrayal in the Philippines*, New York, 1946.

Teodoro A. Agoncillo, *The Fateful Years: Japan's Adventure in the Philippines, 1941-5*, Manila, 1965.

Teodoro A. Agoncillo, *The Revolt of the Masses*, Manila, 1959.

William H. Anderson, *The Philippine Problem*, New York, 1939.

Conrado Benitez, *History of the Philippines*, New York, 1963.

David Bernstein, *The Philippine Story*, New York, 1947.

E. H. Blair and J. A. Robertson, *The Philippine Islands, 1493-1898*, 55 vols., Cleveland, 1905.

H. de la Costa, *The Jesuits in the Philippines, 1581-1768*, Cambridge, Mass., 1961.

Cameron W. Forbes, *The Philippine Islands*, New York, 1945.

Leon Ma Guerrero, *The Young Rizal*, Manila, 1949.

George M. Guthrie, *The Filipino Child and Philippine Society*, Manila, 1961.

D. G. E. Hall, *A History of South East Asia*, London, 1964.

Jose Ma Hernandez, *Rizal*, Manila, 1950.

Ralston J. Hayden, *The Philippines*, New York, 1947.

Robert E. Huke, *Shadows on the Land: An Economic Geography of the Philippines*, Manila, 1963.

Nick Joaquin, *La Navale de Manila*, Manila, 1964.

Nick Joaquin, *The Woman who Had Two Navels*, Manila, 1961.

Teodoro M. Kalaw, *The Philippine Revolution*, Manila, 1925.

Henry Keppel, *A Visit to the Indian Archipelago*, London, 1895.

Frank C. Lanbach, *Rizal: Man and Martyr*, Manila, 1936.

George A. Malcolm, *First Malayan Republic*, New York, 1954.

George A. Malcolm, *The Commonwealth of the Philippines*, New York, 1926.

F. S. Marquant, *Before Bataan and After*, New York, 1943.

Katherine Mayo, *The Isles of Fear*, New York, 1924.

Rafael Palma, *The Pride of the Malay Race*, New York, 1949.

Manuel L. Quezon, *The Good Fight*, New York, 1946.

Carlos Quirino, *Magsaysay of the Philippines*, Quezon City, 1958.

Carlos Quirino, *The Great Malayan*, Manila, 1949.

Jose Rizal, *El Filibusterismo (The Reign of Greed)*, Manila, various eds.

Jose Rizal, *Noli Me Tangere (The Social Cancer)*, Manila, 1956.

Jose Rizal, *The Lost Eden*, new trans. of *Noli Me Tangere* by Leon Ma Guerrero, London, 1961.

Jose Rizal, *To the Young Women of Malolos*, National Library, Manila, 1932.

Carlos P. Romulo, *Crusade In Asia*, New York, 1955.

Carlos P. Romulo, *Mother America*, New York, 1943.

William Roscher, *The Spanish Colonial System*, New York, 1904.

Najeeb M. Saleeby, *The History of Sulu*, Manila, 1908.

William Lytle Schurz, *The Manila Galleon*, New York, 1959.

Ian Shannon, *The Philippines: Australia's Neighbour*, Melbourne, 1966.

R. A. Smith, *Philippine Freedom*, New York, 1958.

George E. Taylor, *The Philippines and the United States*, New York, 1964.

T. H. Pardo de Tavera, *The Character of Rizal and the Legacy of Obscurantism*, Manila, 1960.

Dean C. Worcester, *The Philippines: Past and Present*, New York, 1930.

Gregorio F. Zaide, *Philippine Political and Cultural History*, 2 vols., Manila, 1956.

Gregorio F. Zaide, *Jose Rizal: Life, Works and Writings*, Manila, 1957.

OTHER PUBLICATIONS

A Pilot Study of Communication Problems in the Barrio, Social Science Research Centre, University of the Philippines, Quezon City, 1955.

Asian Studies, various issues, Department of Asian Studies, University of the Philippines, Quezon City.

Comment, various issues, University of the Philippines, Quezon City.

Philippine Studies, various issues, Ateneo de Manila, Manila.

Philippine Social Science and Humanities Review, quarterly, Manila.

The Manila Times Annual.

The files of *The Daily Mirror*, *The Manila Bulletin*, *The Manila Times*, *The Philippines Herald*, *Philippines Free Press*, *The Manila Chronicle* and *The Sunday Times*.

Index